The Book of Timothy

THE DEVIL, MY BROTHER, AND ME
[A MEMOIR]

Joan Nockels Wilson

borealbooks

Book design by Mark E. Cull

Library of Congress Cataloging-in-Publication Data

Names: Wilson, Joan Nockels, 1964– author.
Title: The book of Timothy : the devil, my brother, and me : a memoir /
  Joan Nockels Wilson.
Description: First edition. | [Pasadena, CA] : Boreal Books, [2021]
Identifiers: LCCN 2021019135 (print) | LCCN 2021019136 (ebook) | ISBN
  9781597099325 (trade paperback) | ISBN 9781597099448 (epub)
Subjects: LCSH: Wilson, Joan Nockels, 1964– | Wilson, Joan Nockels,
  1964—Family. | Catholic Church—Clergy—Sexual behavior. | Catholic
  Church. Archdiocese of Chicago (Ill.) | Bible. Timothy, 1st. | Catholic
  women—United States—Biography. | Child sexual abuse by clergy. Brothers and sisters.
Classification: LCC BX4705.W566 A3 2021 (print) | LCC BX4705.W566 (ebook)
  | DDC 227/.8306—dc23
LC record available at https://lccn.loc.gov/2021019135
LC ebook record available at https://lccn.loc.gov/2021019136

The National Endowment for the Arts, the Los Angeles County Arts Commission, the
Ahmanson Foundation, the Dwight Stuart Youth Fund, the Max Factor Family Foundation,
the Pasadena Tournament of Roses Foundation, the Pasadena Arts & Culture Commission
and the City of Pasadena Cultural Affairs Division, the City of Los Angeles Department of
Cultural Affairs, the Audrey & Sydney Irmas Charitable Foundation, the Meta & George
Rosenberg Foundation, the Albert and Elaine Borchard Foundation, the Adams Family
Foundation, Amazon Literary Partnership, the Sam Francis Foundation, and the Mara W.
Breech Foundation partially support Red Hen Press.

First Edition
Published by Boreal Books
an imprint of Red Hen Press
www.borealbooks.org
www.redhen.org

Printed in Canada

For Walter Nockels (February 4, 1932–August 15, 2017)
and Mary Blackburn Nockels (August 6, 1932–October 10, 2015)

con amore eterno per i miei genitori

CONTENTS

ə❧

AH my deare angrie Lord,
Since thou dost love, yet strike;
Cast down, yet help afford;
Sure I will do the like.

I will complain, yet praise;
I will bewail, approve:
And all my sour-sweet days
I will lament, and love.

—George Herbert, *Bitter-Sweet*

PROLOGUE

April 22, 2012 – Sunday

I'm boarding the Leonardo Express, the commuter train from Fiumicino Airport to the Termini Train Station in central Rome. It's four o'clock on a Sunday afternoon, and although it's April, two weeks after Easter, I expect it to be darker outside. This is a distinctive trait of an Alaskan. Despite the change in latitude, I still expect darkness everywhere and every time.

How did I get to Rome? The simple answer is that it took thirty-eight hours with a layover in Chicago, my birthplace, to gather blessings. Or shall I say curses? And isn't life more complex than the Alaska Airlines flight 30 to British Airways flight 4 to Alitalia flight 110 answer? Don't trips like this really begin ten years prior, devouring, for me, my late thirties and making all of the forties I have lived so far a mess for healthy relationships of any kind?

And my brother? His saga began well before, before he really had a chance, behind a closed door that should have been opened, on a twin bed that should have slept one, under the watch of Saint Michael, who supposedly stood ready to battle. Isn't this where tragic stories really begin? Under the theoretical custody of a guardian angel who could not have cared less? Or, rather, under the watchful eye of a wolf in shepherd's clothing? The one who left the ninety-nine grazing peacefully in the verdant pasture to terrorize that solitary, frightened, honey-made lost lamb? In the words of the apostle John, isn't this the true "In the beginning was the Word and the Word was with God" start to it all?

I don't have to say it here, not yet. You must know what I'm talking about by my use of certain words and images. The angel who missed his mark (the actual meaning of "to sin"), the closed door, the wolf—did I say, with the Roman collar?—the small bed, and my even smaller brother. You know the story can't be a good one, but what should be picked up, in case you might have missed the cues, the allusions, not a sin in this context, is the fact that I can't say it, admit it, right from the start. *That* is also the story. Like so many years ago, I'm on the outside looking in, fearful of what I might see. More fearful of what I might say. Even more terrified that I might do nothing.

Yet, today, on the Leonardo Express, I am once again the faithful sister. I'd given up this mantle for a time as well. But after a lawsuit against a priest, a religious order, and an archdiocese that brought no acknowledgment of wrong-doing and at my brother's simple and complex request—so that no other child may suffer alone—I've made telling my brother's story, Tim's story, my personal mission. In this task his story has seemingly become my own. And when it comes to me, I know the ending too well. It can only come with confrontation. With the exception of a trained assassin, who better to confront a serial child abuser than me?

Please let it be noted for I see the folly: I am the only one here, not Tim, on a train to an eternal city without the ability to get on with it. I am the lost lamb with a backpack and a computer bag on a pilgrimage to the Congregazione della Passione di Gesù Cristo to find him—the priest banished to his order's religious headquarters nearly a decade ago.

I ask myself then. Why with this focus on fathers do I think of my mother?

Be careful, child. I can hear her calling. Aboard the Leonardo I've found my window seat, left side—vinyl torn—and I've released the backpack and computer bag tethered to my jet-lagged body.

She calls to me again. *Be careful.*

As the train leaves the airport grounds I want her here, for my own comfort, no one else's.

I open my computer bag, reach inside, and feel for the small portfolio of photos I've carried with me. Here are the reminders of the reasons I need to make it home: my husband, Richard, and our four messy dogs; the Chugach mountains; my Sitka spruce forest of a yard. I pause only briefly at the most important reason, the photograph of my three-year-old daughter, Abbie. With her open arms, she's reaching for me, I can tell. But it seems I'm always a foot away, just out of camera range, life range. Even at this moment, mother that I am, I flip past her. I turn needingly to the photo of my mother holding me.

In it, Mary Catherine Blackburn Nockels is just thirty-two, currently, fifteen years my junior. Her short, cropped hair is auburn. She wears a bright red poppy-colored cotton sweater, and I'm cradled within the crook of her elbow. Mouth open, eyes looking to hers; she's feeding me. I know from another photo that captures that same sweater, kitchen background, and mother's touch that this moment occurred at my sister Teresa's third birthday party. So I, a Thursday's child, am just over two months old. Despite this, my mother appears to be done nursing me; there is a spoon going into my tiny, upturned mouth. The benefits of long-term breastfeeding aside, Mom looks content, as if on this day I am, gloriously, all she ever asked for. I note that until my law school graduation, thirty-three years into the future, this is the one and only photo I have of solely the two of us.

And so for the next thirty minutes, through city outskirts, by cramped, efficient nameless buildings, across the mud-blond Tiber River, this is how the time passes. Just she and I, together. *Be careful, child.*

At Termini, I follow the crowd of casual Romans from track 26, and, with Chicago city sense suddenly engaged, I make my way relatively stress-free through long corridors and down escalators to the subterranean Metro station.

I look over the subway map to find my destination. Here it is. In one direction, Rebibbia; in the other, my other, his other, Laurentina. This is *Linea B.* The Blue Line.

Blue. Blue means careful child, *atento per favore.* Blue means *petrifino* and paralyzed. Blue means anger, revenge, an action loaded upon itself of unadulterated violence. Blue means oxygen-less blood, what I may in fact be seeking. Is this what I am seeking? I must be better than a death wish. Remembering the inscription Richard Rodriguez wrote just a year ago in my torn copy of his *Days of Obligation*—"For Joan, 'Learn not to be afraid.' St. Ignatius."—I will myself back to contemplative understanding.

Blue. Blue means coincidence, calm, and courage. Blue means an act of belief, really an act of resolute faith. Blue means the ending, here at the beginning. And I'm soon to learn in three days' time, from a fresco of the Madonna—*here she is, the mother again!*—beneath the papal apartments, that blue means high holiness.

Purity even.

THE BLUE LINE

❧

March 26, 2002

6:00 p.m., his time, 3:00 p.m., mine.

He was calling from the Blue Line.

When we were kids, the last stop on Chicago's El closest to home was the Jefferson Park station at Milwaukee and Central Avenues. Once we turned ten, Mom never seemed concerned when, unaccompanied, we left home and boarded the 68 bus down Northwest Highway to catch the El into the city. She was a city girl and we were her city children. *Always get a transfer slip just in case your plans change*, she would advise.

By her teaching, we knew when to look others in the eye and when to keep to ourselves. We knew when to give up our seats—*for pregnant ladies and old people*—and at just what moment to rise to catch our stops. *Judge it by the slow of the train. And if you get afraid, just sit in the front car by the conductor.* Watergate and the first Mayor Daley's political machine were nonexistent; our mother had full trust in the cape of authority.

Jefferson Park, Montrose, Irving Park, Addison, Belmont, Logan Square. California, Western, Damen, Division, Chicago, Grand Avenue. Clark, Washington, *change for the Red Line,* Monroe, Jackson, LaSalle, and Clinton. The stops were ingrained in us. Although the El continued farther south and west before its end at Forest Park, UIC-Halsted was as far as my mother ever permitted us to go.

"But what about Comiskey Park?"

"You already have your baseball team."

"Or the South Side Irish Parade?"

"We have State Street."

There was no arguing with a North Sider.

By the time Tim and I were in high school the El was extended to O'Hare Airport, we thought for our convenience. Stations were added at Harlem, Cumberland, and the Rosemont Sports Arena.

Harlem was our stop, one mile from home. Instead of the 68 bus, we took the 90N or simply walked south on the avenue, the city's longest north-south corridor. We passed our church and school, Immaculate Conception, and continued by the Passionist Monastery to the Harlem station located between Bryn Mawr and Higgins Avenues. There it sat, in the middle of the Kennedy Expressway.

The Blue Line. I don't even know if it was called this when we were kids. But by the time I left for Alaska and Tim moved from his Maxwell Street loft to the suburbs, it carried the name. The Blue Line.

I often look for meaning where none can be found—in blue, for example. Not periwinkle or cerulean, just plain, blue-collar blue. That blue means Buddy Guy's wails. It means the haphazard, pin-striped Cubs, and the I. C. (our abbreviation for Immaculate Conception) Cowboys fight song. It followed the tune of a popular march whose name still escapes me, but the lyrics remain: *I. C., the home of white and blue. I. C., on Talcott Avenue.* Blue means . . . Tell me, for I'm no doubt certain the Blue Line has become my undoing.

March 26, 2002

6:00 p.m., his time, 3:00 p.m. mine.

The direct line rang at my law office, where I'd been an associate for four years. I recognized Tim's number and gratefully put the complaint of *Alaska Tours v. Federal Coach LLC* to the side.

"Tim?"

When had we last spoken? Was it when Dad had the angioplasty or Teresa turned forty? Or was it to offer him help to get out of a health club or mobile phone contract? My six siblings called me regularly to talk about these situations. And thanks to them, I'd become an expert on all unconscionable, adhesion contracts.

Then I remembered. Tim had called me right after seeing the ultrasound a few weeks before. He was going to have a son.

"Joan," he said, giving the cough that worked like a stutter after he said my name.

I couldn't help it, at least not then. I went into the full-throttle litigator mode, what my husband calls my most unattractive trait bar none, asking for the details.

He first took it kindly, answering in just as quick succession all my questions. "Is the nursery done?" "Have you decided on a name?" "Exactly how far along is Lisa?" When I asked, "Do you have fears of becoming a dad?" and quickly answered for him, "Of course, you must. But you'll do fine, Tim. You'll make a great dad," his tone changed. Tim started a conversation I shouldn't have led.

"That's just it," he said, "it's becoming a dad that's got me thinking and feeling things I thought were long gone. And I don't—"

The line went dead. I was fairly certain I knew where he was. I knew from conversation he had just passed Jefferson Park, and before I lost him, I heard the squeaks of the El train's brakes. After Central Avenue, the El dips down a small decline below the Kennedy Expressway's road elevation. It was not completely underground. Tim was riding eye level to cars' passing tires. In short order, the tracks would rise again. Next, his signal would get trapped by the combined overpasses of Nagle and Narragansett Avenues. Once he got past Harlem, I knew we would be able to speak.

Oftentimes a memory of Tim can come out of nowhere. At that moment, waiting for his return call, I saw him, covered in baking soda and looking like Casper the Friendly Ghost.

He was eight. I was nine. We were loading our station wagon after a night camping outside Cheyenne, Wyoming. I'd just dared him to set off Dad's extinguisher in the car.

❧

I'll give you a dollar? That's all I'd had to say and bam, the fire suppressant flew out in a gust coating Tim, the backseat, and all the car windows. Enough had covered me that I spit the paste from my mouth for a good hour afterward. Why had I done that to him? Had I been jealous of the one boy out of seven children who could get my father's attention? Did I reasonably foresee the attention would eventually turn to the instigator?

❧

Tim's return call was taking longer than expected. I guessed the El must have come to a full stop, as it often did, before it trundled into the Harlem station. *7200 WEST, 5600 NORTH.* So read the sign passengers saw when they disembarked. We just needed a couple more minutes. He was just worried about becoming a dad. That's all. And so, I waited, thinking this time, had I ever really been there for his worrying?

Not since high school. Circa fall 1982, I became the absent child, the one to go to college and not straight to work in a bank or retail sales like my sisters and even Tim for a while. When I left home to attend the albeit nearby Northwestern University, I told him he could come and see me anytime.

He did once. The doorbell rang at my apartment in Evanston. He stepped across the threshold and stayed for a total of thirty minutes, never telling me why he came. He looked distressed when he said he had to leave. But still, I didn't follow.

After college I moved to Alaska, then Berkeley for graduate school, then Alaska again, then Portland for law school. After all this schooling, I finally returned to Alaska for good in 1996, and, by then, I certainly became of no use to him.

I did hear the stories.

"He dyed and spotted his hair in leopard prints, just like Dennis Rodman," my father screeched. "He rented a loft studio on Maxwell Street in a neighborhood no one feels safe to visit. Then the tattooed hands! What in Jesus's name was he thinking?"

"I don't know, Dad, I kind of like it," I said, more than once, to try to calm him.

Tim started painting too. The work he hung over his bed resembled Edvard Munch's *The Scream*, but the face seemed more magnified and reflected even greater terror. One day, "on the car ride from hell," as Tim called it, Dad asked him if he had a butt buddy. Tim gave Dad a look and never answered him.

Finally, his 847 area code popped into view and I, per usual, jumped in right where I left off. "Tim, I can see why you're nervous, but *please* don't worry. You're a great brother. I know you're an even better husband. You can do this."

"*JOAN!*" When he called my name, I finally stopped. I remember being immediately frightened.

"I've been the reading the newspaper," Tim began. The sarcastic part of me I wished would go away, at least then, thought, *Of course you read the paper. What else would you do on your forty-minute commute?* Yet I knew better. I knew I should wait.

"In the *Chicago Trib*," he coughed, "there's been stories from Boston, about those boys . . . ?"

"There's been stories." I thought of another time his words could have given me a clue.

It was a year before this call, New Year's Eve at the Grand Avenue Café, ten minutes from 2001. We were at the third table from the corner, I think seated under the poster of Tim's long-dead football hero, the Sweetness, Number 34, Walter Payton, running for a touchdown. I know the eastbound wind rushed in whenever the front door to the bar opened, and I pulled my black leather jacket, the one I'd bought at Marshall Field's just before my wedding to a man I then couldn't get out of my mind, closer each time. As a symbolic act for the divorce about to come, I had already cut my long hair pixie short. I drank a '97 pinot noir from the Willamette Valley, not far from where I had attended law school. Tim drank an MGD from the tap and wore a white button-down shirt with a navy-blue cashmere sweater over it. His pants were black denim.

Although 2001 will be remembered rightly for a tragedy much bigger than my own sorrow, at the time I sat with Tim, my divorce was my chief concern. Despite it being clear my husband didn't love me, despite the fact I came home one day to find he had given the family dog away just to spite me, I didn't want that divorce. How could I? As a Catholic girl, even one about to become a twenty-first century one, and the daughter and granddaughter of the long-married, I was schooled to believe marriage was a one-way ticket from the altar to the grave some sixty years in the future. Mine wasn't supposed to end after two years and nine days?

When Tim tapped my shoulder that night, I recall how difficult it was to move my eyes from the Goose Island beer label stuck to the pine-board floor beneath him to his hands. There the tattooed letters on his right fingers spelled out the word PURE, and those on his left spelled SOUL. PURE SOUL. I wondered why he required the reminder. When I finally looked into his hazel eyes, just like Mom's, and saw his angular nose, just like our grandfather's, he started to speak.

"Joan," he said, his voice sounding safe. "I don't know why your marriage ended or frankly why you mourn it. There wasn't much there to celebrate. What I do know is someday you'll lift yourself out of this. When you least expect, when you hurt the most, when you're ready to call it a day, maybe even call it quits for good, something in you will carry you forward. It's then you'll decide no matter what happens or happened to you, you're worth more." He paused. "I think that something is God." Then he stopped. He didn't say how he knew this or why or when he discovered it, but I sensed he spoke from personal experience, that what he said, he had believed for a long while.

There was a long pause before he began again, on his El ride home, long enough for me to try to turn the false bravado I was feeling into something substantial, something that might possibly help see him through.

"It's going to be okay," I stammered.

"I keep thinking about those boys," he coughed again, but this time it sounded like he was trying to catch his breath. "I keep thinking about being their fathers. How am I going to be their fathers?" He started to cry, and so did I.

Then I saw the closed bedroom door.

"Tim?"

"What happened to those boys . . ."

And here was the moment, at least for me—if this could be about me—where the world broke in two.

Before, "You'll be a great dad."

Then after, "Happened to me."

"Father J. B.," I said.

"Yes," he admitted . . . finally.

I don't recall the point in our conversation when I began gathering my own armor, but when I focused, I saw I had pulled out three blue-inked fountain pens and a legal pad. One pen was already in my right hand, cap off, and I was ready to write down everything he had to say, until he said, "There's a lot you need to know, but not just now."

"Tim?"

"Yes?"

We were trapped in a pattern of ebb and flow, me making sure he was still with me, and he, answering, but unsure how long he would stay. I took a moment to find my words. In the silence, my Casper darted into view.

❧

After the fire extinguisher blew and Tim threw the passenger door open, Dad chased him around our station wagon, there in the Cody, Wyoming KOA campground. That is, until Dad suddenly stopped, looked at his crop-dusted son, who leaned first left then right, not sure of which way to go, and let out a full laugh.

❧

"There are things we can do," I began. "I'll call people, get you an attorney licensed in Illinois, I'm not, you know that, and then we'll call the police. But I need to know something." After only six years of practice, I had seen what happened to people in lawsuits. They fell apart, especially when they thought justice was on their side.

"Are you ready for all this? You saw how the Church tried to paint those Boston kids?" I asked.

This time he didn't pause. "Yes."

"Do you think you can handle it?"

Yes again. I'm not sure I believed him.

"Tim?" Wave in.

"Yes?" Wave out.

"Do you have your voice?"

"Yeah, I do."

"Is it strong?"

"It is."

"Can it be loud?"

"Yeah."

"Good," I said, grateful for our legacy. "We'll need a strong, loud voice to speak over them."

❧

After my grandfather, Cletus Nockels, retired from the Chicago Fire Department in 1955, my grandparents left their Northwest side, Eddy Street home to move to what must have sounded like a dream town to them, Lake in the Hills, reminiscent perhaps of their upbringing in eastern Iowa. At the intersection of Hiawatha Drive and Pocahontas Trail they built a raised ranch, with a two-car connected garage—a luxury for any Chicagoan—and a full basement.

Throughout my 1960s and 1970s childhood, that home at 425 Hiawatha Drive felt like what I thought heaven would one day be: perfect. But this should have been my first warning.

It was a repeated ritual. On the last Saturday of July, 1975 in the year of this story, we made our way from Chicago to Lake in the Hills to celebrate the town's Founder's Day. My father knew where he was going, but I, at ten going on eleven, had the northern Illinois map in hand. I took on the role of family navigator in great part to be in the front seat, between Mom and Dad, and closest to the air conditioner, but also to be seen by those parental units; in a family our size, individual attention couldn't help but be a valued commodity.

From home, we took the Kennedy Expressway west to Route 31, which cut north, back then, through cornfields, prairie, and hill after hill of countryside. When the traffic slowed, it was solely to pass through fledging towns like Elgin, West Dundee, and finally Algonquin, each marked by water towers and schools, still family-owned grocery stores and Main Street gazebos. At the Fox River we turned west onto Algonquin Road, north onto Pyott, and then west again on Hiawatha until Dad pulled our Country Esquire station wagon into his parents' paved driveway. Dad parked the wagon on the grass to the right of the pavement so he wouldn't block his parents' vehicles, a Buick of some kind and a powder-blue 1964 Mustang convertible.

Chucka, chucka, chucka—the sound still replays on recall—went the churning water sprinkler, which was to our immediate right as my sisters, brother, one wild springer spaniel, and I bounded out of one car door. The cool wet of the grass under my toes was always a marker for me. Heaven ahead. We had arrived. We made our way down the gangway, by the neighbor's, Mrs. Mueller's, still blossoming lilac bushes to my grandparents' always open, back screen door.

ॐ

Linger here, because I always did.

The river-rock pathway and railroad-tie wall my father and his brothers had built first catches the eye. The pathway led to my Uncle Russell's and Aunt Ginger's house on Pocahontas Trail. The railroad-tie wall kept in place my grandmother's neatly assembled garden of tiger lilies, snapdragons, poppies, and black-eyed Susans. Surrounding all this were six old oak trees, scattered throughout the backyard. Around them, my grandmother, Emma, had planted dianthus and potentilla. The air will be heavy with humidity, the first hint of sweltering heat still to come.

If you look again, you might see my grandmother. From this angle, her large German-American buttocks are encased tightly in white polyester shorts. Her nylon knee-highs, suntan, are rolled down to her ankles. Her gym shoes carry blades of newly cut grass and thick, black soil. She is on her knees, pulling and weeding, lifting and attending, so that even the weakest summer's blossoms could find the light. The wild ducks are with her too. They followed her most mornings, anticipating the squares of dried Wonder bread she kept in the pocket of the apron still tied at her waist.

I opened their screen door and scampered into the basement before it shut behind me with a hollow, tin sound. I felt the cool of the subterranean room's air and took in the wafts of Tide laundry soap coming from the washing machine churning just to my right.

I had a choice there. I could walk into that generously large two-car garage and take a right again into the basement containing my grandfather's tool bench, my grandmother's craft room, floor-to-ceiling shelves of toys, and a pool table. But I chose instead to climb the steep linoleum-covered stairs and hold to its flimsy wooden railing. After my grandmother had her stroke in 1984, my grandfather would install an electric chair here to take her to the second floor. I knew she would hate it. But on this July day in 1975, we were ischemic stroke and arson-fire free. No harm had yet come.

My family had been the first to arrive, but within the hour we had all made our way. Uncle Russ, Aunt Gin, and Aunt Gin's mom Mrs. Golly strolled up the river-rock pathway. Their daughters, Sue and Debbie, were not far behind. Aunt Mary and Uncle Marty had the shortest drive over with cousins Michele, Michael, Melissa, and Maureen in tow. Then Uncle Dan, his shift over at the fire station, and Aunt Mary made it in from the city with Patrick, Russ, and Paul. Who am I forgetting? Aunt Bonnie, Kim and Jenny, of course, returned from the Jewel grocery store, where Uncle Russ still worked as a butcher, with enough popsicles and pop to sustain us through the afternoon heat. And Aunt Vivian would finally finish her morning run just as Grandma and Grandpa completed their lawn and garden maintenance. By midmorning, there were thirty of us filling the den, kitchen, back patio, and backyard. We sprawled really, unfolding long legs and spreading arms, taunts, jaunts, and smiles. This, too, was a *Before* memory.

Much later in the day, I recall, after a parade and beach outing, after lunch and homemade strawberry shortcake with whipped cream for dessert, I made my way through the kitchen and my grandparents' dining room, there quickly passing by the portrait of the mourning Virgin Mary. Uncle Dan, an amateur artist skilled in oils, had painted it. Grandpa told me that one time, when he walked by, Mary raised her eyes from the ground and looked right at him. Frightened still, I scurried past her, head down to avoid her possible, upturned gaze. I reached the living room, my intended destination, and was alone.

Late in the day, the living room was in full shadow and the air was cool. I remember breathing deep and making pretend cigarette smoke circles on the exhale. I brushed at the afternoon's sweat that dripped down the causeway between my shoulder blades. Barefoot still, I stepped up onto my grandmother's brocaded couch to reach the thick wood shelf installed high enough, at least I suppose she thought, to keep any small persons from disturbing it. I know my footprints on her fluffed pillows would mark my presence and that there would be other signs—a dropped Kleenex, a misplaced memento—I had been there, but none of this mattered, even if my usually kind and exceptionally cleanly grandmother could be terse. This was where I belonged.

In the photo before me, set on that high shelf's ledge, my grandfather is in his black dress uniform and hat. His tie is thin and straight. His right index finger rises to a point. With his angular profile, looking like F. Scott Fitzgerald, he turns to Chicago Mayor Richard J. Daley, also in the photo. My grandfather speaks. I was sure the mayor was hanging onto his every word and nodding his approval. "Yes, Cletus. You did a fine job. The city is safe, because of you," he *must* have said. Since Grandpa had retired ten years before, I long wondered how Mayor Daley got along without him.

Beside the photo were seven small plaster-of-paris models of fire helmets. With me skipping rope at his side two summers before in 1973, my father had painted six of the helmets a raven black. On top of the black, he added a white shield and on each shield he etched in gold 32, 108, 58, 93, 16, and 11—all the companies where my grandfather had served. Although not really necessary because of its original color, he painted the seventh one pure white, signifying Grandpa's last rank of chief, and etched in gold the number twelve, identifying the number for grandfather's battalion, which included the four firehouses that then encircled O'Hare during the airport's mid-twentieth century days of operation.

Cornflake-size slivers of white, Kiwi brand shoe polish, once used to bring my grandfather's dress hat to a gleam, fell when I picked up his hat from the shelf. When I turned its equally shining black visor to face me, my ghostlike image reflected back.

After much study during stolen absences from family gatherings over the years, I knew its every part: its braided headband, its shoe-polished surface and Windex cleaned visor, and the once-dank sweatband, which still smelled of smoke.

I next pressed my fingers to its crossed bugles insignia on the hat's central panel. I knew the crossed bugles signified my grandfather's last rank. And I know I made the sign of the cross, and silently mouthed the words, "In the Name of the Father and of the Son and of the Holy . . ." I nearly dropped his hat when I heard his voice.

"Chiefs carried real bugles so they could call their teams to them with a charge."

I turned to see my grandfather. He was still a few months shy of his seventieth birthday then. Except for his black belt and olive-colored tennis shoes, he was dressed in all white. He did that lately, composed himself in monochrome. He next mocked a trumpet hold, curled his right hand into a fist, raised it to his lips, and blew in apparent triumph, "*Brrr, brrr, brrr, brrrr.*" His head tilted back while his left hand rose to hold the cone of the pretend instrument in place. Then he looked at me and smiled. My attention could never fall, not from him.

He walked to my side, put his hand around the small of my back, and helped me jump down off the couch. After bending to pick up the fallen Kleenex, Grandpa pointed to a cushion on my grandmother's still spotless—I had done no harm—gold couch, and we both sat down.

In 1924 my grandfather moved from Decorah in the northeast corner of Iowa to play football for Loras College. I keep a photo of him from this time. He stands with his brother Paul on the sidewalk of some small-town corridor. A street sign I can't read is nailed to a tree behind him. He wears a two-button suit with a white dress shirt and a tightly knotted tie. Because he is slim and muscular, I guessed he played quarterback. He grips his hands low behind his back. His dark hair is parted down the middle, and he doesn't smile. He might have looked mean, even scary, like John Dillinger or Jimmy Cagney, were it not for his eyes. If he weren't my grandfather, I would call them smoky, sultry, and mysterious. I have no doubt that my grandmother couldn't resist him when he slipped a small note into her glove left on a pew during an Easter Sunday Mass. He was visiting a football teammate in her town of Dyersville when he saw her, the beautiful, tall, and curvy brunette. The note read, "*You can put your spoon in my coffee any time dear.*" She must have. They married just ten months later.

On Founder's Day in 1975, fifty years into his marriage, my grandfather's mud-brown eyes behind bifocals still smiled; not mysterious or sultrily, but with the grandfatherly love that I know he doted on each of his twenty-nine grandchildren, none of whom he didn't call his favorite. I could tell. He wasn't angry. Nor was he in a hurry. Instead, he leaned against the couch back and pulled me toward him. I sat in the curve of his right arm, raised my scabbed knees, and balanced his hat on top of them.

Perhaps telling of my future profession, I can still hear myself asking an automatic-rifle series of questions. "Grandpa, did the chiefs yell things?" "Did they scream 'Move that bucket line here,' 'The horses! They're in the way,' or 'Catch that baby'?"

"Yes," he responded repeatedly to each question. "They yelled all those things, all of them, if there were a baby or even an almost eleven-year-old girl to catch." His right index finger, the same one he held up to Mayor Daley all those years ago, tapped the end of my freckled nose. I wanted him to live forever, and I knew at that moment there would be no one I would love more.

"Grandpa?" I snuggled into him. I recall that he smelled like the barbecued chicken my dad was cooking on the grill. "Did you carry a bugle too?"

"No, Joannie. By the time I was a chief, it was 1948. I carried a radio."

"A radio," I think I repeated.

He rose, reached for the walkie-talkie on the shelf, and then handed it to me. I didn't expect to fumble it. It was heavier than I thought.

"Be careful. It's pretty old, kinda like me, I'm afraid." Grandpa took the radio back and placed it on the shelf. The hat soon followed, returned to its original mount. "There now, Mother will never notice," he assured me and with this statement alone swore to keep my secret. He held his arm out one more time, this time for me to stand up. Next he bent to face me at eye level for what, I know he was certain, would be another question.

And so I must have rattled off to get the answer I definitely recall. "Did you yell things too, Grandpa? Things like 'Move that truck,' or 'Hook the line to the hydrant'? I think this is what you would have to say, even in 1948."

He laughed, "Yes, Joannie. That's exactly what I yelled. Exactly," he might have said. In my mind, I see him brushing aside the long blonde bang seemingly always in my eyes.

"But I don't get it," I know I said, nose crinkled. "Why not just talk softly, in your normal voice? You had a radio."

He took his time before answering, just as I would one day do for Tim. And as I think back, in his eyes I adored, was that fear? Or maybe it was confusion about how to explain this to a child. Finally, he lifted his hands to my shoulders and gave me a squeeze.

"Unfortunately, dear, you'll learn this one day yourself." And next he spoke with a determination, which I, a kid who at age eight told her teacher poems didn't have to rhyme, knew hinted on metaphor. He said, "Fires scream and bang and whistle and pierce the air more than you could ever imagine. They have voices of their own. Voices you cannot control. No matter what, Joan, you will always need a strong, loud voice to speak over them. Do you think you can do that, Joan? Speak over a fire?"

April 22, 2012

With the Blue Line conversation marking its tenth anniversary and the death of my grandfather marking twenty, I enter Rome's Metro subway and scan the crowd of passengers for the many pickpockets my *Rome 2012* guidebook says might be my nemesis (if only its editors knew) and make my way, just two subway stops left to go.

First, to Cavour. The automated female voice plays, *"L'uscita é a destra."* Exit to the right? Yes, that's how the subway car's door opens. And, then, the next stop, my stop, his stop, is Colosseo.

"L'uscita é a destra," yet again.
Judge when to rise by the slow of the train.
We, *for I cannot be alone,* are here.

CHINOOKS

How did I get here, to the Colosseo Metro station in central Rome? I blame the Chinooks and all they carried with them.

வ

October 16, 2011

10:00 p.m., my time, 1:00 a.m., his.

By the close of that night, really in less than four hours, I had made my decision: find Ormechea. I shouldn't have been surprised. It wasn't out of character for me to make up my mind so quickly on largely significant matters. Rather, it joined a short list of rapid decisions, such as move to Alaska, marry Richard, and adopt Abbie. Each was made with little deliberation and came as naturally to me as coffee before writing, running long, and, as often as I could, trying to excel. In fact, each decision might have appeared after a cup of coffee, a day of writing, or a long run. That strive for excellence garbage? I really had no choice in that either. It was a coping strategy born of crowded living arrangements. If you want attention in a family of seven children, excel at something. Get a gold star for penmanship. Master the art of skateboarding backwards. Above all, differentiate.

On that October night, a westbound weather front, unusual for mid-October, brought Anchorage's already frigid temperatures into the high thirties and hurricane force winds to the upper Turnagain Arm. These winds, the Chinooks, swelled over neighboring McHugh Peak and followed the cut of Clarks Road until their hundred-mile-an-hour gusts reached the second hump of a hillside, just off the Chugach Range, and my home, surrounded by a forest of black spruce, birch, cottonwood, alder, and sumac, each root system holding to permafrosted soil.

This also was where an abandoned squirrel's drey and a leafless birch tree stood twenty feet outside my living room window, obscured in the darkness and facing a force that should have made them both fail. Like yelling that wouldn't stop or the unresolved grievance before the final slap, the wind was incessant, but I believed in that old tree and the squirrel-less nest clinging to it. They had both seen worse.

That night, a fire had returned to my woodstove through my own machinations: the loose wads of yesterday's *Anchorage Daily News* firmly in place, the pick-up-stick arrangement of kindling, lighting the match, and the five-second wait before the spruce tar hanging from dried needles ignited. Cottonwood shavings and remnants from the two-by-fours used to build last year's chicken coop were also put into place, and it wasn't long before, like that old Rice Krispies commercial, they cracked, sizzled, and popped.

Even though the wild winds rattled my aluminum roof and caused the three-quarter-time crash of the bathroom vent against its metal confines, the house was unusually quiet and finally argument free. Off golfing in Las Vegas for the weekend, Richard decided there would be another day for our discussions, perennially titled "What the hell, *JOAN*, are you doing?" And, after multiple readings of *Art and Max,* the story of two lizards with a penchant for painting cactuses and each other, Abbie, a child who always ran hot, was asleep on top of my bed in only her Cinderella panties. She was a princess ready for her fairy-tale existence, alleged crazy mother and all.

I remember rubbing my fingers against the cat-scratched arm of our way-too-expensive Italian leather couch Richard couldn't even look at any more since I "won" the declawing argument. I sensed something was coming, but I couldn't put my finger on it. What happened? Why this day? Eyes closed. Ears opened. *Crack, sizzle, pop!* When the heat seeped out and the metal of the stove box was too hot to touch, that was when the four dogs jockeyed for the closest place to the fire, only to be beat out by one equally determined calico cat.

The mystics in my Catholic faith—the faith I grew up in, the faith I left at the age of twenty for a bout of atheism, and the faith that was gripping me again—teach of voices that beckon. I didn't need to look further than my namesake, Joan of Arc, for proof. Of course she dropped everything she was doing when Saint Michael, Saint Margaret, and Saint Catherine suggested she reclaim France for the dauphin. For her, there was no choice in the matter, or if there was, the response was innate, a given, even if a burning at the stake would be the requisite result.

On the night when the Chinook winds rose, I heard the voices too, the voices that beckon—but they didn't come as saints. They came as Marley's ghost and the Spirit of Christmas Past with a decidedly Midwestern long *A*—the *traaffic* is *baacked* up on Halsted *Aavenue*—accent. They were, to my recall, forces just as strong as the incessant winds, and forces that came a long way to find me.

First from Chicago. When I closed my eyes, I saw an express train from O'Hare to Grand blow by my Harlem Avenue station, and I stilled my speed-dial thought to jump in front of it, just as Sister Irene had done when we were children. A Belmont bus kicked up gray ice and snow. A police siren wailed. A baseball bat in Wrigley thwacked. In his den at the Lincoln Park Zoo, Mike the polar bear roared. He wanted out. I was sure.

Next came the Nockels. Because of their strength in numbers and the early deaths on my mother's side (the weak Irish, letting plagues and rheumatic fever bring them down), my father's relatives dominated nearly every holiday, birthday, and anniversary. They were of Luxembourg and German descent, and a strong Catholic faith. The men, all of them over six feet tall, each had noses broken more than once. The women with rules and structure could be counted on for certainty on all matters. And all had strong, loud voices capable of drowning out competition, be it a human or natural force.

The firefighters among us, I called to order. My grandfather, Cletus, a chief. Here. My father, Walter, also a chief, son following father. Here, but trying desperately to leave. My uncle Dan. Even still, here. Because of Dan, we learned the dirge of a firefighter's funeral march and heard it long after it was played.

A captain, let's say it's my father, approaches a suspended brass bell the size of two hearts spilled open. He reaches his white-gloved hand for the slight, silver hammer placed on the burgundy velvet cloth just before him, right next to his dead brother's helmet. Despite being only recently found in the electronic store's charcoaled remains, the helmet is polished to a perplexing gleam.

That captain will strike the bell eleven times in total, and after the third and sixth strikes, he pauses long enough to whisper something to me. But what? *It's your turn now?* Or *Can you find him? For all of us?* Short of the questioning, the sequence means this: the fire is out, the heat is subsided, nearly all the first responders are returned safe to quarters, and our brother, our sacred burned and bloodied brother, is safe, home.

Although they were always unaware, I, the firefighters' progeny, was still caught in that unfinished third stanza. I was that twelfth gong waiting to sound. If they looked, they would have seen. When they charged, I followed.

As a result, I'd grown weary of things and people burning.

Last, last came our seeming root, the force that linked us, if I was to dare try, to good Saint Peter himself. And so I opened the church doors and religion came calling. Dad studied briefly in seminary, and Mom long considered becoming a nun before they both chose the vocation of marriage—a lifetime calling—to each other instead. We were children steeped in the sacraments— baptism, first communion, and confirmation, prepared inevitably for marriage or, saints be blessed, holy vows. We were educated in post–Vatican II Catholic schools, first through twelfth. Sunday after Sunday, one holy day of obligation to the next, we filled our church's pews, crossed ourselves with holy water, kneeled, and sang out. *Through him, with him, and in him. In the unity of the Holy Spirit...*

That's why I know. The Church, family, Chicago, and fires; these were the forces and voices, as powerful as an early winter's first Chinooks, which still sent forth a four-alarm call over too many years and too many miles. As their child, I seemed by nature locked in one response. Run always toward the flames and then, of course, always return home. But what if they were one and the same?

It was on brief reprieve from their summoning of me that I looked across the living room to a photo perched on top of my piano. In it, it's an autumn day in 1972, cold enough for sweatshirts and jackets, yet a bright sun streams through the yellowing and burnt-orange leaves of Chicago's Forest Preserve woodland. The neighborhood kids, my siblings, all but Maureen, and I had scaled a fallen oak and pose on the tree's still thick and leaved branches for one parent's camera. I am dressed as I always was. Messy. My green-apple Yogi Bear Campground sweatshirt barely extends over my stomach to reach the waistband of my rumpled brown corduroys. Though just at my shoulder's height, Tim stands tall next to me, looking like he knows something it would take the rest of us years to discover. Legs spread beyond shoulder's width, he seems firmly planted in the past, safe, home.

⮩

When Tim and I and seventy million other Americans were kids, *Sesame Street* ran a little musical segment called "The Fireman." Opening shot: the doors of a fire station rise, and a fire truck pulls on to a busy city street. Firemen stand two abreast on each side of the truck. As it speeds down the road, engine roaring, sirens blaring, the no-wimps-allowed rule must have forbidden all but the driver and captain from riding inside. I knew by training—that is, many visits to my father's firehouse behind the old Gateway Theater—this truck with its cab separated from the main body was a hook and ladder. The name was in reference to the long, clawed ladders the firemen once attached to windowsills and rooftops in difficult-to-access locations like alleys or narrow gangways.

Back to *Sesame Street*. As the hook and ladder makes a tight left turn, an electric guitar and kazoo start playing, and a Simon and Garfunkel–sounding duet start singing in half-note time "Fireman Ready to Go," by William Barnes Brown. They sing about big red trucks and ask who is going to help you when you're out of luck. There's only one answer. *The Fireman*.

All was well and good, I supposed, with firemen off to save the frail, but I always liked the third verse the best, because it spoke to what Tim and I also knew. Fake Paul and Art ask what firemen listen for when they are busy playing cards or cleaning firetrucks. Enter again, musical accompaniment and a "Ring, Ring, Ring, Ring" by an actual one. There again is only one answer. The Fire Bell. Cue, singing along. *The Fire Bell*.

Although it was likely a violation of some unenforced policy, my father often picked Tim and me up from home, in a hook and ladder no less, to take us to Fire Company 108 to spend the night. He kept us largely out of sight and trouble. As captain, Dad had his own room, and except for our permitted inspections of the two trucks—a pumper kept company with the hook and ladder—and one ambulance, in his room we largely stayed. On a shared bed, with spotless, army-tight sheets, we played Crazy Eights or Go Fish. Still, the song was right. Lying fully clothed, yet shoeless, we wrapped ourselves in borrowed blankets and pretended to sleep, waiting, really hoping, for the fire bell. *The Fire Bell*.

When the bell did ring, Dad would lift us into the hook and ladder's cab and once on site, command us to stay put. We were obedient children. We listened to the radio for any orders Dad or the battalion chief might have for the crew. *"Truck 108, we need three men at the ..."* door, window, curbside, hydrant. Although there was a lot of movement outside, usually the only thing I could see clearly was the reflected light from a neighboring ambulance or police car shining on Tim's face in one-Mississippi intervals.

What we came for could have been a burning building, a trapped elevator passenger, a smashed car, or a false alarm, the last the most likely of scenarios. Dad would sometimes come back to the truck furious at the thought that some "hippie asshole" believed pulling a fire alarm for no reason was some kind of entertainment. But he just as usually came back proud of his men (but for the occasional paramedic, there were no female firefighters during the majority of his tenure), pleased they arrived on-site in three minutes forty-two seconds and that they secured the scene in 48.5 seconds. Happy they listened to instructions, took care with the ladders, verified there was plenty of compressed air in their breathing apparatus, and never cracked a face mask. No. Thanks to that fire bell, even in the case of a false alarm, his team could be tested and rise to his highest accolade. "You're a hell of a crew,"—Tim and I included—"for following all commands."

On the night when the Chinooks rose and the specters of my past came calling, I knew I wanted just that: a fire bell to alert me not only to danger but to the chance of danger. Absent that bell, all I had to call me was an inherited vigilance.

In the way of Chinooks, the wind grew silent at times, as if it were trying to determine its next direction. Once decided, it bore down like a blue whale's long exhale, sucker punching the house at its foundation. Shake, rattle, roll went the brittle windows, ill-timed to the "Moonlight Sonata" playing on the stereo. When the lights flickered and I turned to see if the Anchorage skyline had disappeared, my German shepherd, Cletus, raised his head to look at me. Even though he was nearly thirteen and his brown eyes had a cataract shine to them, it was difficult to escape his watch. Sensing he was in my attention as well, the thump of his tail hit the hardwood floor. His panting started and next I heard the strain as he lifted his body by the forelegs. Within seconds his chin was on my lap.

It was shortly after I became certain my first husband was not coming back and, despite my pleas, he would not be returning our dog that I made my way to a local rescue group to pick up what had been scrawny, sixty-five-pound shepherd someone found running loose at Anchorage International Airport. The first rescuers named him Bart, but the name wouldn't stick. I needed to call him something capable of reminding me, at least twenty times a day, I had been loved.

Of course I chose Cletus for my grandfather; Clete for short, and I was right. I said his name twenty times a day, usually with the word *don't* in front of it. In time, I was eventually ensured of both love and blessing.

I'm certain psychologists had a name for what I was doing. Projection, probably. I just called it metaphor. Cletus became my grandfather, my faithful shepherd, my constant friend, and he brought me back, through sheer repetition of his name, to the land of second chances.

As for my other psychological state, my continued vigilance for Tim, for a time it had been useful too. I found him an Illinois-licensed lawyer and counseled him from a distance through both the criminal and civil portions of his case. I identified witnesses, interviewed those witnesses, and, when they gave more names, interviewed more witnesses and victims. I drafted Tim's and my father's legal affidavits and submitted them to Tim's attorneys for further review.

It wasn't enough. To pursue prosecution, Illinois's then applicable criminal statute of limitations required Tim to come forward no later than his twenty-first birthday in 1987, and, like the vast number of child sexual abuse victims, at that age, Tim had no ability to link consequence, a life falling into disrepair, to cause. How could he?

As for the civil lawsuit, I kept my mouth shut when Tim elected to pursue a legal settlement over trial and did my best to explain the clause in the settlement agreement that most concerned him.

"Read it to me," I said.

"Neither this agreement nor any of the terms or provisions hereof shall be construed as an acknowledgment or admission of wrongdoing or liability on the part of the Archdiocese of Chicago, the Passionist Order of Jesus Christ, Holy Cross Province, or John Baptist Ormechea."

"Does it end there?"

"Yes. It sounds like they're saying they did nothing wrong. Not even that Ormechea."

Tim's father-in-law was dying and another baby, the future Cody, was on his way. Tim had decided it was time to settle. It wasn't for me to push back or challenge, and so I told him, "It's standard, Tim. It's in all kinds of settlement agreements. It's the insurance companies that insist upon it."

He swore a couple of times I can remember and said, "So we did nothing to stop them." It wasn't a question.

Encourage him.

"Tim, you did stop him, because of you, he's not a pastor anymore."

"So he gets away with it?"

Keep encouraging.

"No. He can't hurt kids anymore."

I could tell he didn't believe me. Hell, I didn't either.

"If he doesn't admit it, Joan, he gets away with it."

After the settlement, all I had left to offer was my attention. I listened for Tim's verbal cues and took stock of his mental state through conversations with our sisters and the most frequent visits to Chicago that I could afford. I also tried to imagine the best of scenarios for him, as if those well wishes could make things right. On the night of the Chinooks, I imagined Tim in a northwest suburb living in a three-bedroom bungalow he could easily afford. Light music, Rachmaninoff, maybe Mozart, playing as my brother slept. His last words to Lisa before nodding off would have been, "We're so lucky." His oldest son, Hunter, had just mastered his young scientist's test, making snow come out of pressurized water hose, and his youngest, Cody, conked out right after a short football practice, his stomach full from hot dogs, no ketchup, the sign of a properly trained Chicagoan, and macaroni and cheese for dinner. True, Tim's alarm would ring in less than five hours and he'd take the family's one car, in need of a new muffler, to the Vernon Hills train station for the commute to the Chicago Board of Trade where, for the time being, he still had a job. But at this moment, he could get his sleep, without ghosts, and he would wake up fresh, ready to start his day.

If Tim was to have despair, I willingly asked God to give me that despair instead. Did it make sense to wish someone's nightmares and worries on yourself? Of course not. Once described, my therapist initially suggested I suffered from a form of survivor's guilt. Her explanation also empirically made sense of the dreams I had since leaving for Alaska. Backdrop: always a war-torn nation. World War II, Korea, Vietnam, Rwanda. No matter our ever-changing ethnic heritages, Tim and I ended up huddled behind the remains of a building. I would whisper, for fear of detection, "Come on, Tim." In one dream his name was Hans, "We have to go." "Hitler's closing in." In another, "The Viet Cong are here," or "The Hutus have machetes." We were in this together. I wanted him to know I couldn't leave without him and I promised never to do so. But, inevitably when I woke middream, I always had. I always left him behind. I think that's because at a time when I could have made a real difference, maybe even rewritten his story, I did just that. I left him behind.

❧

I remember some details more than it seems fitting, but this no doubt is the nature of memories. The life-altering ones—the ones you wish you could take back—have a way of staying with you more.

It was an early evening on a school night. My parents were in the basement my father had recently refinished. Instead of the exposed load-bearing metal poles and cold concrete floors, which had served well for Tim's and my Matchbox car racing, the room was now carpeted. The paneled walls, a dark sierra, were largely empty, not yet adorned with family portraits still to be taken, but on one wall was a portrait of my mother's father, George Blackburn, as a long-haired, two-year-old toddler. The room was cool and inviting during the summer, but on this day, it must have been late fall, I was chilled just standing in the stairwell.

They were watching television. Dad was in his usual side-job clothing, a paint-stained, white T-shirt and blue cotton pants and Mom wore a white turtleneck with a matching macramé vest. Were they watching *Happy Days, Charlie's Angels*, or *Barney Miller*? If I could remember the show, I would know the weekday, but that detail is gone. The stairs were not, however. I stood halfway down them taking in the new carpet smell. I rested my arm against the high shelf above the stairwell and rubbed my fingers along the monarch butterfly figurine that hung there. My grandmother had made it three years earlier out of shards of orange and black glass.

I know I yelled to them so they could hear me over the blaring laugh track or criminal-chasing music, whichever it was. I yelled, "Where's Tim?" I was fourteen, which would make Tim thirteen, an eighth-grader, a football player, and an altar boy.

On this day in 1979, I needed Tim for something. It must have been important. I asked my parents again, this time succinctly "WHERE IS TIM?"

Dad called back. "Father J. B. is counseling him. They're in his room." I didn't see my father's face because the now panel-encased metal pole in the middle of the room left only his long legs visible.

"Why?" The Magnavox kept drowning me out. "Why?" I asked again. "Why's he counseling him?"

"Tim's upset," Dad answered. "He needs help," he was quiet for a second and then added, "from God." Next, Dad went back to watching TV. I don't recall my mother saying a word.

I walked back up the stairs to the main hallway. Tim's room was to my immediate right. Its door was shut. Who does that? Shut a door with a child? *I guess a priest taking confession*, I must have answered myself. I stood in the hallway for what I remember to be minutes, but it must have been shorter. I focused on the door, waiting for a sound or the turn of its knob. I didn't like this. I had that gut feeling that you know as an adult not to ignore but as a child could make no sense of.

I had noticed J. B.'s eyes kind of glimmer when he joined the boys, never the girls, to play during grammar school recesses. When he patted their heads and pulled them into bear hugs, I suspected something was off. It wasn't right—was it?—that the boys were calling him Father B.J. and Father Blow Job?

Still, there I stood in that hallway, stationary as if long chains reached up from the soil beneath the basement and held me to that place. I heard nothing. I saw nothing. But that's also because I did nothing. I never opened the door! And then, chains somehow loosened, I walked away.

"When you needed consoling as a child, where did you go?" Marsha, my longtime therapist, asked quietly during one of our regular Wednesday sessions in 2011. Her office was a light yellow and it appropriately smelled like lemons. She held herself bad posture free, like the yoga teacher she also was. Her lips were painted in a bright pink lipstick that fit her, always full of spring. Her turquoise earrings matched the flats she wore on her mountain-posed feet. Although sixty, her brunette hair showed no gray and her face was relatively wrinkle-free.

By comparison, I sat curled and fidgety. The business skirt and blazer I wore were too confining. I unbuttoned the jacket and fingered a hole in my nude-colored stockings. It didn't seem to make a difference. My eyes darted to the clock behind her. Only ten minutes were left. Marsha saw what I was doing. There were many times she had to remind me that it wasn't my job to end the session on time, but hers.

I answered, "To books, I loved to read." I then added, "And also, a few times, behind the living room couch," another pause, "or the garage."

She queried further, "Notice you didn't say your parents? You didn't go to them for comfort. Is that the kind of answer you would expect your daughter to give when she's older?"

It took some time to register what she was saying, and I didn't want a name for it when she also said I suffered from what was called undifferentiated childhood trauma. *Undifferentiated* because there is no special event or catalysis; for example, no priest coming into my bedroom for weekly visits. And absent an event I can recall as singular in effect, my trauma began with a lowercase *t*, not a capital one. My parents fed me, clothed me, sheltered me, educated me, and loved me. They might have ignored me a little, left me to fend for myself, but who didn't do that then, especially in large families?

I should have been fine. But the thought was, at least my counselor's thought was, as I aged and my parents became busy with my younger siblings, I became less attended to. They weren't there to pull me out from behind the couch, or even know I was behind it. To cope with parental absence, and, in the end make things worse, I set up my own managers to perform the parenting tasks.

My seeming favorite parent was the taskmaster. When I was asked to visualize her, she was old, mean, and cruel. She held a pointy finger right to my face. When I needed to get out of hiding and do my homework, for example, my taskmaster would grab my hand and tell me, "Get up, you slimeball. No wonder no one cares. You want to be seen? Well, here's how you do it. You have a social studies test tomorrow. Get an A." Then, perhaps trying to show her softer side, the taskmaster would add, "You're not gonna know unless you try. So up and at it. Make a mark."

I listened to her. To increase my value, I set goals and, surprisingly, achieved them. Top grades, not a problem, and long into the future, tough cases, better so. Move to the end of America to prove I could. I'm on it. Choose a husband who looked good on paper. Sign me up. Then get divorced. What? "That wasn't in the plans, but don't mope. How many times do I have to tell you? Get over yourself," the taskmaster would chide.

All this might have been okay if my "feel worthy" drive didn't convert smaller tasks into competitions. To date, I still have to empty the dishwasher without interruption, finish reading any book I start, and check my phone incessantly for work emails. Give me a goal and I damn well better achieve it. And if I don't, anyone out there, you were right not to love me. In fact you should have never tried.

These thoughts were what my therapist called "false realities," but realities to my body and its muscle memories nonetheless. And so, when a workplace criticism or a fight with Richard put me out of sorts, I ended up in one place. I was ten again and hiding behind the couch, waiting for the taskmaster to pull me up.

To her credit, she was an effective manager. While her job was never to love me, it was to keep my body from remembering and feeling long-ago, lowercase *t* traumas. Hence, when I feared failure or lack of love—identical consequences to me—my taskmaster came out to goad me into creating external worthiness. Her aim was simple. To protect me, I must have worth. With achievement, there would be no need to hide behind a couch ever again.

She was not alone. To carry me to adulthood, other managers came forward. When I was threatened, for example, the well-read, defiant, angry teenager who could cut the attacker to the quick with a verbal arsenal appeared. Her skills came in handy in every courthouse or hearing room in which I've appeared. And when I believed there might be something more to this existence than a one-way trip from cradle to grave or that I actually had internal worth, my doubter appeared to question these so-called "facts" and protect me from future disappointment.

When it came to Tim, or my dog Clete, or any other person or animal in need, the most important manager was the rescuer. While the taskmaster was a crone, the rescuer had to be lovely, for her job was solely to interact with those in need. Thus, to me, and to them, I hope, she was beautiful and charming, as well as kind and selfless. Most important, she needed to be a warrior who wouldn't give up even if her intended beneficiaries had. With empathy to the excess, she made it her job to protect others from any perceived harm. Her aim was always the same: she had to open that goddamned door.

I had a perfect role model to emulate, and on the night when the wild winds rose, she was also in ready view. Next to the autumn-day photo of the standing firm Tim and all, I kept the unframed notecard my one surviving aunt on my mother's side—Sister Ann Carolyn Blackburn, Lorraine, her birth name, to me—had sent me long ago. It was small in dimension, no bigger than an index card. On the cover was an imprint of a tall girl-woman dressed in a medieval breastplate and wearing a long flowing skirt, but beneath the skirt, her legs and feet were covered in armor. Her left hand struck a curtsey pose. Her right hand held up a staff that looked more like a cross. From it, a banner flowed straight back. She must have been facing a headwind because her long, wavy dark blonde hair flowed backward as well. And while her nose and lips looked as if they were painted too closely together, her eyes were doe-like and innocent. She was looking up, toward heaven. The halo around her head radiated beams outward as if she were the center of a star. The back of the card told me what I already knew from an earlier day's education. Her banner, undecipherable in the wind, read "Jesus Mary." She was ready to go to battle for them.

Inside the card, in the correct cursive writing style that marked her for life as an elementary schoolteacher, my aunt explained her own personal affinity for St. Joan. She wrote:

> Dear Joan,
>   Here is your loving saint and protector. She did many things beyond what she ever dreamed of. I think she has guided you all these years and helped you attain many of your goals. What a wonderful person you are and meeting so many challenges in this world, in this "now" which is here each day.
>   Love and gratitude,
>   Aunt Lor
>
> P.S. I have a part in Saint Joan of Arc. I was born on her feast day.

I loved Joan of Arc since I first dressed up like her in third grade. While conscious of our dabblings into witch and hobo costumes, the nuns and lay teachers at Immaculate Conception tried to get us back on the Catholic track by requiring us to dress as our patron saints for the All Saints' Day 8:30 a.m. Mass the day after Halloween. And so, I made Joan's armor and shield out of cardboard and her banner out of white felt bought from Van's Variety on Northwest Highway. I sketched "Jesus Mary" out in Elmer's Glue and dusted gold sparkles over the lettering. I borrowed my brother's plastic sword and made my way, suitably armed, to Mass.

Like my firefighter role models, I immediately understood Joan. Just gear up and go, even if it was her own Church that needed fixing. Poor Aunt Lor, giving Saint Joan and not my taskmaster or rescuer the credit. Nevertheless, I did suspect my rescuer was desperately trying to emulate my patroness when she called me that Chinooks night to my holy-hour vigilance.

It had been almost a year since I quit my job at the Anchorage District Attorney's office. Despite constant effort, I think on both our parts, the DA and I never agreed on the way to treat low-level and juvenile offenders. I should've gotten the clue at my interview when her second-in-command remarked my job would be to lock people up in small cages. That was accurate, I knew, for the worst offenders. But prison recidivism rates of sixty-seven percent alone showed that jail wasn't sufficient to stop the next low-level crime. What was really needed, at least in my thinking, were effective substance-abuse rehabilitation programs and the guarantee of a good job. That was me, you see, even rescuing the low-level offender.

About the time Richard left for Vegas, I had just gotten around to emptying the last of my office boxes. Three items from the task were still on my coffee table.

The first was Garrison Keillor's anthology *Good Poems for Hard Times*. I had kept it on my desk, right next to the sentencing guidelines. I was the only assistant district attorney this side of history, so I thought, who relied on poetry to deal with the hourly exhibitions of human frailty I saw in jailhouse courtrooms or in grand jury proceedings. That night I paged through the anthology's selections, wondering what it was at the time about Stanley Plumly's "Detail Waiting for a Train"—

> The main floor of Penn Station, early,
> the first commuters arriving, leaving,
> the man outstretched on his coat,
> wide circles of survivors forming.

—or Rita Dove's "Dawn Revisited"—

> Imagine you wake up
> with a second chance

—that caused me to mark these particular poems on some long-ago day with post-it notes. But before I could recall, out from between the pages fell the second item, my notes from an October 2010 sentencing hearing.

I had been at Nesbitt Courtroom 502 by happenstance. Afternoon felony arraignments had just concluded, and before I could bring my two banker's boxes of charging documents out of the courtroom, about one hundred people walked into it. Solemn faced, casually, but professionally dressed, men and women both, no children, but for two, they filled up all the seats in the court's gallery, and, when there was no more room for them, they opened the swinging gate into the court's well and filled the jury box as well.

A colleague from the DA's office came to sit at counsel table. This wasn't her case, she had told me. She was covering the hearing for her boss. Someone who, we could quickly tell, had cut a deal the victims' supporters did not like.

I walked outside the court's gallery and checked the calendar posted to the left of the door. The next hearing, a change of plea, was for a man whose name had not made the *Anchorage Daily News*. I reentered the courtroom and stood in front of the door well just as the burnt yellow-clad defendant, white, bearded, and well groomed, was led to his public defender at counsel table and unhandcuffed.

Next, a round, white-haired, and usually smart judge entered the courtroom from behind the bench and called the proceeding into order. He gave the name of the offender, informed him of the rights he was waiving by agreeing to a plea deal, and accepted the entry of his guilty pleas. They were to two Class A felony counts for sexual abuse of a minor.

I'm not sure why, but the defendant had scored a sentencing deal that would find him out of prison before his victims—his own daughter and her best friend—graduated from high school. Before the judge could legally accept the plea, the defendant had to face his victims and the adults who knew how to love them. The goal of this group was to try to convince the judge the brokered resolution was unacceptable and an insult to justice. I took out my pen.

On the day of the hearing, Autumn was just thirteen years old. I wish I recorded more about her mental state or if she held her friend's hands or looked toward her father as defendant, but my notes only told me she was pretty, had long brown hair, and was petite. Based upon speeches given that day, I know she sat in the jury box surrounded by a representative from Victims for Justice and her newly adoptive mom, a one-time neighbor and the birth mother of the offender's other victim, Autumn's best friend.

The abuse had started after Autumn's mom died, when the little girl was five. However, the crimes weren't discovered until the defendant added Autumn's eleven-year-old friend and classmate to the mix.

Autumn had been too afraid and nervous to speak, so the victim representative read Autumn's speech into the record. In it, Autumn tried to convey how four years of prison did not come close to atonement for the crimes her father committed. She also said Autumn was not her given name. She had changed it upon her adoption so she wouldn't have to hear the echo of her violator's voice every time her new mom and dad called her to dinner. The victim representative continued channeling Autumn: "I've thought about killing myself. I've hated my life. And I know you don't recover from this. You endure it. It's a conscious choice, every day, every month, year after year."

Although Autumn's words left the judge wiping a few tears, he eventually dismissed his initial reaction and accepted the plea deal. He told Autumn and her friend they were both strong enough to get over this one day and to have happy lives. As for me, I knew better. My shoulders shuddered with emotion no one in that courtroom could have ever understood.

Next, from the Keillor anthology, a poem by Lee Robinson, "The Rules of Evidence":

What you want to say most
is inadmissible.
Say it anyway.
Say it again.

What I wanted to say to that poor ADA sent to the courtroom without any knowledge of the opposition to the plea and to the round judge who told the young Autumn that she would get over this, was "OBJECT." In no way did this plea serve the interests of justice and show society's condemnation for the crimes. "AND SUSTAIN." "Sustain the objection, Judge. Plea deal denied. No easy way out for you, defendant daughter fucker." Why didn't these people know any better? Being raped as a child is not something you get over. It's something that can kill you. Which brings me to the third item on my coffee table. Beneath the anthology of poems was yet another reminder.

Just before putting a rope around his neck, on January 2, 2011, twenty-eight-year-old Princeton graduate student Bill Zeller had elected to post his last will and testament on his web page. Three days later, his brain-dead body was taken off life support. By then his suicide note was trending across the internet. I kept a copy.

In the note the young, promising computer programmer, as he was many times described, admitted for the first time his first memories as a child were of being raped repeatedly. While there were times the aftereffects of the abuse were less intense, he said the resulting darkness had followed him "like a fog." He explained:

The darkness is with me nearly every time I wake up. I feel like a grime is covering me. I feel like I'm trapped in a contaminated body that no amount of washing will clean. . . . So I've realized I will never escape the darkness or misery associated with it . . . I'm just a broken, miserable shell of a human being. Being molested has defined me as a person and shaped me as a human being and it has made me the monster I am and there's nothing I can do to escape it. I don't know any other existence. I don't know what life feels like where I'm apart from any of this.

Bill Zeller didn't make it. Who knew, yet, about Autumn? Would she escape the darkness, make the daily choice, as she described it, to endure? Or was there a rope around a pull-up bar somewhere in her future too? I said a silent prayer for her benefit, but my focus could not afford to be deterred.

11:00 p.m., my time, and 2:00 a.m., his.

On that night, six months before Rome, in a northwest suburb, my brother slept. I needed to believe he was holding on.

So let me speak, even though many have done so before, of the dark night of the soul. Let me correct St. John of the Cross. There is no joy in suffering. Though years have passed and people have rebuilt the best they are able, they know darkness's presence.

It was a cold air that seeped through the uninsulated brick wall of my childhood home. And, on a night when one birch tree and one squirrel's lay took a beating, it had traveled miles to find me. Asking, beseeching to stay, not to be vanquished under the power of acceptance. For just this once, just this night, anger and vengeance wanted to remain.

Don't think we had it beat. For I promise, somewhere, that night, a child closed his eyes and hid in his own shadow. Somewhere that night there was no light, no God, no Joan of Arc breaking through a closed door. Somewhere, that night, the weight on the corner of a bed sunk, a little one turned away, and you, me, we . . . we did nothing to stop it.

Did you recognize it then? Your sheer lack of power? Did you stand at the fence and rattle the locked gate? Did you scream and then howl louder? And even though you couldn't see through the darkness, I know you could sense what was happening? He held his breath. On the exhale, the air disappeared from his lungs, just as sure as the hope from his eyes, the love from his heart, and the faith from his soul.

Tell me about forgiveness, and I will tell you about the ultimate act of betrayal.

HOTEL LANCELOT

෨

Sunday afternoon

To reach Via Dei Fori Imperiali, the Colosseo Metro stop dumps its passengers through an unadorned and utilitarian door looking more fitting as an opening to a latrine than to the Colosseum. In fact, this is how I will recognize it on my future subway excursions through Rome. Look for the place I have no desire to enter.

Once outside, a little after five, sun close to setting, my eyes have little time to adjust. The Colosseum stands before me. And just as Anchorage's late afternoon sun transforms the Chugach Mountains into alpenglow, Rome's bathes the two-thousand-year-old amphitheater in deepening shades of marigold, lemon, and goldenrod.

My hotel's website said, if I'm "feeling energetic," I can walk the four blocks from the Metro station to its front door. Just "head for Via San Giovanni en Laterno and after the Church of San Clemente, turn right toward the steps and a little ahead on the left you will see trees and a green gate." And this is how Italian directions will soon seem to go. "Look for the bread shop and then kitty-corner across the street from it you will find a purple door, go two doors farther." Got it. But when I look up from my handwritten notes taken from that website and scratched on the back of an Alitalia napkin, all I see are minute Italian cars and Vespas leaning into the rounded curve of a crazy careening street I have no idea how to cross. To my left is a more fitting alternative. A sign for a taxi stand.

As I hand the cab driver—a placard says his name is Emiliano—that same napkin, with the hotel's name and address scrawled upon it, all I can think is that cab drivers everywhere must hate short trips. As suspected, Emiliano looks none too pleased and even seems to make a noise like Mr. Snuffleupagus's *garumph*. He turns the steering wheel quickly to the left, pulls us into the roundabout, and we are off to the chariot races.

I catch one more glance of the Colosseum through the taxi's back window. I would say I think inexplicably of Russell Crowe, but it is really not inexplicable. Almost ten years ago, each of my girlfriends and I were equally infatuated with his broad chest, gorgeous kneecaps, and starring role as Maximus Decimus Meridius in *Gladiator*. We even held a birthday party for him, which he understandably could not attend, at my house. The video in my brain would have continued to go on about this—theorizing about what kind of cake we had or whether Anchorage's spring break-up—better known as mud season— had yet started. But in less than two minutes, Emiliano hit the brakes for a fast stop. The green gate, spruce colored to be exact, of the Hotel Lancelot nearly touched the taxi's front bumper. All I can think is *How did I get here?*, then, just as quickly, *It was the Chinooks' fault*.

But maybe not exactly. It was my fault that October night, when the winds blew, for walking toward the glowing apple on the back of my computer, lingering my fingers over the keyboard, and then typing out the inevitable, "ORMECHEA J. B.," on the Google search engine screen.

For years, the retrieved headlines and newspaper articles were the same.
PRIEST REMOVED IN LOUISVILLE
PRIEST'S ACCUSER SAYS HE HOPES TO PROTECT CHILDREN
PRIEST, HIS ORDER FACE SUIT ON ABUSE
TWENTY-FOUR VICTIMS OF VARIOUS PRIESTS SETTLE
Until more recently, when a new set of screens came into view.

At some point around his June 22nd birthday in 2009, Ormechea had set up a homepage on the Passionist Global Network, this a Facebook-equivalent social media site for priests of his order and members of the laity who were their friends, parishioners, or supporters. The website identified him as "John Baptist Ormechea, cp, Rome, Italy," and for an oddly unnecessary reason, added the descriptor "male." Next to his name and gender was a photo.

Judging by the angle, he looked as if an exterior camera had been mounted to his computer. I couldn't help but wonder what other images might be found in his possession, if anyone was overseeing him. But in the photo, his nose is flatter, and his teeth are smaller and more pointed than I had remembered. His cheeks are pudgier. His right eyelid droops behind wireless eyeglasses. Despite the obvious aging twenty years has wrought, time has been kinder to him than I had wanted. He wears a pale yellow polo shirt, and he has a tan. He looks way too happy.

❧

Two of my sisters, Julie and Joyce, were bartenders for most of their twenties, so I know a thing or two about tipping. If you want to be in someone's good graces, even for a short cab ride, tip well. The fare is three euros. Ignoring the exchange rate, I pay Emiliano as if each euro were a dollar and add another twenty percent.

The tip must have done its job, because once Emiliano sees me struggling to open the gate into the Hotel Lancelot's courtyard, he steps out of his taxi to help me. His right hand, well-manicured I see, reaches far to the right of the gate, farther than I would have ever thought to look, for the buzzer. It's hidden under some kind of thick Italian foliage that smells like grapefruit.

"*Grazie,*" I say.

Finally! Here it is, the first word of Italian I've spoken since arriving on Fiumicino's steaming hot pavement a few hours ago. I had no idea when I landed I would descend airplane stairs and step out onto the tarmac. I wondered if in the fashion of John Paul II I should have sunk to my knees and kissed the ground, but I chose otherwise and said nothing. The customs agent just got a shake of my head when he waved me through. And when I was struggling to get a train ticket, no *un biglietto, per favore* could pass through my lips.

For the first two hours since landing, I was stuck between high school Spanish and a level of desperation I wanted strangers to understand by simply looking at me. "*La machina e vechia, la machina e roja, le machina e vechia e roja,*" my *Drivetime Italian* CDs taught me on my commute for the past six months. Why I would need a red, old car was beyond me. But it seemed all my language preparation—that is, since I decided to come to Rome and find Ormechea—never in fact occurred.

❧

There is a bookshelf behind Ormechea in that photo he chose to post. An American flag and a statue of the Virgin Mary are on the top shelf. The next two rows are filled with photographs. I enlarged the image to try to see who was in them, but only got increased pixels as a result. It made no sense for him to keep photos of his victims. Didn't it? Surely his superiors would have stopped that, but they hadn't before. What would make the present any different?

Despite Ormechea's unpunished felonies, the thought occurred that it was me who was the criminal, the cyberstalker, not the old priest. I searched everything he had written and the home pages of all his supposed friends. He had ten, all former or current priests. There were Bill Nash of Ashfield, Massachusetts; Jean Ormechea, his brother, of Flint, Michigan, later, I saw, moved to Arizona. Next, Herman Koten of Palermo, Italy; Homero Filho of Rome, they became friends just two months ago; Felipe Nunes of Jamaica; Father Aurelio, also of Rome; Lukas the seminarian of Warsaw; Father Orven of General Santos City, Philippines; Dan Mailan of Nederland, Texas; and Blaize Czaja of Houston, Texas. Except for Blaize and Jean, most of these men looked to be in their twenties or thirties. For a period of time, they messaged each other.

> September 30, 2009:
> From Enno: "Father J. B., nice to see you here. Hope everything is well in Rome, we had a wonderful celebration last Sunday. Thanks for your prayer."
> To Enno: "Thanks much for the welcome, Enno. Congratulations on your Final Profession. Heard it was a great celebration . . ."

Final Profession? There he was, speaking of priesthood as immutable. But hadn't that been the truth? After criminal prosecution, his order took no further sanction against him beyond sending him to Rome. Abused child after abused child and still able to turn the water into wine? That was about as final as it got.

> That same day, September 30, 2009:
> From Orven: "Hello friend. Welcome to globalization. Hehehe. God bless!"
> To Orven: "Thanks amigo, for the welcome . . . . great song . . . . Hope all is well on the third floor. Hehehe jb"

"Hehehe," huh? And what had happened on that third floor? I could dare to guess.

❧

Emiliano is not the only one to see my gate-opening distress for just as he rings the bell, the smoked glass front door of the hotel opens and out steps a trim, perhaps Middle Eastern man with skin bronzed as if he were fresh from vacation. I'll soon learn I was too far west. The man is of Pakistani descent. He has salt and pepper hair, primarily salt, a sharp nose with a surprisingly bulbous end, soft lips, and chocolate brown eyes that are framed by well-manicured eyebrows and long eyelashes. I hear my mother again in reference to those long eyelashes. *They're always wasted on the boys.* In an olive green tweed vest and tightly knotted maroon tie, he walks through the courtyard, releases the latch on his side, and allows me through. Of the six languages he speaks, he has no troubling discerning which one to use for me.

"Good afternoon, you have arrived!" he says in the queen's English with enough excitement I *must* be a long-lost relative. Like a Disneyland greeter that Richard, Abbie, and I recently encountered at Minnie Mouse's Waffle House, he sounds thrilled that I'm here.

"Yes, I have!" I reply with equal enthusiasm. I'm tricked back into speaking English. As if that were difficult.

My guidebook describes the Lancelot as "a comfortable, yet elegant refuge." What I knew with certainty at the time I booked the room was that I would need a refuge, a soft place to fall, no matter what I came here to do. My as-yet-unknown handsome guide, who smells like baked cinnamon, turns and leads me through the hotel's outer courtyard.

I will notice many things about this courtyard over my seven-day stay, such as how its gray cobblestones pierce through my thin-soled Tevas, most especially after a long day of walking, and how the scent of lilies masks the presence of any cigarette smoker. But most important, I'll think the rain sounds different falling here, kinder in its greeting than I might ever have expected or deserved.

The messages continued:

October 7, 2009:
From Blaise: "John, Hope all goes well there in Rome. I am in Texas finishing some vacation. I head tomorrow for a mission in Cheyenne. We are all in a state of shock over the health issues James Thoman is having. Enjoy the Fall."
To Blaise: "Blaise. Thanks for the message. Good to hear from you. Have also

been enjoying your videos' etc. on the Province Message Board. . . . Never a dull moment here in Rome!!!! Good luck on your mission in Cheyenne. I'm sure it's really changed since I drove through there many years ago. And yes, the health issues of Jim Thoman were a shock. He has our prayers here at the 'Mother House.' Take care."

Never a dull moment in Rome? Somehow the ancient ritual of lions and Christians together in one Colosseum sounded positively inviting.

His last post was to Lukas, the seminarian, of Poland.

Lukas, I was happy to receive your request on the Passionists. Hope you are doing well. You are missed here at John and Paul's. Looking forward to your next visit. *Bueno domenica!*

We are inside. My host is already behind the front desk as I take in my surroundings. A small white-marble-tiled lobby; stairs and an elevator in a corridor behind me; and even farther back, a sitting room with gold-dipped angels who are blowing kisses in my general direction.

"And you are?"

"Joan, Joan Wilson," I say, handing him my passport and keeping my birth name out of it. It has one of my better photos in it. Hiding a neck I think is too thick, I often compensate by tipping my chin too low, but not in this photo. I look seemingly normal, pretty even, with awake eyes and a smile of straight teeth finally in place after getting braces in my thirties. In my driver's license on the other hand, I made the mistake not to smile. I look like one large, sad downturned forehead.

"Yes, Ms. Wilson. I am Faris Khan."

Kubla Khan. I think first of Samuel Taylor Coleridge, but then I recognize the name from my guidebook and the hotel's website. "Oh, Mr. Khan. You own this hotel."

"That is correct, along with my mother. You will be certain to meet her."

He smiles every time he speaks to me. Nothing overwhelmingly, just a slight upturn to his soft lips, a nice trait for a hotelier. He next looks at his computer screen and appears to count the days, tapping his fingers to his left thigh. "I see you will be with us for seven days and six nights."

"Yes, I'm here through Saturday."

"Wonderful! That is a good amount of time to see our city. You will not be rushed. Is this your first visit to Rome?"

I'm so tired that I think I love this man. "It is. I was in Italy before, right after college twenty years ago, but I never made it south of Florence." My Italian really is remarkable.

"Florence is a treasure." When he says *treasure*, he rolls his *t* and *r* together as if he were trumpeting truffles on Trafalgar Square. "But I hope you will find Rome to be without compare."

"Mr. Khan," I say, "I already have."

There is a way for those outside the Passionist Order to "friend" a priest. All a person needs to do is enter their e-mail address, type the words seen above in italics for verification, *upon* or *December*, and make the request. But he'd have to accept me, I mean, the requestor, first.

Perhaps I could have said I was "Carlos" a cousin of "Father Enno." I could add I've heard about the "Mother House" and would love to visit when I come to Rome for the first time, next spring (That's when the thought first came to me. To go to Rome in the spring). I'd add that I heard from Enno *so* many wonderful things about him. One thing I remembered about Ormechea. He loved flattery.

And if accepted, I wondered what I would do next? Would I call him out immediately for all to see?

Hey J. B. hehehe. Still fucking the little boys? Don't even think for one moment I'm not watching you.

"Well, Ms. Wilson. If there is anything I can do to make your trip a success, please let me know."

Perhaps you might tell me where I might buy a .22 caliber pistol?

Mr. Khan is looking at me with his head cocked to the right, just like Cletus back home. I'm so fatigued, for a second, I wonder if I have said this out loud.

When a manager is out, be she taskmaster, rescuer, or an angry teenager with a penchant for swearing, "The human it directs is more in the past than the present," Marsha has told me. The manager encourages a body memory that keeps the human from healing. And so, you are afraid. You fold yourself into the comfort of a fetal curl. You are enraged. Your shoulders broaden and your eyes widen.

More past than present, more past than present, more past than present, until you do one thing. Tell yourself to breathe. It's not the breath alone that moves you forward, but rather the intentional command, even if to an involuntary reflex.

Breathe. Frontal lobes reengage. Breathe. The room I'm in looks familiar. Breathe. Snoring dogs, pleased cat, burning logs. Then go inspect the damage you've done and make amends.

૨⊌

"Ms. Wilson, if there's anything I can do to make your stay just what you desire, please let me know."

"I will, thank you, but as you see," I shake my head like a dog after a bath, "I think I'm falling asleep. I'll be certain to have questions once I have my wits about me." *And they should not involve procuring arms.*

He reviews my passport. "You must be tired. I see you began your travels from Alaska."

"Yeah, I'm from Anchorage."

"I've been there myself, visiting family. I wonder if you might know my aunt? She lives in Anchorage too."

Although part of the least populated state, Anchorage is still a city of three hundred thousand people. We have Walmart and Target, Starbucks and enough car dealerships to line miles of the Old Seward Highway. We are in fact a city on the edge of the supposed last frontier, which, in turn, lost its frontier qualities with the invention of snow machines that go in reverse and semi-automatic rifles that shoot snow geese from high out of the sky. While I might expect to run into a friend or recognize a distant acquaintance at Sea-Tac Airport, the gateway to Alaska, my chances of knowing Mr. Khan's aunt are nil. All this is what I am about to say when he adds, "She runs a marketing business there. My auntie's name is Sarah, Sarah Evenson. Do you know her?"

I nod my head and smile. "I do, in fact, know your aunt, Mr. Khan. I've met her at a mutual friend's home a number of times." I don't add that this was while I was going through my divorce when even my good friends started to avoid me because of my deep depression. I likely made a terrible impression on Sarah. I continue. "She's also the neighbor of very good friends of mine in the Turnagain area of Anchorage. You've been there?"

While I live almost as far up the hillside in Anchorage as one can go and not be in state park or national forest land, Turnagain is the trendy portion of Anchorage, close to downtown. Residents, like my friends Jon and Doug, take 1950s box houses and convert them with thick glass, steel beams, and refined woodwork into potential contenders for the cover of *Dwell* magazine. Sarah owns a lot behind Jon's and Doug's house and will likely build a sparkling, architectural wonder, especially for Anchorage, on a new street with a coastal trail and Mount Susitna views.

"I have," Mr. Khan answers.

Still I change the subject. "I do know your cousin even better," I say. "Garrett, Sarah's son, and I were legislative aides together in the early nineties. His office was right across the hall from mine. That is, back when he needed a job." I'm smiling again like I'm in on something I expect Mr. Khan to know. At the age of thirty-two, Garrett married a seventy-plus-year-old woman, who happened to be an heiress with names like Vanderbilt and Whitney in her background. I banter on, "The last time I saw Garrett was on television at a horse race a couple of years ago. His horse, Lucky Charm, had just upset a contender for the Triple Crown. Dang that Lucky Charm." Mr. Khan looks away and I suddenly realize, again, that I'm making no sense. Whatever I'm to do here, I just need to shut up for the time being.

I hit the red *X* and sent Ormechea's homepage back into the ether world, then stood and walked to my piano.

"Not only play majestically, but be majestic," my long-ago piano teacher Mrs. Malley once told me over its very keys. I leaned into the images above it. Tim on fallen oak. Joan with her unseen, but expected, Jesus Mary.

The thoughts came to me in a flurry.

The darkness is with me nearly every time I wake up.

I've hated my life and I know you don't recover from this. You endure it.

An already-made decision. Like Alaska. Like Richard. Like sleeping Abbie. Make a victim's impact statement.

If they don't admit it, Joan, they get away with it.

Be heard. Be seen. Rome in spring. Seek the truth. From *Father Hehehe Bueno Domenica Ormechea* himself.

Not a bad idea. Majestic even.

❧

"Well, this is indeed a small world, Mr. Khan."

"Yes, it is. And please call me Faris. Now, is there anything I can do for you at this moment?" He can help the lost feel found.

"Mr. Khan, I, I mean Faris, thank you for your offer, but at this moment, the best thing I can do is sleep."

❧

In a northwest suburb, my brother slept, peacefully so, hopefully so.

❧

"Of course. I will have Antonio show you to your room."

Just as Faris speaks, I hear shuffled, soft-soled footsteps to my immediate right and see young Antonio is already present. He carries a silver tray with a bottle of water on it and reaches for the room key Faris is extending.

"Let me offer this advice, Ms. Wilson," Faris continues, "it is just after five. Why don't you rest for two hours? We will ring you for dinner. As you probably know, we sit down for a prix-fixe menu each evening. You can then get a full night's rest afterward. This will set you up for a good tomorrow. In addition, I am the chef and hope you will enjoy the meal I'm preparing." That explains the smell of baked cinnamon.

"I think I can manage that," I say. "Thank you, Mr. Khan."

"Faris."

"Yes. Thank you, Faris."

The elevator was slow to arrive, so Antonio and I decided to walk up the spiraling staircase instead. He carries my computer bag while I hold on to my backpack by its handle. On the second floor, he opens the first hotel room door that faces us, room twenty-three, places the bag on a nearby chair, and turns, not even waiting for a tip. Julie and Joyce would be disappointed I don't chase him with a euro in hand, but I'm too tired for any pursuit.

With his departure and the silver tray now in my hand, I look over the room. It's no bigger than the outdoor sauna at our house. Still, with a twin bed, a nightstand, a chest of drawers, a chair, and a small writing desk, it has everything I need.

Above the writing desk is a framed lithograph captioned VEDUTA DI PIAZZA DE SPAGNA, a view of the Spanish Plaza. I think of Audrey Hepburn skipping down the Spanish Steps with a vanilla ice cream cone in hand before Gregory Pecks bumps into her, accidentally on purpose, of course. I also think of Abbie.

To prepare for my visit, in addition to *Drivetime Italian* CDs, she and I watched movies filmed in Rome. *Eat, Pray, Love. Return to Me. Cinema Paradiso.* And even *Angels and Demons* with its scary self-flagellating priests. But *Roman Holiday* always made the top of the list. Abbie and I watched it together at least three times.

I would try to say things to ease her, like, "I need to go to Rome for a little bit, my darling, so I can find where we will both go together. I promise to be right back."

"Oooh," her toddler-pitched voice responded. "But I want come with, Mama."

With each repeated request to join me, I petted her soft brown hair incessantly, still not believing, a year and a half after the adoption, I get to be her mom. My answers to her requests rarely varied. "No, not this time my sweet, but soon, I promise. I'll find the best places for us to go together. Like the Spanish Steps, where the princess in *Roman Holiday* got her ice cream."

I reach out to the lithograph and peer closer. No ice cream there. The Spanish Steps are still being constructed within it. Next, I place the silver tray on the bottom shelf of the nightstand. On the top, I put my phone and photo album. Its cover is thick cardboard, so outer photos stand like they're in a frame. In the one facing me, Abbie is dressed as Snow White for a Halloween-themed kids' running race. She's holding up her candy cache. Richard leans toward her. Both are gooning happily for the camera. I meet them with a frown. "I'll come home," I promise, not acknowledging the anger I feel welling, especially when I'm so close.

I take a drink of water. It seems to keep an oncoming headache at bay. "Remember to hydrate," I told myself, three flights ago. I stand and open the window, which faces the interior courtyard below. Italian words—*necesario, blanco, finestreno*—stream in. Someone might even be arguing, but I'm without any context to interpret intonations.

I lean my head into the bathroom and see just what I need. Soon I'm standing, eyes closed, letting the high-pressure shower take away the sweat and dirt extended travel brings. The lilac-scented shampoo falls into my eyes but doesn't burn. I hear the crunches in my shoulders and backbone as I try to unwind them from too many hours of sitting erect. My right hip, always the worse for wear, seems to pop back into place.

It's then I drift back to the conversation with Faris. How did I choose this hotel exactly? It was one of two closest to the Curia. I know that. No more than a ten-minute walk. A requirement. But I tried to book at the other hotel first. I only chose here after learning the Nicolas Inn was sold out.

"I wonder if you might know my aunt?"

"I do in fact know your aunt."

A small thing, I know. But when you're traveling alone, about to face a man who has taken so much from so many, small things matter. Small things make the difference between having courage and having none.

"And what else was odd about my day?" I say, willing myself to a recollection I'd already checked off, thanks to my doubter, as mere coincidence, but perhaps I was wrong. It was on the plane from Madrid to Rome. Our flight had been delayed before we boarded. A crowd at the Barajas Airport gathered around the gate agents, who had talon-like nails and looked as if they could not have cared any less. That's when a man, looking perhaps like the pilot, stepped forward. Initially, I thought he was Spanish, but he spoke Italian in a soft and confident voice. I think he said *"tarde"* and perhaps *"idiotas,"* but I may have made that up in my mind because I was more interested by this fellow's bravery. Every word he said was met in response by a pummel of Italian expressions and gestures from his mixed audience, businessmen, a few priests, I think, a group of college students, and well-dressed, quintessential Italian women in exceptionally tall heels.

After the pilot man spoke, I heard another man looking to be in his early forties and with close-cropped hair explaining in English to a British couple the reason for the delay. Our flight was three hours late departing Milan. Once it arrived, we would board quickly and perhaps make up some time.

Two hours later, that man ended up sitting in the aisle seat across from mine. But on this plane, the center aisle was so narrow we could've been seatmates.

Like Faris, he had a kind face. Even though dressed casually in khaki pants and a walnut brown blazer, I had the distinct feeling he might be a priest. I smiled at him once or twice. I'm not sure why. Since 2002 I looked at all priests I didn't know well as potential pedophiles. Anyway, about halfway through the flight, whether priest or not, the man reached for his briefcase and took a Bible from it.

He turned to a specific page, he was not simply browsing, and started to read. From my viewpoint, I could easily tell the text was in English. I could just as easily tell something else.

"To Timothy, my loyal child in faith," the facing page and epistle from Saint Paul read, "Grace, mercy, and peace from God the Father and Christ Jesus our Lord."

He was reading from the Book of Timothy.

My Tim was born breech on the last day of January 1966 during a cold spell that sunk Chicago temperatures to well below zero for one week straight. From what my mother told me, however, my relationship with Tim began long before his birth and those frigid days. When his hands and feet punctuated our mother's womb, she said she told me, her feeding baby, "He's reaching toward you, Joan Mary, his Irish twin," a term for children born in quick succession of each other. Although two generations removed from the home country, my mother was still a Celtic charmer. Once I finished drinking and my sucking sounds were replaced with rhythmic breath, she would remind me we rested together, my brother and me, in double-decker slumber.

Both obedient Catholics, my parents searched the January calendar of saints' feast days for my soon-to-be-born brother's name. They did the same for a girl, just in case, but with two daughters already they were hoping for a son. John was a possibility. So too were Francis and Aiden. If they dared, Bobinus, Tarskius, and Saturninus could also have been in the running. Instead they chose to name him for Saint Paul's faithful servant, Timothy.

The Greek origin of the name Timotheus is said to mean either "honoring God" or "one honored by God." To be the faithful servant or to be bestowed upon. My brother as it turned out would lose both chances.

What I fear the most today are a failure of words and the resulting inability to justify my choices. Will a future reader or faultfinder think there is a critical disconnect between subject—me—and object—revenge for Tim. For if anyone were to think my brother was not worth what has amounted to struggle after struggle over the last ten years of my life, I would have done Tim a great injustice. Ten times ten years. That is his worth. So, as you see, I've only just begun.

The house Tim first came home to was short on floor space, but excessive in plastic-covered furniture and light shades of green—I heard we shared a crib for afternoon naps and slept together head to toe. My hand instantly wrapped around the arch of his foot like an involuntary reflex, "Nearly every time," Mom said. From his birth, my mother told Tim, "Be comforted, dear one, your sister can't let you go."

We lived then . . .

When Tim was just one and a half and I was pushing three, I stood next to the tire swing hanging low to the ground from a single Dutch elm on our front lawn. There, Tim made his way through the tall grass that was in need of a cutting. With each movement the blades engulfed his lower body. When he reached me, he grabbed onto my legs and tried to hang on. I bent down to lift him but fell on top of him instead. We rolled gently onto the lawn. When the wisps of Tim's translucent blond hair tickled my nose, I let out a child's giggle. He smelled like a honey-made graham cracker and became my first memory.

In 1969 our family moved to the suburbs of Chicago. Tim and I filled our days with constant patrols for the salamanders and chameleons that lived in our basement window wells and any other place where floodplain waters, in this new town built atop a one-time cornfield, still might gather. When we found our wiggling friends, we carried them to the ripple of a creek, which we insisted on calling the big river, behind our home. On the way back for lunch or supper, we always stopped to feed carrots to the neighbor's horses. It was there I told Tim, the first person ever, "I love the country much more than the city." And he replied, "I know, country mouse. I know."

I was five and Tim four. His wisps of translucent hair had morphed to thick, dark blond. His bangs, slightly parted at the middle, reached just past his eyebrows. His eyes seemed darker then, browner then. His nose shared the same shape as mine, a small upturn at the end, but it and his cheeks were a mask of freckles.

"Can I connect them, Timmie?" I would look at him with a green magic marker in hand, pointing at his face. With a smile and quick sprint, he'd soon be out of my reach—exactly where the sound of his laughter, the vibration, the tenor, currently resides. "For me, it was like a spring of fresh water in the desert."

That's what Saint-Exupéry's pilot said about the Little Prince's sound of glee. I know it was the same for me too.

For Tim and me, our story of faithfulness was born on long walks to the big river and the small subset of years when it seemed it was just the two of us.

Was it just us? If so, I wonder how could it ever have been? When my cousin Carole's mother died and the little girl came to live with us as a sister, it was seven children who filled the dinner table and station wagon, not two. It was seven of us who crowded around the television set for Saturday morning cartoons and who played long games of Monopoly late into the Saturday night evening. Nevertheless, it's Tim who stands out in my memory, who was always at my side.

❧

Well, at least before we were teenagers. It was Tim's thirteenth birthday, and we hadn't been that close lately. My family was gathered at another table in another house, after our move back to Chicago, to watch him open a small pile of presents.

"Pretty soon you might need this to keep the girls away," my father joked. He used Tim's new tennis racket to strike at the pretend contenders for his boy's affection. Our Springer spaniel Spot nearly knocked over the dining room table thinking a ball might be coming his way.

He is here.

"Here, open this one next." Father J. B. pushed a ribboned and bowed box toward the boy dressed in jeans and a Steelers jersey. Tim ripped both off and opened the box. He eventually pulled out a thick, burgundy red dinner plate and looked at it queerly. The words *You Are Special* were painted in gold and cursive style along the plate's edge.

J. B. reached for the plate.

Perhaps my recollection has been influenced by reality for no one, other than John Wayne Gacy (who at the time happened to live about two miles away) looked better to play the part of child predator than he did. In 1979, J. B. was forty-two years old. He was of eastern European stock, just shy of six feet tall, and, I expect, around two hundred-twenty pounds. When he wore his black priestly garb it slimmed him, but his stomach was soft. So were his hands. Not a single callus. Despite that, his skin had the bronzed color of a working man's. His relatively full head of dark brown hair was parted at the far-left and swept over his wide forehead. His gold-tinted aviator eyeglasses cut his thick sideburns in two.

Behind those eyeglasses, I wasn't quite sure. "He smiles too much," I once told my father. "And when he does, I think he looks wrong." Because he said it on more than one occasion, I'm certain Dad's response was, "He's filled with joy because he's God's representative on earth. Who can ask for a better job?"

"You see, each of you can use this," J. B. said, focusing on the plate and actually looking at me for a sustained moment, a rarity for him to even pause over a girl, "when you have your own special day. Say, a birthday or you get an A on a test, whatever it might be. Let your mom and dad decide." His attention soon returned to Tim. Next came a pat, a seeming constant to Tim's shoulder.

"Thanks, Father," Tim muttered, quickly turning to his next gift, which was from me and Mom. When he opened it, I volunteered, "It's the baseball glove you wanted, Timmie. I figured we could take it down to Wrigley to see if Buckner or Macko might sign it." The gift had been my idea, some way to reconnect.

Since 1972, when I was eight and Tim seven, we had lived on a street called Palatine, named for one of Rome's seven hills, on the city's far Northwest side in what was often called policemen/firemen's corner, because there were so many of them we called neighbors. Our houses were built after World War II in the city's expansion to the west. These brick four-bedroom, two-bath homes came with unfinished concrete basements and overworked furnaces that could barely keep their new inhabitants warm.

Unlike our country home by the big river, where only one boy named Fritz lived nearby, Tim had his pick of playmates to choose: the Antkoviaks had two, the Tierneys and Pennacchios each had one, the Stantons four, and the Branders five. Count them, at least thirteen boys in a two-block radius. And so when the back screen door would slam shut, it was usually Tim off to some sport with Stan, Steve, Charlie, Joe, Mikey, Billie, Tommie, Jimmy, Billie Two, Mikey Two, Jimmy Two, Tommy Two, and Danny.

By the age of thirteen, Tim didn't join in, but he didn't defend me from taunts about my looks from the boys either. Even if I were being kind to myself, I'd have to say I was going through a homely puppy stage. By the time of Tim's birthday, my hair had finally grown out of its Dorothy Hamill cut, and like J. B., it seemed, I'd chosen a far-left part for my dark blonde hair, so it covered the acne on my forehead. In doing so, my lengthening bangs were often swept under the round plastic frames that were at least eight times the width of my eyes. My cheeks were round, and I no longer smiled open-mouthed. When my dentist asked my mother if I was going to be a model, she replied with what I took as a "do you see what I see" look, and he confidently announced I wouldn't need braces. And so, I hid my inward-turning front teeth behind closed lips. I hid myself too, in any book I could find.

Despite my at times faltering relationship with Tim and J. B.'s seemingly more constant presence, I still knew the priest was right about one thing. Tim was special. He was still the boy who assembled model airplanes whenever he could. Smelly glue scented his fingertips even after a good washing. He was the fastest of all the kids on our street. And before Chicago streetlights turned bright amber, he was the first of us each night to point to the rise of Venus on the horizon.

He was primarily kind. When the rest of us complained, Tim said he liked Mom's chocolate chip cookies, especially the burnt ones. He never wanted her to go out of her way, insisting, for example, that each birthday a Sara Lee pound cake would be perfect for dessert.

Even in these days of early adolescence, we did have one last just-between-us ritual in place, courtesy of Deborah Kerr and Yul Brynner. I'd grab the album, turn the front-room record player on, and drop the needle to the tenth groove of Rodgers and Hammerstein's "The King and I."

I looked at Tim, half hidden under a table or behind a couch, and raised my arms. He rose, grabbed my hands, and with each beat of the orchestral music that once joined Miss Anna and the King in an acceptable embrace, we pushed and pulled each other into our own version of waltz, weaving between and jumping over pieces of furniture as necessary.

This is when he laughed the laugh I can't remember . . .

This is when we danced.

Are you ready? Because, I'm still not. Not just yet.

Between Tim's thirteenth and fourteenth birthdays, Ormechea's visits came with greater frequency. They must have been more difficult for Tim to predict, because even if Dad were spending the night at the firehouse, Ormechea would still show up for dinner. He didn't have to ask. Ours was an open door. He was even welcome the five days before payday when grocery shopping was off limits and Mom scavenged the cabinets for something nutritious to feed us.

"So Mary, I was wondering..."

On one such night when Dad was at the firehouse, J. B. sat in an armless chair upholstered in the yellow and brown checks of our country themed kitchen. He leaned forward and rested his left elbow against our sunflower-yellow countertop. Mom stood at the kitchen sink washing dishes in scalding hot water with Palmolive soap, no gloves. She regularly looked out the window over the sink to the gangway between ours and the Antkoviaks' house, but turned back whenever he spoke.

I was her official dish dryer that night, with seven of us, we equally shared the chore, and turned toward him as well. The lemon-yellow kitchen curtains, even brighter than the countertop, reflected in his eyeglasses. He sat comfortably slumped in the shape of a letter C and turned in such a way he could easily monitor any movements, perhaps, to him, even invitations, emanating from my brother's closed bedroom door, just down the hall.

I don't recall what he said next, but I have no doubt he spoke in his animated, sing-song voice or that he giggled, somewhat like a little girl, or that he kept my mother engaged. If I were to guess further, I would have to say he was saying something about God because he always talked about God, especially to her. Man, he was a master. "Oh, Mary..." He spoke in a tone that said, "I get it, I've been there, and so has God."

At a certain point, after the dishes were dried, Mom would've noticed Father's coffee cup was half empty and would've filled it with the decaf drip remaining in the percolator. Before sitting at the kitchen table to join him, she excused me. Before heading upstairs to finish my homework, I knew I should talk to Tim. Something about that April day had been bothering me, and I thought he might understand.

I opened his door quickly after just one knock. I don't think he even said "come in." I noticed his lights were off, so I switched them back on. At their first flash, I saw Tim sitting on top of his comforter, but braced like he was ready to leap off it. He had the look of a scared snowshoe hare. He was dressed, still in his Notre Dame High School junior varsity basketball shorts and jersey. Although he was still a couple of years away from his growth spurt, he was muscular. I was prone to challenge him to arm wrestles I would always lose.

"Whoa, calm down, it's just me, Timmie," I remember saying. I laughed a bit, and then I saw him sigh. Even though I could've caught him doing the things all manner of thirteen-year-old boys must do, he seemed relieved it was me. He gave a casual lift to his chin and motioned his hand for me to come farther inside. I'm not sure why, but I shut the door behind me. Relief again crossed his face.

Tim put another pillow behind his back and sat up straight. He leaned against his helm-shaped headboard and the stormy-ocean-blue wall behind it. He raised his knees. White tube socks, with yellow stripes, rode halfway up his calves.

Questioning my choice and uncertain of his interest, I stammered. "Sorry to bother you." I sounded a bit like a waitress trying to close a tab before the end of her shift. "But I came here 'cuz I was wondering if you remember what today was?"

He gave a blank stare that said no.

"It was eight years ago today, April seventeenth, that we left Crystal Lake and moved back here to Chicago."

"Eight years to the day, huh?"

"Yup."

"How do you remember things like that?" He sounded interested. Did I tell him? Name the date. Papa George's death. Then Aunt Pat. I record every time we lose someone.

"Because it was the day Cha went missing." This was a reference to my cat. He tilted his head, puzzled. "It's not like we didn't find her, Joan." It was Tim who did. He heard her in back of the moving van and brought her to me once we reached the city.

"I know, but it wasn't my choice to leave her behind." I tried to explain that Mom and Dad got tired of looking for her, and added, "It was my job to keep her safe."

He seemed resigned to help. "Got it, Joan, but she was found, and she is still here, I bet on your bed. It all worked out fine." Next he changed the subject.

"So," Tim asked in a voice I now recognize as pensive, "is he gone yet?"

"Nah, he's still in the kitchen talkin' to Ma. I think it'll be soon though. I heard him say he has the 6:00 a.m. Mass tomorrow."

Tim turned toward his nightstand and rustled through his top drawer. "Then do me a favor. Stay here for a while, okay?" He pulled out the deck of cards he was looking for.

"I got an idea. To celebrate our eighth anniversary here and Cha being safe," he pulled out the cards he found, "let's say we play Crazy Eights?"

Only after the front door was deadbolted, with Ormechea outside of it, did our game finally end. These are the things I take stock of now. Recording what I've lost . . .

When he was alone and ravaged.
   Don't think we had it beat.
   When he thought no one was on his side . . .
   Stand at the fence and rattle the locked gate.
   I wish I could have told him . . .
   Scream and then scream louder.
   "I'm here, I see you, and we will bring this to an end."
   Why I didn't? My only explanation is my hand slipped. That's the only reason I would ever let him go.

PENCIL ERASERS

Sunday night

I'm late. By the time I've made it to the Hotel Lancelot's dining room, just the other side of the kissing angels I first saw two and one-half hours ago, the salad plates are being removed. Faris is pouring wine for a table of guests across the room. He looks in my direction and points to the single empty chair to my immediate left. According to the hotel's website, a distinctive feature of a stay here is the communal meal "where hotel guests eat, sharing tales of their lives and their travels." As I near, the five seated people look up almost simultaneously.

"Hello," I say to the man closest to me, the best dressed among us in his white shirt and a olive-green tie. I managed to dress for dinner as well, but I'm too far down the jet lag scale to look refreshed. I apologize for being late, explaining neither a wake-up call nor phone alarm managed to rouse me. Before Robert, that's his name, lets me know he's just transferred from a World Health Organization post in Gambia, his home country, to WHO's Roman headquarters, Faris has seen to it that a green salad and fresh baguette are placed in front of me. I eat quickly so as not to slow up the *secondi piatti* for my tablemates.

Robert will explain what I think I read on the hotel's website as well.

"The owner of this hotel. Have you met her yet?" he asks in even more perfect Queen's English than Faris's. "Her husband had worked for the WHO. Now many of its diplomats stay here on their way to and from assignments. I myself will be here for a week, before I move to an apartment here in Rome."

"We have that in common. I'm here a week as well." I smile and, even though I didn't intend this as an invitation, so does he.

Besides Robert, my other dinner companions are all traveling together from their home parish in South London. To my immediate left are Barbara and

Douglas, a sixty-something couple. Barbara has a beaklike nose and is exceptionally exuberant. Douglas, who shares his wife's nasal design, wears his baby blue, button-down shirt a little too unbuttoned to reveal a large golden cross and graying chest hairs. The cross is knobby and molten, just like the golden nuggets sold from the rows of gift shops lining Anchorage's Fourth Avenue.

Barbara and Douglas seem kind. They've brought their college-age children along on the trip. Barbara points to her son's and daughter's chairs in the far back of the room, where Faris had been pouring the wine.

"Melissa has already been a handful," Barbara explains, "asking for this and that and seeming to forget she is here out of *our* good graces." Douglas nods in agreement. I let her know that while going to college, I thought the world was all about me as well. I even asked my parents if they ever entertained the thought of not having children after me or at least Tim. Then, I argued, they might've had money to help me get through school.

On the other side of Robert is Samantha, a thirtyish African English woman new to her parish. Over a plate of pasta, which keeps an unending smile on my face due to the six tablespoons of butter in its sauce, we compare notes. She's left her four-year-old son home alone with her husband for a week and just called tonight to check on them.

"No crisis yet," she explains sounding like Princess Kate.

"None on my end, either." Although Richard once preferred not having children after his son and daughter with his first wife, Abbie has her father entranced.

Samantha is also a runner. She tells me, "There is a beautiful park just uphill with very nice pathways."

"Celimontana?" I ask.

"Yes, how did you know?"

The honest answer would be, "Why Samantha, I've plotted my path to and from Ormechea's door for months. And should I need to leave quickly, this park will help do the job. It's right by his door and will make for a fast getaway." Instead I tell her I saw it on the walking map Faris provided me when I arrived.

Next to Samantha is Vivian. She's Barbara's age and is dressed like a post–Vatican II nun in a long, flowered skirt and matching sweater set. She's polite but says very little by way of introduction. Like Samantha, she travels without a spouse or partner. Judging by her grimaces when Barbara or Douglas speak, I tend to think she's not enamored with either of them.

The Brits, there must be thirty in their group, have all returned from a day spent touring St. Peter's Basilica. Barbara points to a man at the head table and explains that he's their guide. I see only the back of his head. Although he wears his gray hair short, it's balding in a monk-like fashion.

"It was hysterical. Matthew—that's our guide's name, Joan—wore a blue and gold tie to Saint Peter's today. It was *absolutely* identical to the ties the Vatican police wore. They thought he was one of them."

"You mean the *gendarmerie*?" I ask, thinking of my movie-watching training, this time from *Angels and Demons*. As if my brain is short-circuited to visual entertainment, I also recall my sister Julie's favorite line from *Moonstruck*. "It's Johnny Cammareri," someone with a steady increase in pitch and nasal tone says when Danny Aiello's character comes back from Rome to break up with Cher.

"Yes, well I think so," Barbara says ignoring my internal monologue. "And that Matthew! He spoke with such authority!" When she said this, she tossed her short red hair back in a way that made me think it had once been long. "I truthfully believe those officers would've done anything our Matthew asked of them."

Aha! I can see. She has a crush. When he turns to profile, Matthew looks a bit like Michael Caine. He's more handsome than her husband and likely more educated as well, at least when it comes to Italian history.

Once the main course of white fish, roasted carrots, and squash arrives, previously silent Vivian points to a tiny sort of man sitting next to Matthew. As I look, he stands and clinks his wine glass in an attempt to bring the room to silence. In his early fifties, he has a warm face, rugged chin, and sexy eyes, all of which, despite the height difference, remind me of Richard.

"*That* is Father Stephan, our pastor," Vivian says. At least I think she called him Father even for an Anglican order.

When the room is quieted, Father Stephan announces, "Everyone, after dinner please join us in the parlor." Such an appropriate word for this converted villa. "Our organist, Thomas, and his wife, Beatrice, will be entertaining us. Beatrice is an accomplished opera singer. You will not be disappointed." Then he sits and looks highly entertained by their Matthew, who manages, at least once, to smile in Barbara's direction. I don't think he knows he's encouraging her.

Through the main course and the custard dessert, our conversations do not go into any great depth. From me, only simple questions need answering.

"How was your day?"

"What do you do?"

"Are you the equivalent of a solicitor or a barrister?"

As always, Alaska gets some attention. The usual line of queries about the frigid temperatures and long nights, I'm happy to answer. I note, however, no one asks about the unending hours of sun during the summer, and I chalk that up to my pasty skin. Even in April, I must convey winter.

At coffee, the conversation slowly turns to our plans for tomorrow. Robert will be reporting to WHO headquarters and then viewing two apartments—the first by Termini, the second near Centro Petro on the outskirts of town. The Brits will be visiting three churches, Saint Paul in Chains, Santa Maria Maggiori, and just nearby, the church I was to walk past on my way here, San Clemente.

"Matthew knows everything there is to know about each of them," Barbara declares fawningly, sneaking a peek his way, "He's been directing Roman tours for five years."

"That sounds lovely. I'm sure you'll enjoy yourselves." I say, meaning it.

"And what will you do?" Samantha asks.

"Me? I'll go for a run, come back, clean up, then find a park and write a letter to the priest who abused my brother. He lives here, not too far away."

After keeping my eyes closed a beat too long, I look up and indeed I have Barbara and Samantha's attention. Vivian is listening too. Barbara taps Douglas's shoulder. Why am I such an idiot? Why can't I just be the woman traveling alone who's always wanted to see the Colosseum? I had to chalk it up to fatigue. I could think of nothing but the frigging truth.

"Douglas, did you hear?" She gasps it out like a surprised juror. "She's here to find the priest who abused her brother." Then, she gives me the look I don't want, one of pity. Thinking of her crush, she calls out, "I know. Matthew can help you. Matthew!" she yells for him to hear.

"No! No need for that," I say and shake my head. To show I have some control, I reach for her hand, look right at her, and say, "I am genuinely sorry. I should not have taken this very good conversation in this direction. I have everything taken care of," I lie. To show I really mean it, I add, "Everything is okay. I just have a few things to do here in Rome, which do not permit a touring agenda. But I will see some sights. I'm really looking forward to going to the Trevi Fountain. Have you been there yet?"

I don't know why, but it's Samantha who rescues me and answers, "No, we're here mainly for the churches. After a few more days in the city we leave for Assisi, but I hope one night to get to Trevi and, of course, the Piazza Navona."

"Yes," I say thinking of the closing scene in *Return to Me*. "I would like to go there too."

When we walked out of the dining room, I was ready to shrink away and hide from these people and my unintended admission. But then Faris tapped me on the shoulder.

"How was your dinner?" he asked.

"Excellent. You're a fantastic chef."

"The fish. It was not too dry?"

"Not at all."

"And the custard?"

"Very good."

"Lovely."

Then a little woman sidled up to him. She appeared fresh from the beauty parlor. Although I did suspect dye was also in her recent history, not one strand of her black hair was out of place. Her chocolate brown eyes were encircled with thick, black eyeline liner, like a 1970's Elizabeth Taylor, and her lipstick was ruby red. "Ms. Wilson, have you met my mother yet?" Faris asked. "This is Helen, Helen Khan."

I had trouble believing she was old enough to be Faris's mother until she said it was true. I let her know I could see the family resemblance, and Faris gently reminded her I was the woman who knew her sister. Soon a member of the wait staff walked up and Mrs. Khan and Faris excused themselves, which is why I now find myself, unable to escape, on an overstuffed sofa parallel to the parlor's piano. I fit myself in between the rose-and-gold armrest and Vivian's slender frame. A large vase of long-stemmed orange and yellow flowers is to my right, and I'm careful not to knock them over.

"Good evening!" Thomas announces as if he's done so many times before. "We are so pleased to be able to perform for you tonight. We do so out of abundant thanks to Father Stephan; Matthew, our glorious guide; and Mrs. Khan who has made our stay here so refreshing and personal." The three of them, sitting next to each now, stand and give fake bows and a curtsey. "Now, may I introduce you to my wife. Beatrice, darling, say a word."

Beatrice is dressed in black from head to toe, and her auburn hair carries on in long waves halfway down her back. She's beautiful. She seems to have borrowed Ms. Khan's lipstick. Their shades match to a T. She's ivory skinned and although larger boned—the stature one would expect for an opera singer—she looks fit.

Her mood is as light as Thomas's, and she works the crowd like a cabaret singer. "Thank you, dear. How wonderful it is to be here in Rome amongst such good company, old friends and new. As Father Stephan told you, I sing a bit of opera and would like to share a song or two with you this evening."

As the crowd applauds, I look around the parlor. The floor is a gold-tinged marble. The end tables and coffee tables are loaded with books on art, music, and Roman mythology. In the corner, an ecru-colored bust of a Roman boy lowers his chin. I can see his grin, he's laughing and beguiling. Like the Tim I sometimes remember.

Thomas begins to play with heavy hands that nevertheless strike each necessary key precisely before Beatrice strikes at the crescendo. She's singing Puccini's final aria from *Turandot*, "Nessun Dorma."

I'm no opera expert. In fact, when my parents caught me as a teenager watching some opera on public television, my general recollection of their reaction was something like "who do you think you are?" I would turn the channel quickly and there went my training for the "polite" society I would one day encounter as a "professional." That said, I made up for it a bit during law school when Sunny, and a few other friends and I would get discount tickets to the Portland Opera. I know the aria Beatrice sings is intended for a man, and I know the opera is a story of a tested love and an unwillingness to accept that love, until, that is, the very end.

Beatrice begins singing the title in repeat as the melody demands. Spoiler alert. Princess Turandot is a bit of a bitch, but she has a reason to be. Anyone who wants to marry her has to answer three questions. If they fail, she beheads them. Apparently, however, she's so beautiful her suitors think the potential prize is worth risking their lives. Perhaps, I think, turning morose, a bit like me getting what I really want from Ormechea.

Enter the disguised Calaf, who is the Prince of Tartar. Despite the protests of the two people who know who he really is, Calaf places his head on the proverbial chopping block and submits to the princess's three riddles. Calaf, however, correctly guesses the answers deal with the subject of revenge. Turandot does not want to weaken her kingdom and further desires to defend the honor of a once-violated and vanquished queen. Answers correct, Turandot must marry him, but seeing her disappointment, Calaf gives her a get-out-of-marriage-free card. If Turandot can guess his real name by sunrise, she may choose to behead him instead. The ability to defeat her suitor riles up Turandot and she orders *nessun dorma*, "none shall sleep," until his identity is discovered.

Calaf hears the order and shows no concern. In fact, he's confident no one shall know his name. When the sun rises and he kisses her, she shall be his. I have to admit it. Here in Rome, steps from Ormechea, I understand Turandot's resistance to love. Together, although I did not seem to truly intend it until I got here, we are the embodiments of revenge.

When Beatrice stops singing, Vivian looks at me. She's says I'm crying. I raise my index finger to my eye, the way Abbie does with my hand to her own face when she wants me to know she's genuinely moved. I try to wipe the tears away, but they keep coming. What is happening to me? Am I finding joy in Ormechea's destruction? "Yes, yes, I am."

I feel like telling the truth again. *Vivian, part of me is ready to kill.* But I resist and say instead, in explanation of my tears, "I just can't believe I'm here, in a parlor, with all of you from England and Italy and Ghana," I see Robert out of the corner of my eye standing and clapping, "listening to Puccini, being part of something so beautiful. This doesn't happen back home."

I rise before Vivian can ask another question and say, "And on that note, I think I need a little time outside before going to sleep. *Buona sera*, Vivian."

"*Buona sera*, Joan." I distantly hear as I make my exit pass the kissing angels.

In the fashion of older European hotels, I turn in my hotel key to the front desk—I think to the cute Antonio—walk through the Lancelot's courtyard, and let the gate that once confounded me shut behind me. I knew before leaving that I needed green space and a bench. I knew I would find both in the direction of Celimontana, but that would mean being too close to the Curia. I wasn't ready. Not tonight. So I turn right, not left, walk down the hill, not up, in the general direction of anywhere but there. Via del Queceli looks pleasing. A young couple walks in my direction with a little girl, a little older than Abbie, just behind them.

Suddenly, the gray wool sweater covering my shoulders feels thick and unnecessary, and I realize I am in a very different place than home. Warm air on skin at night, no less, is one of the oddest sensations for an Alaskan. But, unlike my daughter, I'm not really one. I know that. As a child, I never asked for my hat, gloves, and bear spray repellant so I could go play in the woods in the middle of July. Nor did I peer longingly at my pet goldfish and ask my mother when it would be big enough to eat. Instead, I was the bare-shouldered girl equipped with a week's supply of tank tops and bathing suits. I swam at night and sat on my front porch on a towel.

Although not the same volume of heat that gathers and holds onto the sky with little reprieve during Chicago summers, I know this Italian night, this warmth, these embracing city streetlights, the combined smell of sewage and gasoline fumes, and this encounter, for the second time today, with city-sense direction. I know if I keep walking downhill and then let's try here, across Via Labicana, by the florist shop and the small bar, and now to my right and up an unnamed street, I'll see an old man and his beagle coming toward me. I'll observe their stiffened gaits and rightly assume they didn't walk for long, just a slight veer to my left and up this stairwell, and there it is: a park, spanning a city block, with a single paved pathway and a row of benches on each side.

The sign announcing park hours says it closed forty-five minutes ago but that hasn't stopped the man on his bike who sails past me or the old couple a few strolls ahead. I walk a third of the way into the park, close enough to still see the stairway and the lights of the unnamed street below, and sit to rest.

My taskmaster is quiet, but my doubter is out. She asks over and over again, "Why are you here? Why are you here? Why are you here?" Although I recently confirmed with Reese Dunklin, a *Dallas Morning Star News* reporter who had once tried to interview Father Ormechea in Rome, that Ormechea is likely still living at the Passionist headquarters, no intelligence tells me he's here this actual week. Perhaps he's visiting Florence or Venice. And if he isn't here, what am I supposed to do? Talk to his barber? Stake out where he gets his coffee? Figure out where he buys his kiddie porn?

And what if he is here, just up the road, readying for bed, just like that old man and his beagle are? What am I supposed to do next? "Wait a second," I think. Did I look closely at that old man? What if the General Curia keeps a beagle the way my dad's firehouse once kept a dog? What if the beagle's favorite food is Kibbles and Bits? How the hell are they going to find Kibbles and Bits here? What if Ormechea brings it with him, every time he gets to go to America, which is never, right? They would never let him back, not after what he did, not only to Tim, but the other boys? And if this *is* happening, if he does get to go home, they would want me to stop him, right? But how?

"Just get it done, Joan," it's the taskmaster's turn. She's short on love but dedicated to mission.

I know what she means. If I didn't have Abbie, would I be able to do it? Kill Ormechea? What if I was prepared? I would've studied the Italian justice system and confirmed there's no death penalty in Rome. Perhaps I would only looking at a life sentence. Maybe they would send me to Cappane Prison and I would be cellmates with Amanda Knox. In the best scenario, I would work in the prison's library and bone up on the local language by reading the same text, say *Pride and Prejudice*, in English and Italian side by side. It couldn't be all bad, Amanda and I could be friends, assuming, of course, I could kill.

Be careful, child.

Breathe. Tell yourself to breathe, Joan. Although diminished by the city's lights and a full moon, the stars are still visible. I think of Beatrice singing, beseeching the stars. Their light is how I make out the Metro police starting their patrol at the far end of the park in my opposite direction. Unless they get distracted or don't care if an American fresh from the plane and with little sleep is plotting a homicide, I'll have to go soon. But those stars. They remind me of Dad.

It was eleven thirty some August night in 1974. Dad and I were the only two awake on a long car ride through Wyoming, the same one, where earlier in the day, Tim had released the fire extinguisher. We still had ninety miles to drive to get to Moran, where Dad planned to get a motel room. If all went well, we would reach the Grand Tetons by noon the next day.

The two-lane highway we traveled was poorly lit, but the stars were something. They were everywhere. Sitting in the front seat between my parents, I leaned against my mother, who was asleep with her book, *The Lighthouse*, falling slowly down her chest. I turned to Dad.

"See that, Dad," I pointed out the windshield and outlined the shape with the back end of the flashlight my mother had been using to read. "Those stars look like a kid, with a ponytail, riding horseback." No answer, at least to me. It was the era of "Convoy" and Breaker Breaker 1-9. Dad grabbed the speaker from his CB and announced, "This is Long Pockets," a reference to his five-foot-nineteen-inch height (another of his jokes). "All is quiet on Route 287. No gumballs, over and out." He clicked the CB off and asked me to point out the shape once again.

"See, right there," I said, outlining the stars. "But I think instead of a ponytail, she's actually wearing pigtails."

He looked in the direction I'd pointed. "I see it, Joannie. I have to tell you. You have the best imagination."

At last! What I was seeking. Recognition! I couldn't help it. To maintain my accolade I pointed out every star-outlined figure in the sky, even if it wasn't really there.

"Look, Dad, a clown, and there's a giraffe." Thirty seconds later. "Ooh, there's a dachshund eating a hot dog and a ketchup bottle is right next to them. They just got out of that red pickup truck."

Dad held it together for another five minutes, saying "uh huh," or "no, I can't quite make that out." Then he was quiet. He turned the CB back on, but there was nothing but static on all the channels.

"And there is a cat sitting on a beach ball."

"That's enough, Joan. I have to find the turnout." No he didn't. Chief navigators like me knew the turnoff was still thirty miles away. I closed my eyes and pretended to sleep until I actually did and Dad was alone, just as he probably wanted to be long before.

Every time I see him of late, however, he doesn't seem like my father at all. The last time was just twenty-four hours ago on my Chicago layover.

"Joannie, you're here." His voice was weak and gravelly.

"Hi, Dad," I'd said standing just yesterday in the doorway to his bedroom. It took a few moments before I could acclimate to the urine smell coming from his sheets thanks to incontinence, which was in turn thanks to prostate cancer or rather its treatment. We're now lucky if Dad gets out of bed every fourth day.

His decline was gradual. Just eleven years ago, after retiring, he was still walking five miles a day, that is, until he called for Mom to pick him up. His heart was racing and it was hard to breathe. The angioplasty seemed to help. But then came the prostate cancer and next the kidney cancer and the laparoscopic surgery to fix it that went so long he woke up with a pinched nerve in his neck, which we mistook as a stroke. Then the spinal stenosis set in. After that came the quadruple bypass and the neuropathy, caused by unregulated diabetes, which made it impossible for him to feel his feet, let alone stand.

He used to get so tan working outside. Instead, his legs, right ankle crossed over his left knee, were the color of alabaster ivory. Bone color. Sick color.

"When does your next flight leave?" At least he knew why I was here and remembered it was temporary.

"In about six hours. How are you feeling?"

"Same, same," he smiled. I should've picked it up from his lisp. He still hadn't put in his front teeth in today. He gave the gapped grin of a seven-year-old child and eighty-year-old father.

"Do you want to come into the living room, Dad?" I had no idea this would one day be an accomplishment.

"No, not today. I was up yesterday," he said. He lowered his leg and his sheet sagged, revealing the tube from the catheter he wore full time.

I decided to go in. The bedroom was recently painted a chipper yellow, which I hoped had made him happy. A year ago my parents replaced their king-sized bed with a queen, but there was still little room to maneuver between it, two dressers, and the TV table, which held Dad's pills, water glasses, and crossword puzzles. A make-believe painting of the Blackburn farm in Mayo County was on one wall. A large banner imprinted with an image of Mom and Dad walking down the church aisle on their wedding was on the other.

Mom had moved a chair in from the dining room. A bit more used to the scent, I sat down on it and stretched my long legs, which I inherited from Dad, toward the bed. I carried a small, red, leather-bound notebook in my hand and a pen.

Dad had told me just a week before he tried to write Ormechea, but he just couldn't do it. He was having terrible dreams instead. Julie next told me in an e-mail, "Mom and Dad decided not to write anything. They're letting go of this and their anger and you should too. Do not upset them anymore!"

That's the way it was now. A long-ago promise I had made to Tim had somehow morphed into this quest for his abuser. A person with a fine life before this shit, I am the one who can't let go, who causes disturbance for everyone, even Tim. He was supposed to have a note for me too. I was supposed to pick it up from him at his son's baseball practice, but Tim hadn't returned my calls and practice was long over.

Oddly, I felt like they both, Dad and Tim, owed me. They shouldn't send me to Rome on my own to express the tsunami level of damage Ormechea did to our family with nothing for me to show him. But they didn't send me to Rome, did they? I did that all by myself.

I was more timid than I thought I would be. As if I had pointed out one too many star shapes, I asked shyly, "Dad, I know you couldn't write a letter, but maybe I could just write down a few of your thoughts so I get them right. Just tell me how you feel, that's all." I thought of how Abbie finally convinces me to offer her a second popsicle and see that same look of parental acquiescence in my Dad's face, even though his daughter is forty-seven. He knew I wouldn't go away unless he tried.

"Okay, Joan. Get out your pen. Here goes." Surprisingly, he dictated his thoughts like a letter, and I wrote them down, word for word.

Dear Father,
I do not even know where to start. I continually do not have rest in my mind. What you have done has been an evil ordeal to my family, as a whole. I continually have to resist the notion that this is what God wanted His Church to be like. I believe the evil portrayed by you and others like you had been put in place by the evilness of the evil, the devil, of whom you have fallen in league with. I will not and cannot take part in this by acts of violence to my God. It destroys all notions of what I believe and why we existed. You have terribly corrupted the notion of the goodness that God wants us to be. We are taught to forgive one another of our sins but how can we when you offer no apology to so many you have hurt? Especially, first, Tim, and our family, of whom you many times took refuge.

Took refuge? His words seemed so medieval. But perhaps this was what my father had become, a relic of old-school Catholicism.

Dad continued, "Thinking of the shame you have brought still brings tears to my heart. But I stand resolute in my faith and even pray, somehow, that you will find forgiveness."

Then he stopped, seemingly done. So I asked, "What about when Tim was sixteen? When he tried to tell you. Do you have anything to say about that?"

How can you not, Dad? I thought. How can you not admit you didn't believe your own son when he tried to tell you what was happening? And when the hell was I ever going to forgive you for that? *Then*, we could have made a substantial difference.

Dad took a wheezing breath at the prompt. Why was he not wearing his oxygen again? He began with explanation, "Mary and I could not believe a priest would do this. And I now continue to suffer the pains of rebuking my son. I grew up with the notion that our faith was a treasure of joy and hope. Your hideous acts of defilement have destroyed that notion. And I believe so much that man was put on this earth and that one of the first things we learn in catechism as to why we are here is to know, to love, and to serve God in this world so that we may be with Him in the next. Without Him life has no other purpose and will become shallow."

He looked at me again. "Is this enough?"

As the good speech writer I said, "I think you need a conclusion." When did this become an assignment? Perhaps when I made it one.

"Okay," he said, and added, "Even now, I pray for you and all victims in this act, which I totally blame on the evil one, who does exist, the Devil . . ."

"Good, Dad."

I handed him the letter. He scribbled in a broken signature still recognizable as his. "Yours in Christ, Walter."

ð

A few stars are peeking out to the left of the moon. They make the shape of a Christmas tree. "Look, Dad!" I almost want to say.

The police are closer and it's time to leave. I begin the walk back to the hotel following the careful directions I've kept in my head. Cross Via San Giovanni en Laterno (I never would've found it earlier), right on Via dei Querceti, then left on Capo-d'Africa until I come to the green gate with its easy-to-locate bell.

On the way home, I mimic Prince Calaf's and Beatrice's sung conclusion. At dawn, I will win. Whatever this might mean for me tomorrow, I sure hope so.

But it's only 1:00 a.m. It was Lorena who buzzed me through the gate about an hour ago. I had seen her before I left. She was a small woman with dark hair in a high ponytail. She was getting the hotel bar ready for after-opera drinks and was next working the front desk when I arrived back. She handed me my room key, and asked, "How was your outing?" Her face was youthful and, I swear, she wore the same ruby-red lipstick of Helen Khan and Beatrice. I was beginning to think this is the only shade sold in Rome.

"I had a pleasant walk. It's beautiful out."

"A few hotel guests are still at the bar," she volunteered. "Would you like to join them?" I had peeked down the hallway and saw the backs of Father Stephan and Matthew. A red-bearded man, he could've been the face of Brawny paper towels, looked my way. He raised a highball glass to his nose. Before I could see if it was an invitation or just a sniff of brandy, I had turned back to Lorena.

"No," I shook my head. "I think I just had the illusion of a second wind." Did she even know what that meant? "Not a real one. It's time I try to get some rest."

"Very well. *Buonanotte e buoni sogni.*"

"*Grazie.*" Good, Joan. Keep up that Italian. My fourth word in the language was the same as my first.

Back in my room, I flopped on top of the rose-colored comforter, which matched my bed's padded headboard and the upholstered chair next to the courtyard window. I snaked out of my dress and left it and my bra on the floor before I scrambled under the covers.

Maybe I should've gone to the bar, because I still can't sleep. It's 1:00 a.m. I do the math: ten hours. It's three in the afternoon back home, which explains my beyond-all-desire wakefulness. The thought occurs to call Abbie's Montessori. She would've just woken up from her nap. But whom am I kidding? It's Richard I should be calling. I've been tiptoeing past him for three years.

I'm wearing a black tank top and salmon-colored panties. The lighting in my room is subdued; perhaps I should woo myself. That might help me sleep. But ask Richard again. Any interest in a sex life, with him or alone, has withered like the branches of my favorite birch tree over those same three years. It may be hormonal. I'll add this to my to-do list and check it out when I get home. Order Estradiol. I hope it's mere exhaustion. With a full-time legal practice, a three-year-old, and a vendetta to settle, I think I have a right to shut down that side of myself. It's not that I'm not sexually attracted to my husband. I'm just tired.

He had kissed me, almost eleven years ago, even before he introduced himself to me. Because he had the good looks of a Dallas Cowboys quarterback and eyes that were Tahitian blue, I had no choice but to reciprocate. Then, on our first date a few days later, I reached over, touched his hand, and told him, surprisingly—post-divorce and before Tim's admission—I was a genuinely happy person. Add to this a tall, now pretty blonde and a lawyer? I could tell. I had him hooked. We were married within the year.

During our almost ten years together, he's shown his character. He's a man who doesn't give up on me, ever, well, at least not yet. It's like he still expects the woman who told him how happy she was to just show up. I think he hopes she went to the grocery store and will be home any minute. Then again, he knows I would rather eat a can of tuna over the kitchen sink than go grocery shopping. I must be somewhere else.

I had wished Richard out of thin air. One year after my separation—on the Camino de Santiago, somewhere east of Burgos, Spain—I took pen to paper, yet again, and wrote everything I wanted out of a new man in my life. The hokey ones and unnecessary, sought-after physical qualities were there, but so were the real tests. Like the ability to take me as I was, all baggage included, and the concomitant desire not to change me. I asked for a man who would believe and trust my belief and knowledge of myself were true, even when I didn't know exactly where I was going. Just as important, I wanted him to love his own life, have worth on his own, and be sure of himself. Still, he couldn't be so arrogant to believe there was just one way to see the world. I implored, "Make me smile. Make me laugh. Above all, be peaceful to me."

He was and largely still is. But a little less than two months after our wedding came Tim's Blue Line call. It took no more than that to bump Richard from the first most important man in my life to at least the third, behind my also emotionally ailing father. Richard could get by until I was done, I had thought. But ten years is too much to ask for one person. If I don't finish this soon, I'm going to lose him. Everyone, especially the dreamed-up one, has his limits.

Knowing I won't be able to move Richard up that list while I'm trying to sleep, alone, on a twin bed in a Roman hotel room, I reach over to the night table for anything to read. A guide to Rome and a companion *Italian Phrase Book and Dictionary* are there to scour. I could read about the Vatican Museum and learn how to properly ask, "*Dov'e il Belvedere Torso?*" "Where is Belvedere's Torso?" So too is the city map Faris gave me. As I told Vivian I had already done, I could plan out my morning run. But beneath them both is the newspaper my mother handed me before I walked out her front door to return to O'Hare and catch my flights to Rome.

I grab it for a closer look. It's a yellowed May 2002 edition of the *Catholic New World*, a newspaper for the Archdiocese of Chicago. Despite its color, it's in nearly perfect condition. It's so flat. I wouldn't be surprised if she'd been ironing it once a year.

On its cover is a full-length color photo of Pope John Paul II, current, as of this writing, saint. Parkinson's had set in, but in the image, he's not nearly as disease-scarred as he would become his last year of life. He wears a white cassock with cuffs embroidered in the pattern of ocean waves. The cassock is the same color as his cap and his thinning hair. His outer robe is a complementary cream.

JPII's hands are folded together, left hand cupping the right, in prayer. A gold ring with a large Celtic cross upon it faces the camera. It's on his ring finger above the folds of his reddened and wrinkled old man's hands. The fingernails on his left hand look like they should be clipped. Still, the photographer's focus must have been on those praying hands, because the pope's forehead rests upon them. His chin is turned downward, completely out of view, and only the top half of his right ear is visible. He's supposed to be looking sincere.

These words are plastered in a twenty-four-point bold Times New Roman font beneath his image.

". . . there is no place in . . . religious life . . . for those who would harm the young."

I'm more intrigued by the text the ellipses exclude than by the meaning these conjoined words are intended to offer. Everyone who cares to know knows it. John Paul was no champion of clergy sex abuse victims. As Michael D'Antonio wrote in an article entitled "The Man Who Would Be a Saint, John Paul II and the Era of Scandal," John Paul's spoken word in response to the crisis, indicated "It was the scandal, not the rape and molestation of children, that was the main problem." For that, the dead pope blamed the free American press.

And so, sleep deprived, still angry, and angrier here, in the city that is supposed to bring peace, I see his image and imagine what his ellipsed sentence might really have read in full. Perhaps:

> If we are *not* speaking of the thousands of priests whom I have protected through use of archaic Canon code no one, in fact, deserved; if we are *not* speaking of them, well there is no place in what some might consider a religious life for those who harm the young. For those thousands of priests I have protected, I'll find room. They have my promise.

I am a cynic, but for my mother, those emblazoned words written beneath JPII's image must've seemed like they were spoken by God in heaven and delivered through the pope straight to her front porch steps, not more than four weeks after she learned, for the second time, the abuse of her son was true. It was an *Alleluia* miracle.

"My mother is not a simple woman. She's complex and caring," I tell this to myself, even when I seek to separate from her. She's devout and has been so since she was the smallest of girls growing up in a three-story walk-up next to her Catholic Church. She's also the daughter of devout parents, and that devotion was passed down to her like an inherited great-grandmother's emerald broach.

Devote, derived, from the Latin word, *devovere*, meaning to vow or consecrate. She did and still does. If there is a holy day of obligation that requires Mass attendance, even the odd one celebrating Jesus's circumcision, she's present. If the Holy Eucharist requires adoration from 3:00 to 4:00 a.m., she'll sign up as well. Delivering communion to the sick, helping the homebound with their dishes, training young girls in the ways of *Puella Maria*, my mother is, and has always been, the first in line to vow her life to the Catholic Church and to give service. In so doing, the Church has provided her a routed course and a sure-fire path to get to heaven. Still, her devotion is real, and her sacrifices are pure.

That's why I know that when my father asked Tim on an Easter Sunday, not three weeks after his and my Blue Line call, if what Tim tried to tell him so long ago was true, when he saw my brother's face and knew there could be no reason to doubt, when he called my mother to him with a cracked one-syllable, "Mare," and when she heard what Ormechea did—the polite, censored version, that is, it must have sounded like a pronouncement that the aliens had indeed landed. She had no means to cope. No means, that is, other than this: with John Paul by her side, she could, perhaps not easily, I'll give her that, forget.

I hate to write about my first marriage. It was a mistake. It's over, but in explaining its pageantry beginning and humiliating end I can explain my mother.

Just know this. When I finally convinced my first husband he should marry me, my next call was to my parents to plan our wedding. Because I had seen my father sell his riverboat for one sister's wedding and take out a home equity note for another and there were still four girls to go, I suggested perhaps my youngest sister Maureen, who was already engaged, wouldn't mind if we doubled up. Where there was one bride, why not plan for two?

The wedding was a younger girl's dream. A horse-drawn carriage carried the two brides to the church. Our bridesmaids, three for each, so we did not co-opt the altar, wore complementary shades of celery green and lilac. Following the exchange of vows, an Irish bagpiper led us down Immaculate Conception's long center aisle and into an eighty-degree September day. The photographer's camera flashed, the drinks were drunk, and soon after my sister Julie scrapbooked together a photo album of the best wedding moments. She gave it to my mother.

When I came home to Chicago two years and ten days later to recover from my husband's announced departure, I looked for my mother's scrapbook wedding album, but it was nowhere to be found. One year later, however, I found it, back on its honored shelf in the grandfather clock with all the other wedding day photos of Teresa, Tim, and Julie.

This time, it looked noticeably different. The front page of the wedding album in its altered state now read:

THE MARRIAGE OF   AND MAUREEN AND STEVEN ZINK—
SEPTEMBER 5, 1998.

Liquid paper had been doled out thick and straight in an apparent three lay-ers to cover David's name and mine. But for the champagne glasses and joined hearts, which remained glued to the edge, the first page of photos was blank. The same could be said for the second page. Zippo. However, Maureen was on the third. Under the power of an entranced sun, the sparkle of her sequined wedding gown reflected in her exuberant brown eyes. And there she was on the fourth and fifth pages as well. There she was on all of the pages, except for those that once were mine.

Wherever I had been, the page was, in turn, doctored. Second bride extract-ed, reference to her removed, even if the scrapbooked caption's grammar suf-fered. "Here Come the Bride"—liquid paper—lacked verb-object agreement. Then there was, "The Time Has Come and She"—handwritten in—"Look"—liquid paper— "Beautiful."

On each of my visits back to Chicago between 2002 and 2005, I couldn't help but be drawn to that wedding album's pages. Not out of sadness, but really out of fascination. Perhaps that's why my mother finally told me, reluctantly (though did I hear a hint of mixed pride?), "It was me, Joan Mary, your own mother, who removed you and any reference to you."

That's why I know. If I were to follow my mother's example and be that joyous woman Richard once met, I would do so by extraction, removing the names—first, middle, and last—erasing invitations, "you are cordially invited," and deleting stored memories one at a time, just like unnecessary excesses on a gorgeous wedding day. My mother, Mary Catherine Blackburn Nockels, can do this, without discussion, without ever looking back. One day, September 5, 1998, the events and people were there. The next, they are all gone, sent into another world, without any need for return, my friends.

I recall sitting at her kitchen table in 2009, the day before the Chicago Mara-thon I'd come to run, drinking the coffee she made for me from the Starbucks beans I brought home for her nearly two years before. I was just waking up, still out of tune with the Chicago time zone but ready for her stories.

"Hey, Ma?" I asked. "Do you remember when you took Buck to Anti-Cruel-ty and they wouldn't give him back to you?" Buck was our second-in-line family dog who succeeded our first perfect dog, Spot. Unlike the ancient coffee I had raised to my nose, Mom was fresh and peppery. She had just returned from eight-thirty Mass at I. C. and had changed from her brown suede heels to what we each—after twelve years of Catholic school education and gymnasiums— still called gym shoes.

At my question, she sucked in the air way too quickly, sounding just like her dead sister Pat once had. I could see, the Celtic charmer had returned. She was ready to regale me.

"Well, you remember how Bucky would just drive me nuts. As soon as you and your brother and sisters left for school, he would jump over the backyard fence like it was nothin'. By the time I got to him, he was always on the other side of Harlem. How that dog never got hit by a car? St. Christopher must've been his crossing guard."

As she spoke, I listened for the hard and long *As—aas, waaz.* They announced her as lifetime Chicagoan. Her Celtic cross was stuck on the collar of her white blouse and it pointed to me as if in accusation even before I had committed a venial sin. *Do not make fun of your mother, Miss Joan Mary.*

She continued, "One day I just had enough. Bucky jumped the fence for the fiftieth consecutive school day. I went right to our Buick LeSabre. You know? The copper-colored one that *your* father made us buy." She emphasized "your" as if my siblings and I had more than one dad. "God, how I hated that car. I followed that dog all the way to the Norwood Park rocket slide before he finally jumped in. Then, I just decided. Just like that. It would be straight to the Anti-Cruelty for him."

At seventy-seven my mother's face then wore the endless and sinking lines of a woman who birthed six and raised seven children over two full decades. Her sharp hazel eyes stood out like they didn't belong alongside all those markers. But when she told this story in particular, one of her favorites, her wrinkles seemed to disappear and a shimmer of her once Mary Martin clean and fresh good looks came through.

"I says to the man at the check-in counter, 'I found this dog lost in my neighborhood.'" *I says,* the one tense misalignment neither the nuns nor I could cure. She mimicked her long-ago hand gestures of surprise, paused, and then looked up to her kitchen wallpaper—brown and yellow checks replaced, it was a dusty blue then, with overflowing fruit baskets bordering the ceiling's edge. The bananas and pears looked too ripe to eat. Then she turned and looked at me, ready to re-enlighten.

"Well, when you kids got home from school, you were all beside yourself." I didn't tell her I was out of the house already, in college. In her mind, I think she thought it was better that all of us stood as her witnesses.

"I says to you all, contrite, heartbroken, 'Bucky is missing.' And here is where I had my comeuppance. What did I think you would do? Nothing? Terri and Julie started canvassing the streets and alleys, putting up signs. Joycie, Carole, and Maureen, and, I think, you knocked on doors looking for him. And Tim?"

"Yeah, Ma?" I asked as if I didn't know the answer. "What did Tim do?"

"Tim said we better get in the car and go check for him at Anti-Cruelty."

Mom shook her head from side to side, grunted, and wiped her forehead as if she had been caught all over again. "So we're in the Buick, Tim and me, and for cryin' out loud, I could hardly say a word to him the whole way there."

Mary Catherine turned to me, her own coffee raised, and said, as if she'd been waiting forever to tell me, "So we get there. I let Tim off at the door and go park the car. That was my first mistake. I should've stayed with that lousy car. By the time I walk to the check-in counter, I hear the officer say to Tim, 'A dog matching Bucky's description was brought in this morning.' Timmie is beside himself, happy, relieved. But then the man looks up, squints his eyes, points to me, and yells—I swear for all in the room to hear—'by that woman!'

"Next, Tim looked my way and called out, 'Ma? You've gotta be joking me!'"

To act out Tim's part, she dropped her shoulders and eyebrows and turned her mouth into the shape of a large letter O.

"I swear whenever that boy looked at me over the next hour, as Anti-Cruelty decided what to do, he had this 'How could you've done this to me, Ma' look on his face. It hurt too much to see him like that."

Something changed next. Her shoulders fell and her reenactment stopped. She lost her words. I noticed the sounds that replaced her storytelling. A garbage truck rolled down the alley and its brakes squeaked when it reached the neighbors'. A single pigeon flew to the top of the phone lines. Mom's fingernails chipped the frosting remains of an Entenmann's cheese strudel out of the kitchen table's joint.

She looked down to her left gym shoe and then to the right and my eyes followed suit. This might have been the time to say, "I haven't forgotten either, Ma. It wasn't your fault." But, in truth, I believed it partially was. She had to have known anyone, priest and God included, could go off script.

Next, she grabbed her spoon, stirred her coffee, and looked to me. I smiled. I still can't tell you why I smiled. And the moment passed. She said, "Finally the nice man at the counter decided to release Bucky to the crazy lady on the understanding this was a one-time deal." We both let out laughs, and together Mom and I turned and looked to the back door as if we both expected Buck, dead for seven years, to walk in, for his pat and our forever endearment, "Bucky, you were such a good dog after that. You never jumped the fence again."

ॐ

I am shoulder. I am arm. I am beheaded. I am veil.

ॐ

On my last visit to Chicago, the one prior to my Roman revenge mission, I stole the wedding album. It was my intent to add in the wedding photos of Richard and me onto its empty pages. Our outdoor, matching-running-shoe, bonfire-breathing, frozen-lakeside wedding photos would have looked out of place, I know, when placed in the context of the church wedding photos. But something told me my mother deserved completion.

Despite my desire, I couldn't replace the lack of me. On close inspection, my all-out absence or partial presence fascinated me even more. When total obliteration would've ruined a lovely shot, I saw she chose to leave bits and pieces of me in place. On page three, in the photo of my sister riding in the horse-drawn carriage to the church? I'm the cathedral-length veil sitting next to her. On page eight, I'm the decapitated bride in a tight-bodiced, white silk gown standing on Passionist Monastery steps behind the bride who is complete with head. On another page, my right hand wraps around Joyce. We are about to dance to "We Are Family." And in the shot that would've made the family portrait wall, but for the unfortunate circumstance of two brides in full regalia, I'm the bare left shoulder and embracing arm peeking out from where we all gather.

Teresa, Tim, Julie, Joyce, Carole, Maureen, and partial me—*sing us like we are an octave rising*. We're next to a light post with a sign reading, THE NOCKELS. Dad had installed it on our front lawn too many years ago to remember. That bare left shoulder and embracing arm are cradling an old and graying Buck. I know for sure I would've been excised altogether if my mother didn't have the good sense to keep the family dog, even the one she tried to give away.

I once told this story about the wedding album to a friend of mine named Judith. When I finished, she asked if my mother and I still spoke. "Of course, we do," I muttered. "I mean, this is nothing." Judith raised her eyebrows and pursed her lips, looking at me as if I were in denial.

So how to explain? If I were to follow my mother's example, I would do so by extraction, removing from an otherwise pleasing life the pieces that don't fit. Snip, snip, gone, finished, just for that moment, and then, perhaps, if we are lucky, for a lifetime.

For here is what she seeks. A time when daughters don't cry over ex-husbands. A calendar month when dogs don't jump fences. And three years, three years in which her own son . . .

I was fairly sure. This was how she did it. Not thinking, even once, of another man whose name, like my ex-husband's, she had purposefully forgotten, the one who in priestly white and gold married her daughters to their betrothed.

Father John Baptist Ormechea.

That's why I know. If *he* had been in even one background shot? One sparkle of an eye? One slimy hand reaching out? One thumb? One fingernail of a pinky? She would've taken the scissors to him. All of him!

Family dog be damned.

⁊

I am shoulder. I am arm. I am headed. I am unveiled.

⁊

My great-grandmother was a master quilter. She took the discarded suits of the working men of Dyersville, Iowa, and cut them into strips and squares. When the 1938 St. Francis Xavier Christmas Pageant concluded, she did the same with shepherds' robes and the star of Bethlehem. She combined gray tweed and persimmon felt, copper-colored wool, and orchid-yellow silk. By the open fire in her home on Victoria Street, she chose her design and set to work, fragment by fragment, square by square.

One photo memorializes her efforts. My grandmother used to keep it in her den on a wall right above the television set where we watched so many Cubs games together. I used to call it "the wall of the dead," because only when a family member passed away would their photo jump from "the living wall" across the room to this burial ground. As a child, the photo of my great-grandmother terrified me, probably because I was afraid I might one day look like the tall, broad, and ancient woman it captured. In it, she was close to ninety. She wore a polka-dotted long-sleeved dress with a Christmas-wreath broach at the neckline. She sat round-shouldered in an embroidered chair between two windows with wood-slat horizontal blinds. She didn't look at the camera. No, behind her thick-lensed horned-rimmed glasses, she focused on the patchwork quilt that covered her lap and flowed down to the floor. Her wrist tilted. Her hand bent. And between her right index finger and thumb, a threaded needle joined.

❧

And I am burdened.

❧

I'm still shoeboxes full of photos, file folders of newspaper clippings, and bankers boxes of litigation filings. What my mother has removed, I have gathered.

On trips between Chicago and Anchorage, I've filled suitcase after suitcase with fading Polaroids, home movies, and carousel after carousel of Kodak-moment slides. I did so, I thought, to say at least one person has not forgotten, at least one person has the self-assigned job of remembering not just the good—that's the easy part—but the parts that burn.

My inventory is divided into two categories: *Before* and *After*.

Before. Eight-millimeter film of thirty-five-year-old parents pulling their three-year-old son's sled down an unplowed Meade Avenue after an unexpected early April snow. They lift the boy into the air and swing him in everlasting circles. Each of their smiles tells me they never saw this coming. *After.* The father's arm around his sixteen-year-old son's shoulder on the night of the boy's junior prom. The boy bristles at the touch.

Before. A black-and-white photograph of my grandparents raising glassfuls of warmed brandy to welcome whatever New Year was captured. *After.* Ormechea sits on a green upholstered chair in their den. It's Christmas. A child's hand—face out of frame—reaches toward him.

I could keep going, sorting memories into their separate heaps, but a time will come when he is everywhere. My parents' twenty-fifth anniversary. My brother's high school graduation. My grandmother's wake. My uncle's funeral. Hell, even my wedding. In the years before, he is what's to come. He's the reason Tim can't look at any childhood photo of himself without crying. Should his smile be captured, say an absolute moment of joy being knocked from an inflated tire's inner tube and into the pool, he runs, screen door still thwacking at his ever-present exit.

There is a first rule of litigation: develop the timeline because law can't operate without one. Facts must be applied to the legal elements. You need the *actus reus*, the "guilty act," to have, in fact, occurred. But if the records Tim's lawyers had gathered were to be believed, my timeline was unreliable. They showed Ormechea arriving at I. C. in 1979. This would make it impossible for my recollection of him coming out of the rectory to join the boys for a school lunch recess to be true. I would've been in high school by then, not at I. C. to see Ormechea's eyes sparkle and something sick in him arise. It was only my mother's copy of the book *Immaculate Conception Parish 1904 to 2004, A Century of Grace* that saved me. The page entitled "Pastors and Associate Pastors of Immaculate Conception Church" confirmed Ormechea as arriving in 1976, giving me three more years to acquire the *After*, making my memories reliable.

When he did arrive, parish secretary and bookkeeper Joan Troka knew something was off. Ormechea decorated his rectory office with sixty individually framed photographs of boys, all aged thirteen. When she asked him about these, he told her they were eighth-grade graduation photos of his altar boys from his previous parishes, St. Agnes in Louisville, Kentucky, and Saint Mary's in Fairfield, Alabama. That's one reason she told me, granted, twenty-four years later, "That's right, my boss was a pedophile, and I knew it." I could've corrected her. Because Ormechea was sexually aroused by the just pubescent child, he was technically a hebephile. A simpler way to say it was that he liked young teenagers. He fascinated himself with fresh, undefiled meat.

Of the child victims at I. C., by all known facts, Tim was the first. Grooming and abuse years: 1978 to 1981. Ormechea's second victim overlapped Tim. Abuse starting: 1980. And how we found him in 2002? We had one person to thank: my father. After Tim's Easter Sunday admission, Dad became a private investigator himself, querying any parish member with preteen sons during Ormechea's reign and asking them if they had ever witnessed anything odd concerning the former pastor. Dad asked this of Helen Tierney while she was checking out his groceries at Evening Hill's. She told Dad to call her ex-husband, Eddie. Instead, Dad tasked me with that job.

"It happened when we lived on Heart's End," Eddie told me. His thick brogue unintentionally converted Hartzell Avenue to what it really was. Heart's End. The Tierneys were Irish immigrants; Eddie was from County Mayo and

Helen was from County Clare. As such, Charlie and his sister, Bridget, were first-generation Americans. When Charlie turned thirteen, his grandmother became sick, which required his mother to return to Ireland for a long period of time. She often took Bridget with her. This meant, in the summer of 1980, Eddie and Charlie were left largely alone.

"Charlie was no bigger than a thumb, even in high school."

"I remember, sir." My mind flashed to Tim and Charlie sitting in the back-seat of our station wagon. I was a newly minted driver at sixteen, and, for some reason, I was tasked to take the two of them to Notre Dame High school for Boys, where they were freshmen.

"At first it started innocently enough. To help me out, Father J. B. would drive Charlie to his football games"—he meant soccer—"and take him to a movie now and then. I was pretty busy with work and didn't mind. And then on other days, he would join us for dinner. I first got the inkling somethin' was wrong when the priest would go into Charlie's room and shut the door behind him. 'Who shuts the door to a little kid's room?' I thought."

Though we were talking by phone, I heard Eddie take a long drag from his cigarette. I imagined a brown one, the More brand, which constantly hung from my own Irish uncle's lips. I also remembered how Mr. Tierney looked. He was small, skinny, and balding. He wore a blue suit to every Sunday 9:30 a.m. Mass.

"Mr. Tierney, how long did this go on?"

"At least a year, I'm sure of it. But it finally got to the point that every time Father J. B. came to the front door, Charlie would go out the back. One time, in '81, I believe, Charlie was gone five straight days. I later learned he was sleeping in the gangway and bathing in a neighbor's pool. I can't tell you the exact date, whether it was due to Charlie coming home late or performing poorly in school, but I do know I asked him, 'Son, what is going on?' That's when he broke down in tears and told me Father J. B. had been touching him where he shouldn't."

"Did he say what J. B. did to him?"

"That's not my place to tell you, Joan Mary." The Irish in my neighborhood still added my middle name, as if they were beseeching the Virgin herself. "You'll have to ask Charlie. But I will tell you what I did."

"Go to the rectory with a gun?"

"It would've been a good idea," he laughed. "No, I sat down to write out a note. I told the Father he betrayed our trust and I never wanted to see him by my son ever again. I told him never to step through our front door. I showed

Charlie the note. He approved. Then I stamped it and had it delivered by certified mail. About four days later, I got a reply letter from Ormechea. He also said
he would respect my wishes."

"He wrote you back?"

"Yeah, he did."

"And the letter from him, was it typed or handwritten?"

"It was in his handwriting. But I see where you're going. I read the note,
showed it to Charlie, and then I tore it up."

I didn't want to appear accusatory, but I had to ask. "Mr. Tierney, did you
ever think, back then, of going to the police?"

He laughed a little and took another cigarette drag. "No, I didn't. I think
it was because I thought of this as a private matter, best forgotten. I mean who
talked about this stuff then?" No one. I knew that for sure. "Our way was for
Charlie to never have to think of J. B. again. I buried it too. I wanted to close
the whole chapter; not open it anew with the police."

My mother had taught me never to question motivation, especially of someone in distress. That's why I didn't say, "But Mr. Tierney, how could Charlie
ever get over this by you doing nothing? And you knew how popular Ormechea
had been. Did you ever think there might be another boy who needed your
protection, who needed you to speak up?" I imagined those lost years, just post-
abuse, for Tim. At least those could've been reclaimed. Instead I thanked Mr.
Tierney for his time and asked for Charlie's number.

"Hi, Joan. Tim said you would call." His cadence was quick, as if he were late
for a meeting. On my notepad I wrote out the words, "Charles Tierney, Abuse
1980 to ___?" and was about to ask a first question when Charlie volunteered,
"I know I'm only going to be able to say this just once. Do you want that to be
with you or someone else?"

I didn't think twice. The interview with the assistant state's attorney was
scheduled for the following week in October 2002. I would hear the details
from her. But I told him to stay on the line just a little longer; I didn't want to
end the conversation just yet.

The last time I had seen Charlie was when he was in high school. Even late
into his junior year, he had thin arms and knobby shoulder blades. Bono-like,
his hair grew in a thick mane, almost to his shoulders. His eyes were the cobalt

blue reserved for the Black Irish. His skin was freckled, just as Tim's had been. Ormechea must have had his standards.

I imagined the day we spoke he was looking a little like my husband, with graying hair and piercing eyes. I heard he had gone into a trade of some kind, operating engineer most likely, that he was married and had a daughter. Like Tim, he had just turned thirty-four.

"How are you doing?" I asked.

"Okay, I guess." The words rolled out quickly, like he was still late for that meeting.

I had been hoping for a real answer. Tim told me Charlie had called him a couple of nights before from a bar. Charlie's speech was so slurred, Tim was surprised he could even dial the phone. After a few tries, Tim finally made out that Charlie had never told his wife, but his own mother just had.

"I can only imagine how difficult this is for you, Charlie. You must've been surprised to get your Dad's call, then Tim's, and, of course, mine. But I hope you know you're not alone. You have Tim, and you have me."

All he could offer was a speedy thank-you.

"It's somehow much more shameful for a male to admit to being abused," Dr. David Reiss, a psychiatrist, once told *ABC News*. "It not only stirs their sense of weakness about being victimized but also the whole issue of sexual attitude and identity." If a young body reacted in any way connoting pleasure, a boy's immediate fear was that he was gay. As adults, child sexual-assault victims often suffer from "affective dysregulation," what Dr. Reiss defined as an inability to be close to someone without feeling danger at the same time. Charlie was afraid his wife would reject him.

When Charlie did talk of it once, to the assistant state's attorney, he told a story that began when he was a freshman and spanned two years. As Ormechea had done with us, Ormechea ingratiated himself to the Charlie's family by taking Charlie to soccer, filming many of his games, and regularly returning to the Tierney home for dinner. On the auspices of saying good night, Ormechea regularly entered Charlie's bedroom and then closed the door behind him. Over time, the kisses progressed from pecks to lip locks. Ormechea then moved to the penis, bringing the boy to erection and ejaculation. After time, he requested and received the same from Charlie.

While Charlie and Tim were receiving the brunt of Ormechea's attention, the stories of two other families were playing out under almost identical circumstances in the 1981 to 1982 timeframe. Ormechea must've never had dinner at the monastery because in addition to frequenting our homes, both Robert Bauer and Cory Conrad reported to the assistant state's attorney that Ormechea was a regular dinner guest at their homes as well. Each recalled receiving hugs and kisses in their bedrooms, which made them feel sick. However, the key factor saving both of them was the presence of brothers. "Without my little brother Greg in the same room," Cory said, "J. B. would've definitely tried to go further." As for Robert, he and his brothers made a pact to never allow one of their number alone with the priest.

And so, from Tim's eighth-grade class came a minimum of four boys who piqued Ormechea's interest. Since two had brothers to protect themselves, Ormechea was tasked to find new victims to take their places.

Enter a former priest and a former nun to explain who came next. His name was Kurt Wilowski. It was Ormechea's unusual behavior at Kurt's funeral that led them both to believe something was very, very wrong.

That priest, Steven Edison, will tell Tim's investigator he first met Ormechea in 1973, when they were both serving at a Passionist parish in Fairfield, Alabama. Edison was just ordained, and they served only a small amount of time together before Ormechea was transferred from Fairfield to a parish in Montgomery, Alabama. Edison wouldn't meet up with Ormechea again until 1984, when they were both assigned to I. C.

Even working together, Edison recalled that he and Ormechea were not close. There might've been some jealousy on Ormechea's part because the teenagers of the parish had taken an immediate liking to Father Steve. As our neighbor Jim Brander explained to his mom, "We would never become friends with Father J. B. like we did with Father Steve. J. B. was so creepy." On Edison's part, he admitted that one of his first disagreements with Ormechea concerned proposed funeral arrangements for Kurt. He was perplexed when he found out Ormechea was ordering balloons and even considered hiring a clown, for a theatrical enactment of "Send in the Clowns," to perform during the Mass.

Edison recalled how close Ormechea had been to Kurt and his family. So too did former Sister Jennifer. When she called me in 2002, I was surprised when she then identified herself as Patricia Sprague.

"I never knew you were a nun," I said.

"Well, I came to I. C. as Sister Jennifer in 1970. Two years later I left the convent to date the man who would become my husband."

And that's just when we moved to the parish. I remembered her. She was the tall, pretty brunette with a Dorothy Hamill haircut, who stood at the altar after our daily school Mass and taught us songs, like "Day by Day" and "Eagle's Wings." She was our own Maria Von Trapp.

"Where to begin?" she said. "Like you remember, I stayed on at I. C. as your music teacher but left in 1975 when my first child was born. My second child, David, was born in the blizzard of '79. You must remember that, don't you?"

"All Chicagoans do," I replied. "I think we got three or four snow days from that one storm alone."

"Yes. Well, our son David was baptized that summer. J. B. officiated. I remember him coming to our home afterward and how we were so taken by his charisma." That's what the adults called it then. Charisma. "From 1979 to 1984, I primarily volunteered at the church. I organized and planned the program for the huge liturgical celebration when J. B. replaced Father Jerome as pastor. Do you remember it?"

"I do. It went on for hours." I also recalled Tim served as an altar boy that day.

"I returned to work at I. C. to teach music in 1984. Soon after I came back, I regularly heard the kids on the playground calling Ormechea 'Father GayB' and 'Father BJ.' Teachers knew about the nickname. The sisters knew it. Priests knew it. But we all made light of it. We thought the kids were overreacting. There was *a lot* of denial; a lot that was unspoken. I think it was because he had so much power."

She tried to explain what Catholics of my generation knew of hers. Eddie Tierney had told me the same thing. My parents and all my aunts and uncles had as well. "You trusted the Church," she said. "You just didn't question it or its pastor." But with time, she said she realized, "The more I saw the nuns and priests as people, the more I saw human weakness." She became silent, analyzing her own blind spots. "Looking back, there were several red flags that J. B. was harming children."

She listed how frequently J. B. surrounded himself with young boys. She would walk into the rectory, and they'd just be hanging out together. He stocked his office refrigerator with pop and sandwiches for them. She especially noticed how he gravitated to the eighth-graders, laughing and hanging out as if he were one of them. "Never with the girls," she said, echoing what I already knew. "He looked foolish. He had no sense of boundary or propriety."

As she continued, almost in monologue, I had to ask only very few nudging questions. She said she thought about all the boys she did nothing for, like the child of a single parent I. C. schoolteacher. Her son was neither popular nor athletic. "J. B. used to come over and watch television with them. The teacher would go to bed, and then J. B. would stay alone in the room with the boy for who knows how long."

There was also Freddy Thompson. When his mother became increasingly debilitated with multiple sclerosis, and his father ended up leaving them, Ormechea tried to fill the void. One day, Ormechea called the boy out of class, and asked him to sit down with him in his office. When Ormechea sat next to him and tried to put his arm around him, Freddy screamed at him to stay away. Ormechea backed off, but only after admitting to Freddy that he was perplexed why the boy was so angry with him.

Then, there was Kurt. Repeating Edison's statement, Patricia Sprague offered up, "J. B. spent a lot of time with him and his family. Poor Kurt died not long after learning to drive. He ran into a tree on Bryn Mawr Avenue, right behind his house. Weather wasn't a factor. I always wondered if he was trying to escape something, if his death had been deliberate. J. B. said his funeral Mass. Did you know he wanted to bring balloons and circus performers in for a 'Send in the Clowns' montage?"

Kurt died in 1987. He had a younger brother, but apparently Ormechea's relationship with the Wilowskis changed after Kurt's death. So Ormechea moved on. He returned to a prior family he had visited frequently. Cory Conrad was off in college. His younger brother Greg was still at home, alone.

Greg was Maureen's classmate. Their 1985 eighth-grade class photo captured him as he was. Like Tim and Charlie had been, Greg was small and thin with a strap of biceps just starting to show where his shirt sleeves ended. His hair was golden-blond. He smiled with a wide grin. Jim Brander recalled that while Greg was two years older than him, they both hung out at I. C.'s teen center and became good friends. Jim started to notice how much time Greg spent with Ormechea, even going away on weekend trips with him.

Steve Edison would also admit to witnessing their unusual bond. He said that as priests they were taught to set boundaries with parishioners, and Ormechea had clearly crossed the border with Greg. He recalled the many times Ormechea closed his office door when Greg was visiting. He also said this: "I never investigated what was going on, probably because it was one of those things the Church didn't want to talk about."

Edison left the priesthood in 1987. He said he did so because it was too daunting to care for more than a thousand parishioners and preside over a hundred and fifty funerals a year. Before he left the priesthood, he recalled speaking to Joan Troka, who had become a friend. She told him she had concerns about Ormechea's involvement with young boys and specifically mentioned Greg. Not only that, she said she had taken her concerns to the Passionist's then-Provincial Superior, Father Sebastian MacDonald.

Joan Troka had initially been reluctant to return my calls, most likely because of her strained relationship with my father. As bookkeeper, she had seen some of the tax-diverted salary, such as free gas and tuition for my younger sisters, sent his way, but likely didn't realize this was Ormechea's way of grooming my dad in addition to Tim.

After dropping her opening line about her boss being a pedophile, she blurted it out, "From the minute Ormechea took over, I could tell the finances would be creative. I'm sorry, dear, but I saw how your father was paid and that was only part of it. I knew something was fishy when Ormechea wouldn't let me count the Sunday collections until he was done with them. And for a man who took a vow of poverty? He always had cash on hand. He was doling it out to young boys with gifts you wouldn't believe. By the time Greg came around, he was handing out television sets, Nikon cameras, and stereos."

Recalling what Edison had said, I asked if she recalled Greg and Ormechea alone in his office.

"Oh yes, but Greg wasn't the only boy. Ormechea had *real* problems." She recalled when Norma Bauer, a woman who was "One hundred percent of the time sweet and considerate," called the rectory, upset, and asked her to relay a message to Ormechea that he was not to come to dinner that night or any other night. Robert Bauer also recalled that call. He said he and his brothers got the nerve to tell their mother how uncomfortable Ormechea made them feel. She surprised them by doing something about it.

Joan Troka next explained how giddy Ormechea would get when a young boy came around and said there were several times he would bring children into the rectory she had never seen before.

"One boy, he brought home from a South Side shopping mall. He looked dirty, as if he was living on the streets. There was another time he and I were driving together to attend a meeting in Old Town. We were stopped in traffic and next to us was a young boy with a driving instructor. Ormechea rolled down his window, gave the boy a big thumbs-up, and said, 'I'm so proud of you!' When I asked him who the boy was, his expression changed from excitement to denial. He said he didn't know the kid. That man was strange, but I didn't get direct confirmation he was a pedophile until 1987. Actually Loretta Finger got it, and there was no reason to doubt her."

"Does this have to do with Greg?"

"Yes, it does. It was the summertime. Loretta and I were working in the rectory when Ormechea came in all cleaned up. He was wearing a new sports shirt and smelled of fresh aftershave. He seemed giddy, excitably happy, and kept glancing out the front office window like he was expecting someone. Come to think of it, he was acting more like a schoolgirl waiting for a date than a priest. Then Greg Conrad walked in. He would've been in high school by then. Ormechea shuffled him off to the rectory assembly room downstairs. I looked at Loretta. She looked at me and said, 'Let's go down and see what they're up to.' Fearful I might lose my job, I told her no, but Loretta went alone. When she came back upstairs, she was shaken. She said she'd seen something she wished she could unsee. Ormechea was holding the boy in a passionate embrace and kissing him."

"And that's when you went to his superior, Father Sebastian?"

"No. It wasn't. Later that day, Ormechea spoke to Loretta. He told her she misunderstood what she saw. He said he was merely providing counseling to the boy, who was having trouble at home with his parents. Heck, at the time, his parents were J. B.'s best friends, especially the wife." Joan next explained how both she and Loretta needed their jobs. "My husband had passed away. Hers had too. I had four kids to raise. She had two daughters. We kept quiet, and Ormechea left us alone." Like Mrs. Sprague's pause while analyzing her own complicity, Joan did the same thing. I heard her sigh before offering, "This sounds like an excuse, I'm sure, but you have to remember what we knew. It was like a brotherhood with those priests. Even if we did come forward then, Father Sebastian wasn't going to believe a couple of women."

There's only one explanation for what happened next. Ormechea must have been in love, because he was getting reckless. Despite being found out by Loretta Finger, he didn't back away from Greg. Patricia Sprague found them together the next time.

Before describing what she witnessed that same summer, she had to give me a little history. "I went back to school in 1985 to get a master's degree from the Catholic Theological Union in Hyde Park. Father J. B. even offered to subsidize my education. He said it would be good for the parish. I now realize that all he really wanted was the upper hand. But one night, a couple years into my studies, I was coming home late from school. I realized I hadn't left J. B. the notes he said he required for the next morning's Mass. It was 10:30 p.m. on a Saturday; no, it was 11:00. I remember that now. I was driving on the Kennedy, so I got off at Harlem, and pulled into the rectory parking lot. Remember the parking lot?" she asked. "There was one light on the east side of it. Sometimes it was on, and sometimes it was off; it was unpredictable."

"Yes," I told her. I tried to further picture what seemed so innocuous; a parking lot with seven or so diagonal spaces about a hundred feet from the rectory door.

"Well, the light was off that night, but parked right under the light pole was a van I thought I recognized. When I pulled into the lot, my headlights came down on its interior. I saw the silhouette of two people in the front seat, sitting very close to each other, like they were on a date. Because times had changed since I was a girl, I initially thought nothing of it. Two school kids maybe, borrowing their father's car. I parked curbside of the rectory, got out of my own car, and used my master key to get in."

I guess to sufficiently orient me, Patricia Sprague quizzed me again on layout. "Remember the rectory? How there were two sets of doors?" she asked.

"Yes." The large, aquamarine exterior doors opened to a foyer that had a split stairwell. From there, you could go down into the rectory assembly room, or up three stairs to the main office, which was behind another locked door.

"Well, I was bending over to slip the notes under the second door and into the main office when I felt a presence behind me. It startled me, and I turned. It was Father Ormechea."

She said how odd he acted, like he was trying to figure out what she had seen. "I'm just here to drop off your notes," she said she stammered. He gave no explanation for his appearance and expressed no gratitude for her courtesy, especially at this late hour. "Then, we both went back to the parking lot," but as she opened her car door, it hit her. The van belonged to the Conrads. "He walked right back into that van, right in front of me. I saw, for the first time, the other occupant of the car was young Greg. What was he? Sixteen? As I pulled away, I began to think. What was *I* doing at the rectory at eleven at night? No, what was *he* doing in *that* van at eleven at night? I began to suspect, though I should've suspected much earlier, Ormechea was abusing Greg."

Thanks to her professors at the Chicago Theological Union, Patricia Sprague began to put a couple of more things together and became more of a detractor of Ormechea's efforts for parish control than she ever thought herself capable. Without really knowing it, she began her efforts to protect the next victim, whoever he might be. So, when Ormechea insisted I. C. students attend Mass every day, she questioned him and told him it was unnecessary. He was flummoxed. "He said he needed the children there. Now, I see why," she told me.

In 1988, Patricia Sprague reached the point where she just couldn't stand to be at the parish any longer. In addition to Ormechea, she had witnessed the school's principal, a nun, struggle with alcoholism and increasing violence toward students and faculty. There was no reproaching her because the nun and Ormechea had a tight bond. Patricia Sprague also remarked how the two bragged when they caught the young man—"they never said who"—responsible for a series of break-ins into Ormechea's office.

In the end, it was always Father Ormechea's deviant behavior that was chief among Patricia's concerns. Perhaps in her despair she sought more allies. Without going into detail, she confided her concerns to one nun, Sister Mary Pat, and to two mothers, Mary Lou Murphy and Patricia Heidkamp. Both moms were starting to take seriously the nicknames the parish children had for Ormechea and had also noticed his close bond to the Conrad boy. Patricia Heidkamp's son had also worked in the rectory in the evening answering phones and had become an unintended beneficiary of some of Ormechea's largesse. When Ormechea bought a new camera to film Greg's wrestling matches, J. B. gave his old camera to him.

There was finally a "showdown" at a parish council meeting that Sister Mary Pat, the Murphys, Patricia Sprague, and her own husband attended. It dealt superficially with the Ormechea rumors, and it was decided. Sister Mary Pat would talk to Father Sebastian.

The record of the meeting Sister Mary Pat held with Father Sebastian isn't clear. My efforts to reach her were always unsuccessful, and in 2008, she died. But Patricia Sprague shared what she knew. She explained it was Confirmation Saturday in March of 1988, and she had only a moment of Father Sebastian's time before the bishop was to arrive.

"I just remember telling him there is so much that should concern him." Because she still believed she couldn't take on the institution, she admitted her statements were more "implied than expressed." She discussed without specifics the dishonesty she witnessed. She said Father Sebastian listened to her, but said nothing in response.

Should the opportunity have ever arrived, I would have asked, "Isn't it true, Father Sebastian, that you failed to mention that just seven months prior to Ms. Sprague's comment, parishioners Patricia Heidkamp and MaryLou Murphy took you to lunch at the Blue Angel. There, they told you all about Ormechea paying too much attention to young boys, particularly with Greg, and that they needed you to 'avert a scandal?'"

His never-existent, "Yes."

"And isn't it true again, Father Sebastian, that even before this lunch, Sister Mary Pat had already spoken to you about identical Ormechea concerns?"

I'll assume he refused to answer.

List them before they fall away. Sister Mary Pat, then Patricia Heidkamp and Mary Lou Murphy, and then Patricia Sprague; Father Sebastian must have been a good poker player. If he is to be known for anything in this odyssey, it was his bluff face and skill at keeping secrets. Of course, reporting Ormechea to the police would have never been on his radar, but even he had his limits. In 1988, it was time to quiet the rumors and transfer Ormechea. Yet, Steve Edison's request to leave the parish had to be handled first. Transferring Ormechea somewhere else? That had to be a matter of good timing.

And when that time finally arose, Ormechea didn't want to go. The twenty-fifth anniversary of his ordination was coming up and he wanted it celebrated at I. C. He didn't get his wish. Not because of the four women who came forward (we must assume Sister Mary Pat was just as telling), but because in 1988 the Archdiocese of Chicago compelled his removal. That wouldn't have happened without Ormechea making one additional reckless move. He tried to fire Joan Troka.

During the fall of 1987, Ormechea made work difficult for her. He increased her work hours at the same time she was recovering from a quadruple bypass. He tore up her doctor's note in front of her face when the physician had written those additional hours would be injurious to her health. Finally, when he thought he had caught her making a deposit error she had already corrected, he instructed the parish's youth director to fire her.

In an effort to save her job, Joan Troka called Father Sebastian. Unlike what Steve Edison recalled, she had not brought up her concerns of Ormechea's pedophilia at that point. It was financially supporting her family that mattered. Since she was technically an employee of the Archdiocese of Chicago and not the Passionist Order, Father Sebastian instructed her to call Vicar Charles Cronin on the compensation board and request arbitration. Joan Troka followed Father Sebastian's advice. Vicar Cronin in turn told her to report back to work and to try to work things out with the pastor. When she reported to work as instructed, Ormechea began screaming. She explained Vicar Cronin had told her to report. Troka told me, "Ormechea became flustered and yelled, 'How dare you talk to my friend Charlie Cronin. He has great respect for me. You are fired!'"

Joan Troka's last day of work was February 26, 1988. After nine years of employment, she was owed two weeks' regular and three weeks' vacation pay. Ormechea shorted her, writing a check for only $1,000, and then canceled it before she could even deposit it. It was enough. Joan Troka went to an attorney for the first time in her life.

Troka admits her focus remained with recovering the money she was due. But during her consultation with the attorney, she told him everything. She spoke of the three thousand dollar check Ormechea had cut to himself to pay for his mother's funeral, the checks he would also write to cover his credit card payments, the missing cash from Sunday collections, the lavish gifts for Greg Conrad, and, finally, the witnessed embrace. She said she told her lawyer, still remarkably uncertain, "This is possibly why I lost my job."

During discussions with the archdiocese, her lawyer in turn told them everything. Joan Troka was witness to an April 14, 1988, exchange between her attorney, the archdiocese representative, and a Passionist representative. "In no uncertain words," Joan Troka recalled, "a man working for the archdiocese stated, 'if the Passionists don't get rid of him,'" a reference to Ormechea, "'we'll take that Church back!'"

On June 16, 1988, Joan Troka's attorney wrote to the general counsel for the archdiocese demanding an independent financial audit and an immediate removal of Ormechea from public ministry pending a full investigation of his sexual assault of children. That same month, Ormechea was removed. Joan Troka's lawyer was informed that Greg denied being abused. So, based only on the word of a scared sixteen-year-old boy, neither the archdiocese nor the Passionist Order launched an official investigation.

One has to wonder. In July 1988, when my father found Father Sebastian strolling the monastery grounds Dad usually tended, when my dad beseeched the Provincial Superior not to remove Father J. B., saying "he was a good man the Church needed," did the thought of any other victim, besides Greg Conrad, cross that flawed Provincial Superior's mind? It should have. Five women had told him their concerns were not limited to one child. They were concerned in general about Ormechea's interactions with young boys.

And with this in mind, how far should Father Sebastian have been from asking my father, "Walter, it's true you have a son? What can you tell me about him?"

If he had, my father might have said, "My son, Tim? He's just turned twenty. He never could apply himself at school. We tried to get Ormechea to help him, but it didn't work. Perhaps you heard of that unfortunate incident? It was my own son who was using my keys to break into Ormechea's office to steal the cash the priest had on hand. But I promise, I paid back every last penny. Should I go on? Father J. B. and Sister Joan Mary stayed up all night in the rectory waiting for the thief. You should have seen the sadness in Father J. B.'s eyes when he had to tell me it was Tim who was stealing from him. He even promised not to take it to the police."

Dad might've continued, "I don't know if I should tell you this. Tim was probably just trying to take the attention off himself, but he said he stole the money because, for years, J. B. had kissed and touched him in ways that made him sick. Don't worry. I told my son he was wrong. I told him J. B. was just effusive and misunderstood. Then I told him never to talk that way about a Catholic priest again."

There might have been still more Dad could have said. If he searched under Tim's bed, he might've found the beer and whiskey. If he talked to Tim, he would've known he dated as many girls as he could so he wouldn't have to think of a man's hands down his pants. He might have understood Tim's anger that came from nowhere and the fear that crept up on him in confined spaces. He could have learned of the grime that covered him, the darkness that enveloped him, the choice he constantly made to just endure.

❧

The timeline is composed. First Tim, then Charlie, then Kurt, then Greg. 1988 is the marker, a date well within the Illinois criminal statute of limitations to convict, if anyone had said one single word to us.

As for the women who came forward to the leaders of the parish, but not the parishioners, my biggest question is this: shall I forgive them? How could they think all they had to do was tell the one priest who treated Ormechea like a son? Their goal should've been to create a scandal, not avert one, to shout, "Has Ormechea hurt you?" or at the very least, call the Chicago Police.

But this I do know. They are full of regrets. Patricia Sprague said it best. When she left I. C., Ormechea wanted to throw her a going-away party. She declined saying there was nothing there to celebrate. She was also angry. She said she didn't know it then, but the child in her was angry for the children she didn't protect. "Every time I think of those boys," she wanted me to know, "my heart is heavy." Then she apologized. "Your brother? Tim? What did he look like? I can't even remember what he looked like!"

When she asked the question I didn't have to struggle for an answer, just as I don't have to now. "About as beautiful as any child could," I told her with my own voice quivering. "He had dark blond hair he combed in a long bang from left to right. His eyes were hazel and big as a cow's. He had beautiful eyelashes. Freckles stuck to his nose like whipped cream on a pie. His teeth were perfect even without braces. He smiled a lot, until he stopped."

Once Tim's name and the removal of John Baptist Ormechea from his position as pastor of Saint Agnes reached the Louisville, Kentucky, and Chicago newspapers on December 14, 2002, there was still more to learn. Joan Troka will recall the certified letter from Eddie Tierney that arrived for the pastor in 1982 or 1983, but she'll remind me, "Ormechea ordered me never to open his mail." Then will come her recollection of a psychologist who attended a weekday Mass Ormechea had officiated. He'd come into the rectory angry, wanting to know why the priest was playing music at the service "more fitting for a slow dance with a wife than for church."

"Something's with that priest. Have him call me," he said handing her his business card. When she passed along the card and message to Ormechea, Ormechea said he would do nothing of the kind.

In 2003, I. C.'s pastor, Father Michael Houlihan, will call for a parish meeting. He'll tell the five hundred assembled, for the first time ever, that upon leaving I. C., Ormechea was sent into treatment in 1988. He'll add that Ormechea was sent into treatment once again, in 1993, when the parents of a mentally disabled child brought a claim that Ormechea once took their eight-year-old boy to his office and asked the boy if he wanted to be greeted the way Jesus greeted his apostles. When the child said yes, Ormechea fondled his genitals. However, the brain-addled child will admit under much pressure that he may have been mistaken, that it could have been some other priest who did this. When that occurred, Ormechea was cleared as good to go and put back into public ministry.

Although Father Houlihan didn't say it in front of the assembled crowd, he will also confidentially admit to former Parish Council member, Judge Bill Ward, that there were several past allegations of abuse within the Holy Cross Province of the Passionist Order because Houlihan himself had signed several of the settlement checks.

Can I figure out those recipients, at least for Father Ormechea? Besides Tim and Charlie, Robert, Cory, and Freddy, another victim will come forward, one I don't know, alleging abuse from 1981 to 1986. One boy can't come forward. It's impossible to do so from the grave. Another boy, Greg, despite everything, still won't. And many likely wouldn't have said anything, if it weren't for Tim.

❧

If I were to follow my great-grandmother's example, I would collect. I would gather witness statements and newspapers clippings. I would comb through forensic reports and develop timelines with a borrowed copy of *Immaculate Conception Parish: 1904 to 2004, A Century of Grace*. I would deal out people, places, and events into two categories: *Before* and then *After*. I would peer into miniature frames in search of explanation or some detail I might have missed. I would listen. I would analyze. When I might come to a perceived barrier, I would push forward, still search. I would ask, why couldn't they have done better? Why couldn't they have done more?

Of the people I would study, my grandparents and parents, Immaculate Conception faculty and staff, other victims, other witnesses, anyone who knew anything, I would gather up their choices, one by one, and link them to their most significant consequence: my forgotten brother. I would assemble and reassemble, pattern and blend, contrast and characterize—to figure out how we got here. How we built a Church so ready for the destruction of children. And then, with a computer keyboard slipping under the soft side of two wrists, I would join one choice to another, one fragment at a time, square by square, until what is created explained. No, it must do more. It must say, never again.

EGERIA

❧

Monday morning

The Parco di Porta Capena is small, only three blocks by one. Mediterranean cypress, oak, and Italian pines dot its expanse, and a lawn covers its remainder. While a sidewalk lines its edges, just twenty feet to its interior is a dirt track. My running shoes are on and my feet are on the earth, a more comfortable location for this trail runner than the concrete and pavement that got me here by way of Via di San Gregorio, past a Benedictine monastery and the Roman headquarters for Mother Theresa's Missionaries of Charity. A few exposed roots upheave the soil and make for careful foot placement.

Like me, park patrons are the running-shoe, moisture-wicking fabric–wearing, exercising kind. A pull-up bar and sit-up bench are near. There, a man in a red jogging suit is coaching two women through a series of core workouts. Three men are running ahead of me. A woman and a teenage boy aren't far behind me. A few bicyclists ride on the neighboring Via di Valle delle Camene. The air is city fresh and the temperature is in the midsixties. A slight wind from the north blows gas fumes my way from a stream of cars making their way through the Circus Maximus during this Monday morning's late commute. When the traffic light at Via dei Cerchi is red and the cars only slightly mutter, I can make out the sounds of scampering birds and my own footfall.

The park commemorates the Porta Capena, a gate in the Servian Wall that enclosed Rome and its seven hills for nearly nine hundred years. Oral history or myth, take your pick, says that in a one-time forest near this gate, King Numa, successor to Romulus, snuck away most evenings to meet his consort, a nymph and minor Roman goddess named Egeria. Egeria was the whole goddess package. She was imbued with Jupiter's greatness, Minerva's wisdom, Venus's beauty, and Juno's love of nature, most especially for water and oak trees. And at her nightly meetings with Numa, she offered him wisdom and prophecy in exchange for libations of water and milk. It is from her, legend-keepers surmise, that Numa developed the Sacred Books, the original framework of laws and rituals that governed the kingdom.

King Numa is said to have ruled over Rome for a long and prosperous time. Under Egeria's guidance, he built temples to Fides, the goddess of faith, and Terminus, the god of proper boundaries. He set up priesthoods, designated holy days, and instituted burial rites. Numa loved Egeria and she him. When the king did die, even at an old age, Egeria's tears were still ceaseless. According to Ovid's *Metamorphosis*, Diana took pity on the nymph and turned her into a spring. From her, the Vestal Virgins fetched their water for sacred rituals. All in homage to Egeria, mother of the law and keeper of grief. Her park holds memory.

So too does my body. Sleep finally came last night, but only in a round of short intervals. My first-arrival shower had released only half the kinks. The untapped remainder was still there, holding what they always held: fear, criticism, judgment, and the electric frenzy of a mind seeking to devise alternative plans, A through D, for how to approach Ormechea. This was why a run was in order, and as is usual for me, when endorphins rise and the routine of heel-to-toe footsteps bring me to a contemplative state, hope sometimes comes too.

"Good things can still happen," I reminded myself by my fifth lap. I was recalling my last run in Anchorage the morning before my departure. I had planned to take first Cletus and Emma out for an off-leash run around a nearby park about the size of Parco di Porta Capena and then return for round two with the younger dogs when I made out shapes in the park's still-dark parking lot. "Those can't be cats?" I thought until I saw my eyes weren't fooling me. One black cat with a ruff of white fur still slept on the small bed someone must have discarded from a car, along with her. The other was trying to drink from a frozen puddle. I walked up to the first cat, the one in the bed, and reached out for her. She grabbed onto my neck and placed her hind legs in the crook of my arm. When I reached for the second cat, she didn't hesitate either. I walked home with one cat holding to a shoulder and the other in the arm where she first planted herself, dogs on leash ahead of me, as peaceful as possible, as if this kind of intervention happens every day. Before I left for the airport that evening, all online and pound ads for lost cats had been reviewed, both cats had been to the vet for medical assessments, and I had found them at least temporary homes until my return. Who can do that in less than twelve hours, still pack a bag and feed a child, unless, perhaps, she was there at the right time for just this purpose? Ah, the runner's high. With it, God and faithful intervention are very much possible.

Then, again, there was the appearance of the Book of Timothy. Right time, right place, right seven-page epistle out of a seventeen-hundred-page Bible. The thing was, this hadn't been the first time it appeared unbidden.

"You need to go to confession and pray for their souls," my friend Linda once commanded. Under a mound of blonde curls and in the company of perfectly white teeth, her blue eyes gave a death-grip stare. She looked at me like not only their souls depended upon it, but mine.

The souls to whom she was referring were those of my five embryos. Four years into our marriage, Richard and I had taken a go at in vitro fertilization. As such, I had one, okay, maybe five, chances of becoming a mother.

"Nah. I saw their photos," I told Linda. After the injection of the embryos into my uterus, the doctor gave me a three-by-five glossy of them. The two-celled blastocysts all posed so nicely together, but in the picture, I noticed their cell membranes had a lot of bumps and what looked like open-air pockets. They looked nothing like the healthy cells—the ones that became actual babies—I'd seen in the advertising brochure for the Seattle-based fertility clinic we had selected. The IVF doctor suggested we try to implant them all anyway, to see if any might stick. "I've seen it happen," she had said, less than enthusiastically. I told Linda, "Besides, I'm pretty sure they were just opportunities for souls, rather than souls themselves. They never did implant; never did grow."

"No, you need to go. You mess with nature, and you have to pay the price." Linda looked as if she were trying to grab my hand and take me there herself. Where I took many of the catechism's instructions as guidance, she took them as holy script, not to be defiled or ignored. I had left the embryos' souls unprotected, destined for limbo. "You're committing a sin," she said.

If I desired to argue, I would have told her, even if I had done wrong, I didn't believe a priest had any more power to petition God for my forgiveness than I did. But I also knew, before I even gave Linda an opportunity to respond, she would remind me those five little beautiful embryo souls had no such ability to argue their case. Who, besides me, their mother, could petition to save them from the vast, eternal nothing? Finally, I relented and said, "It's been twenty-one years since my last confession, Linda. Where would you like me to go?"

Linda recommended a young Benedictine priest, Father William, from Holy Name Cathedral, in downtown Anchorage. I called him the next day to make an appointment for a "reconciliation," the new name for the sacrament I had only known as confession. I saw him within a week's time. There's no distinct feature, physical or spiritual, about him that I can recall. He was a beige man, who I think might have worn a beige, checked shirt. I met him at the archdiocese's white office building behind the cathedral, and he summoned me into his equally nondescript office. There were two chairs; I took one, he the other. His was on wheels. A low, round coffee table was between us. I remarked this was difficult for me. While he might have thought this was a demonstration of my true remorse, that I believed five embryos needed me to be sorry, what I meant was, this sacrament was difficult for me and sitting before him, then, was even more so. Tim's lawsuit had recently settled, and I really knew how the Church valued him. I had already placed about the same value on Father William. He was worth the yearly premium for a term life insurance policy.

Father William suggested, "Well, we should begin with a prayer." Then he wheeled over to the Bible he kept on his desk, wheeled back, turned the Bible to one page, then another, and then a third, and stated, "I think this might be fitting." He read: "To Timothy, my true child in faith. Grace, mercy, and peace from God the Father and from Christ Jesus our Lord."

I asked him why he chose that selection. He said he didn't know. I said that's my brother's name. He said, "Oh." He knew no story of Tim; nor did I share one. But here he was with us. Timothy.

At the end of my confession, I mean reconciliation, after I was forgiven for messing with nature and after Father William suggested I think of each of my embryos as a child I will meet one day in heaven, I might have said, mockingly, "Perhaps I'll name one Tim." But I'm sure I left that office as a believer. God saw my need, saw my brother's need, and reached out to me the best way he knew possible: through my first-memory brother. I clung to God the way that cat held onto my neck on the way back to my house. I wasn't going anywhere with anyone else.

In addition to teaching Numa, Egeria also protected pregnant women and helped them bring their babies safely into the world. That's why her name shares the same Latin root as the verb *gero*, meaning "to bear" or "to carry." Egeria is also said to have used her gift of prophecy to foretell the future of each baby of her followers. I wonder how she might've handled IVF. Could she prophesy which blastocyst might implant and which might not? Or were her talents left for the actually born kind, the feet-first brother, the bedridden father? And what might her prophecy have been for me? If it were that I was to fall in her park, she would've been dead-on.

I didn't see the root that caught the tip of my shoe. I made wide arm circles, trying to right my equilibrium, but the forward momentum was too great. I landed on my right side, upper arm hitting soil first, then hip, then quad, and rolled next onto my back. I could tell I wasn't hurt. My shoulder moved just fine. Only a light layer of soil, no blood, coated my arm. My ankle adjusted back and forth. My knees bent and hips loosened. Still, I stayed down, looking up at the sky that poked through the oak trees' canopy. The cumulus clouds made the shape of connected elephant trunks. Colonel Hathi's elephant march from Disney's *Jungle Book* played in my eight-track brain.

After a minute and a wave to the red-suited coach to tell him I was indeed okay, I sat down on a bench facing the Tour di Via di Valle delle Camene bicyclists, who stood leg-sprawled in a circle over their road bikes. It was there I made myself remember what the Book of Timothy actually said. If I was to believe in prophecy, whether from Egeria or Jesus, what could the man on the plane be foretelling?

Front page to last, the two epistles that make up the entire book of Timothy take up seven pages in my *Catholic Women's Devotional Bible*, and this is with introductions to the chapters and two instructional pages on Mary of Bethany, Martha's fun-loving sister, edited in.

The First Epistle starts off well enough with the words partially read to me in confession: "I Paul, an apostle of Christ Jesus by the command of God our Savior and of Christ Jesus our hope [write] to Timothy, my loyal child in faith, grace, mercy, and peace from God the Father and Christ Jesus our Lord."

The editorial introduction to the text explains the Book of Timothy is not like the other epistles, which were written as letters to specific congregations in the emerging Christian church. Rather, the books were personally addressed to Timothy to assist him with his newest assignment in the Roman Empire's then fourth-largest city, on the western coast of what is now Turkey, Ephesus.

Timothy was the grandson and son of Lois and Eunice, two early Christians who had converted from Judaism. Timothy's father was Greek. Paul soon concluded that this combined heritage made Timothy a perfect emissary to the Greek and Hebrew populations of Asia Minor. As a young man, Timothy had joined Paul on missions around the Mediterranean. He may also have been imprisoned with him a couple of times. Titus notwithstanding, Tim was Paul's favorite.

Some writings say Paul circumcised Timothy when Tim was an adult so that Timothy would be more persuasive when converting Jewish believers to follow Jesus. I had a hard time understanding this particular litmus test. How, in fact, would the crowds of Hebrews have any idea that Timothy was or was not circumcised? When he addressed them in markets or house churches, did he add, "And do I have something to show you?" But be that as it may, it is a small footnote. What is major history? Paul asked Timothy to move to Ephesus and become its bishop. The epistles were meant to encourage and guide Timothy when, at the time, he was dealing with discontent.

Paul's epistles to Timothy are known for providing pastoral leadership instructions for the Christians making up some unknown portion of Ephesus's then two hundred thousand residents. In my reading, however, the majority of the epistles' guidance equaled nothing but misogynistic malarkey. Women were all over it and the word to them left me wanting. On first read, I knew that even with the introduction, there would be no long-time home in the Book of Timothy. Paul first instructed Timothy to tell women to dress modestly, not wear gold, pearls, or pretty dresses and not to braid their hair. The braided hair restriction puzzled me. Paul, it would appear, never struggled with hard-to-control wisps. Paul next said that once a woman's good deeds become her wardrobe, she best not talk about them. And the biggest proscription? While she is permitted to learn, she must do so in full submission. Once taught, she must not teach or have any authority over a man.

Why so harsh? Paul had an explanation for that too. He said, "For Adam was formed first, then Eve, and Adam was not deceived, but the woman was deceived and became a transgressor." Perhaps in its most perplexing and heretical passage, Paul stated there was hope for women, but it wasn't through Jesus Christ. Rather, it was through childbirth and not the Egeria-protected kind. "Stay away from false gods, women, and make another Christian, hopefully a son, and you just might be heaven bound."

Paul's instruction to Timothy had a few more gems, primarily against widows and later against slaves. If you happen to be a widow and have a family, the epistle informed, do not come to the church for help. It's your children's job to take care of you. And, if you are a young widow, even if you don't have a family, don't come to the Church either. Get remarried instead. And if you meet a young widow who doesn't want to get remarried? Tell her to get her act together. Uninstructed, these nonmarrying young women are prone to be idle, gossipy, and pretty big partiers that walk from house to house wasting other people's time. This refrain repeats in Book Two. Beware the weak-willed, silly woman during the end days, Paul said. Just like Eve, she will be the one to let the godless and boastful sinners into the home.

Wow. In all of my favorite books, I could easily turn to loved passages. But in the Book of Timothy it was more like the worst knowledge to pass along to any woman or any man. Not only did the book make me feel bad about the message, but it carried over to the men stating it. When I thought about it, I couldn't help but wonder what Father William may have been told in advance of my confession. Could Linda have vaguely warned him about me? Was this his way of picking a passage that would help him put a foolish woman down? Come to think of it. Did I have braids in my hair that day? And what of that nice English-speaking, potential priest across the aisle on the plane? Maybe he was female destructive as well. "Have no authority. . . . Learn in submission." If the confession and the plane were God moments, which my heart still hoped to be true, why the Book of Timothy? The only answer I could peacefully settle upon was God loves irony.

The woman and her teenaged son run by. They each give me the runner's nod; this, our universal greeting when we pass each other. It means, "I see you out here, running, taking command of your day. Good job." Since I remain seated, I have the breathing power to greet them with an audible *"Bon giorno."* I stand to stretch. My ankle still bends. So does my shoulder. A robin eats the mid-morning worm. The elephant trunks continue their mad-sky march. I return to running laps, recalling, unfortunately, derision.

From my parents to my sisters and friends, conversation after conversation followed a similar trajectory.

"You're doing *what*?"

"I'm getting on a plane and going to Rome to find Ormechea."

"Why?"

"To talk to him." I didn't add, *And perhaps kill him.*

"Why would you want to do that?"

"I need answers."

"Why do you need answers?"

They must have known by now. I'm the one that holds, that gathers, that reminds you of the 1974 Oil Embargo, Sunday Bloody Sunday, and the 1981 Republic of Ireland Hunger Strike. This is my identity. The holder-onner, the never-forgetter. It's why . . .

"I want to know what Ormechea was thinking, why he did this, if this had been done to him, if he tried to stop, how he felt when he almost got caught, did he have a runner's high, what was his favorite position, did he think of them and what he was doing to their souls, does he think of them still, does he wonder what scars he left, can he name each boy, would he name each boy? I want to know what he did with all the church money he took. I want to know how he cemented his power, how he groomed each parent, how . . ."

My loved ones interject, "Do you even know if he's there?"

"I'm not sure."

"So the whole trip could be a waste?"

"Maybe."

"And it's worth it to you? Leaving Richard? Leaving Abbie?"

"At least I get to see Rome."

"Well, if he is there, there's no way he is going to talk to you, ever, or listen to a thing you have to say."

"Why do you say that?"

"Why would he?"

"Because he's old. Because he's running," forward momentum, wide-armed circling, leg collapsing, "out of time, here on earth. Maybe he is ready."

"For what?"

My silence.

"For what?"

∂♥

King Numa's last testament required that the Sacred Books be buried alongside him. At the end of his life, they spanned twelve, thick volumes. As if he were burying Egeria herself, to keep her near, each book was entombed in its own stone coffin, and each coffin surrounded his body, which, against custom, he forbid to be burned. Five hundred years later, still one hundred years before the time of the common era, *anno domini*, a huge rainstorm pummeled Rome and the stone coffins were unearthed. At excavation, the one holding Numa's body was full of dust, but the Sacred Books survived intact. That is, until the Roman Senate ordered them burned. The reason? Within those five hundred years, the Romans had introduced superstition and demagoguery into their social order and religious ritual. Any casual reader of the Sacred Books would have easily uncovered this. So, rather than share their teachings, the senators ordered them gone. Egeria's wisdom was said to be lost forever, gone away with you, my friend. That is, unless one considered the still-adored goddess Diana.

As sister in message, all that was the wisdom of Egeria could be said to have continued through her for Diana too was endowed with Jupiter's greatness and Minerva's smarts. Often accompanied by hunting dogs or the great stags she would not kill, and, in kinship with Juno, she was the goddess of nature. Like Egeria, women who wanted to be pregnant worshipped her. Once pregnant, they offered libations for an easy delivery. For their children they asked for prophecy. Diana held a special love for young girls and often offered them her protection. In Rome, the cult of her followers was as old as the city itself. King Titus Tatius built a shrine in her honor. In the country, seventeen miles to the southeast of the city, Romans venerated her in a grove of oak trees beside the water-filled crater of an ancient volcano, Lake Nemi. Coincidently, it was to Lake Nemi that Egeria fled following Numa's death; here that the spring that is Egeria, whose waters the Vestal Virgins gathered, still flowed.

If I were to follow my own example, I would slow, mid-run, and then bring myself to a halt. I would raise my head and look for the seven-hill horizon. I would listen for the church bell's call and the rain that might lightly fall. I would feel the sweat beads gathering at my temple. I would taste the salt on my skin. And I would try to answer that last question, here, on Italian soil. Maybe he is ready, because he never got the last word.

❧

Like many deities of similar Roman and Greek mythology, Diana was more than a Roman goddess. In Greece and Asia Minor, she was known as Artemis. The Artemis of Asia Minor, in turn, shared root with Cybele, the mother goddess of Egypt and Asia. Thus, the farther east one traveled, the cult statues to her differed in form. When in Rome and Athens she was depicted as a hunter with a moon diadem on her forehead and a bow and arrow at her side, in Asia Minor, she stood in an Egyptian sarcophagus stance. Numerous nodes, some say breasts, others bull testes, both signs of fertility, covered her chest. On the front of her skirt were the rows of animals she protected. On her sides, were bees and rosettes. Young rams kept her company.

In Asia Minor, one city was her stronghold. From the time its Amazon warrior founders placed a shrine to the great mother of the gods in an oak tree and built a great temple in her honor, her people cried out, "Behold Diana, nay, Artemis, goddess of all."

During the time of Saints Paul and Timothy, Antipater of Sidon, one of the original contributing Hellenistic authors to identify the "Seven Wonders of the Ancient World," had this to say of temple in Ephesus built in Artemis's name:

> I have set eyes on the wall of lofty Babylon on which is a road for chariots, and the statue of Zeus by the Alpheus, and the hanging gardens, and the colossus of the Sun, and the huge labour of the high pyramids, and the vast tomb of Mausolus; but when I saw the house of Artemis that mounted to the clouds, those other marvels lost their brilliancy, and I said, "Lo, apart from Olympus, the Sun never looked on aught so grand."

But what else of this ancient city of Ephesus? In *I Suffer Not a Woman: Rethinking Timothy 2:11–15 in Light of Ancient Evidence*, authors Catherine Clark Kroeger and Richard Clark Kroeger describe it as the city of philosophers and the learned, of equal heritage to Alexandria and its grand libraries. Ephesus's first century population was estimated at two hundred thousand people. Because intellectual snobbery and devotion to Artemis abounded there, both authors concluded Ephesus "was not an easy place in which to bring the Christian message."

Nevertheless, around AD 55, Paul arrived there. The Acts of Apostles (19:28) propose that any Greek or Jew living in Ephesus was sure to have known his name. As the Acts further chronicle, one follower of Artemis took notice that Christianity might potentially deal his goddess harm. It is written:

A man named Demetrius, a silversmith who made silver shrines of Artemis, [noticed Christianity] brought no little business to the artisans. These he gathered together, with workers of the same trade, and said, "Men, you know that we get our wealth from this business." You also see and hear that not only in Ephesus, but in almost the whole of Asia, this Paul has persuaded and drawn away a considerable number of people by saying that gods made with hands are not gods. And there is danger not only that this trade of ours will come into disrepute, but also that the temple of the great goddess Artemis will be scorned, and she will be deprived of her majesty that brought Asia and the world to worship her.

When the gathered tradesmen heard this, they were enraged and shouted, "Great is Artemis of the Ephesians."

Shall I announce here, when finally understanding that my key to reaching Ormechea is to appeal to his tainted image and his need for that repair, that it has to about him, that I dare to shout, "Great is the Holy Trinity—the Artemis, Diana, and Egeria—of the Ephesians." That in response to an epistle that values subservience, there is a goddess who will take none of it, who forms the law, who instructs the king, and who is made with human hands only because those hands are imbued with her. A true immaculate conception.

And what of the Epistle's Timothy? His name appears as the coauthor of Second Corinthians, Philippians, Colossians, First and Second Thessalonians, and of Philemon. Paul once wrote to the Philippians about Timothy, "I have no one like him." No one.

Paul installed Timothy as bishop of Ephesus in the year 64. Legend has it Paul wrote the two epistles to Timothy, first in 64 from Macedonia, and the second in 65 from Rome, while imprisoned and about to face his death.

Despite the Artemis stronghold in Ephesus, there, Timothy had either a fifteen or thirty-two year run. This is because some place his death in the year 80 and others in 97. And just as there are two potential years of death, two different reasons for its cause are still in circulation. The first is that the Roman Emperor Nerva's emissaries killed him. The second, the more popular legend, is that a procession of people taking part in a five-day celebration in tribute to Artemis dragged Timothy's weakened body through the streets and stoned him.

Under either version of his death, in Christian history, Timothy was a martyr and thus a saint. But in the second story, by putting himself in harm's way, I have to believe Timothy became a foolish one. He must have been angered by what he saw. Some describe the festival of Artemis, known as Katagogi, as an orgiastic parade. But what about picking one's time and one's battles? Isn't the message of Jesus as savior more effective after the crowds have really screwed up and determined the celebration left them feeling empty? Isn't it easier to grab the few discontents as they walk home than it is to stop them before they've understood they've done any wrong? One would think. But Timothy jumped in that believing crowd early and the result was anger: anger and death by stoning.

Moreover, Timothy's sacrifice appeared in vain. By AD 163, the people of Ephesus still declared their allegiance to Artemis by official proclamation. A plaque then read:

> Since the goddess Artemis, leader of our city, is honoured not only in her homeland, which she has made the most illustrious of cities by her own divine nature, but also among Greeks and barbarians, the result is that everywhere her shrines and sanctuaries have been established, and temples are founded for her and altars dedicated to her because of the visible manifestations effected by her. (Horsely, ed., *New Documents Illustrating Early Christianity*, 4:75)

And so we have it. First, the Roman Senate, next Saint Paul, and then Saint Timothy; each trying to bring that holy woman trinity to an end. Yet they were vanquished. The mother goddess wasn't going anywhere any time soon.

But I am. En route to the Parco di Porta Capena, I purposely avoided Via di San Paolo della Croce altogether and elected instead to pass the Arch of Constantine, the ruins of Palatine, and the church of Saint Gregory the Great, with its twelve-step entrance and its signs in English that marked its longtime link to the Camaldolese monks who once evangelized Great Britain. But returning to the Hotel Lancelot—to home, I might have even called it—I had the strength born of endorphins, of green space, of pathway decided, and maybe even of Egeria.

Long before arriving, I had memorized the location of the General Curia from every direction. With the Colosseum in view to the North, I know to take a right on Clivo di Scauro, such an odd street that feels more like I'm running up someone's alley. I pass the fence surrounding the Cathedral of San Giovanni e Paolo and mask myself, for the moment, behind the gate of Viale Spellman, one entrance to Celimontana. I watch what look like embassy employees walk in and out of an undesignated building within Celimontana's perimeter. It's flagged with cherry-red and sunflower-yellow banners as if it's an embassy of some kind. The men out front, all dressed in black, look like unarmed guards. I play the part to which I've been assigned, runner, lean against the stone post, and pull my left knee into a quadriceps stretch. Then I bend down to tie my right shoe.

I raise my head and look toward what I am seeking. The open gate to the Curia, number 13 San Paolo della Croce, is right before me.

There's a problem. It's so apparent that the editors of my Catholic Bible even acknowledge it in the introductory text to the second epistle to Timothy. They remark: "Though this letter may have been completed after Paul's death . . ."

After Paul's death? It didn't take much research to see I wasn't the first reader puzzled not only by Paul's ability to write from the grave, but by the Book of Timothy's focus on the silencing of women. A silencing, by the way, that took women out of the equation to answer these questions. "How shall young boys be spiritually nurtured?" "Shall we permit one-on-one counseling between a priest and young altar boy?" "What is a proper relationship when there are to be no relations at all?"

So what was the need for the back-from-the-grave pronouncement? Before the epistle's woman-silencing trajectory, the Gospel writings were full of proof Jesus had many free-thinking, creative, loyal women in his band of followers. His mother for one; with him to the end, and, some say, buried in Ephesus. Mary of Magdala, also present when the men fled and the first person to whom Jesus appeared after the Resurrection (Side note: it's a late-written Gospel of Luke that tries to doctor this by making Peter the first recipient of a risen Jesus's greeting). Look also to Lazarus's sister, Mary, who sat by Jesus's feet forsaking the dishes, and Martha, who dutifully did the dishes. And next to Johanna, Susanna, Salome, and the Samaritan woman who gave Jesus water. They were just as much students to their teacher as Peter and John had ever been.

The same might be said of the women of the real Saint Paul, for recall what he told the people of Galilee:

> So in Christ Jesus, you are all children of God through faith, for all of you who were baptized into Christ have clothed yourselves in Christ. There is neither Jew nor Gentile, neither slave nor free, nor is there male and female. (Galatians 3:26)

Thus, if we are all one in Christ Jesus, why the later instruction to silence half the human population?

Sister Chris Schenk, a sister of the Congregation of Saint Joseph and an eldest daughter of an Iowa farmer, was the first to set me straight. In her lecture to FutureChurch, "The Silencing of (Catholic) Women: Then and Now," she quickly dismissed any likelihood Paul penned the epistles to Timothy. An analysis of use of language and terms more appropriately marks the writing as occurring sometime in the fourth century, more than two hundred years after Paul's death. So the next question becomes, "Why the need for these instructions to the women of the fourth century?" The most logical answer was to curtail what was, in fact, occurring. Women were indeed teaching.

In opposition to the Book of Timothy's proscriptions, the frescoes and mosaics of the first Roman Christians show women very much in the forefront. In the Catacombs of Priscilla, for example, a fresco painted at the end of the second century depicts a Eucharistic banquet in which women are consecrating and breaking the bread. And, on the catacombs walls displayed at the Pio Cristiano Museum, an aristocratic woman named Crispina cradles the Scripture, while Cissa, with hands in a teaching posture, is about to preach. Sister Schenk had explained: "The sarcophagi," she said, "of these largely wealthy women with the power to leave a message tell us how they wanted to be remembered. They are speaking from the grave." Egeria's ever-flowing, water-rich grave.

Listen. Only the footfall of the perhaps embassy personnel is behind me. Feel. The slight breeze at this near-noon hour is at my back. Look. The gate to numero 13 is open, but the pathway to the Curia's front door is empty, devoid of humans. Ormechea does not depart for his morning cappuccino. Neither do the priests, students, and superiors, that must enter and exit constantly. The front door remains closed, and I do know this. Running-shoe wearing, moisture-wicking apparel clothed, the means for conversation only beginning to develop, I am in no position to enter. Not yet. Still, shoulders squared and chin raised, I stand. That is, until I run, but not away. Not anymore.

There is another history this story cannot fully tell, such as the rise and fall of Gnosticism (in Ephesus, yet again, a stronghold), the replacement of the home church with the public gathering place, and, as result, the movement of Christianity from a religion of women and slaves to a religion of empires and kingdoms. To gather the aristocracy and their concomitant influx of stoicism, women had to be diminished. In time, they were deleted from apostlehood, disciplehood, priesthood, deaconhood, and the altar. Finally, to keep the neck from turning the head as a character in *My Big Fat Greek Wedding* would say, women were also deleted from any kind of marital union with priests. This was the ultimate separation of sexes, which, in time, led to a prohibition against sexual intercourse for clergy; that is, if you don't count the little boys. But even absent this lengthened history and discussion of cause and effect, there is something I hope we all can agree upon. For the two chapters of the Book of Timothy, early church leaders were working really hard to put women in their supposed place. Again.

Back in my hotel room, I kick my running shoes under the bed and grab the Bible I brought along. Even in the days of Kindle, I just can't help it. My luggage is always half books.

Catholics are often accused of never reading the Bible cover to cover, and, in my case, it was most definitely true. The first time I read the Book of Timothy was after my confession with Father William, which got me thinking. Never in my twelve years of parochial education did any Sister of Providence or Resurrection ever once mention the epistles or its instructions against women. Nor did the book reach my Aunt Lorraine's list of bedtime stories to read to Teresa and me, when we spent the night at her convent.

Instead the teaching sisters, my aunt included, spoke of a Jesus who does not subjugate and of the women that were his friends. Not just of Martha, Veronica, and the long list of Marys, but of the women of the widow's offering, the mother's faith, the sick's confidence, and the little girl raised. The teaching sisters, especially through their silence about the Book of Timothy, did what the Vatican was too weak to recognize. They controlled the message.

And, now, they've been found out. Just two days before my departure to Rome, the Vatican announced it would be appointing an American bishop to oversee the Leadership Conference of Women Religious (LCWR), this, the representative organization of eighty percent of American nuns, because of "serious doctrinal problems." Not through open teaching but through their silence, the sisters were accused of challenging church teaching on homosexuality and the male-only priesthood. Their "radical feminist themes" were deemed "incompatible with the Catholic Church." The Vatican further reprimanded the nuns for making public statements that "disagree with or challenge the bishops, who are the church's authentic teachers of faith and morals." This appeared to be a reference to the women religious who ran hospitals and backed the Affordable Care Act at the same time bishops preached against its contraceptive-access provisions.

While the first public words of the nun serving as director of the LCWR were, "I'm stunned," a leading member of the conference was more direct. She stated, "The church in Rome believes in the patrimony of God. But we believe that God created men and women equally." She added, "What woman do you know who truly believes she is not equal to a man?" The sisters seemed to know this was a battle as old as the Book of Timothy itself.

And, no matter how much the Vatican might have wished otherwise, I was the nuns' creation, not the Vatican's, which meant one thing. I couldn't play the fool, but I could play the part, the part that one hiding predator priest might even expect of me. What if, in talking to Ormechea, I were respectful and humble, a midwestern girl in need of refuge (my father's word) and ready to forgive? What if I become his friend, sympathize with his emotions, cajole him to admission, and ease him so gently he never realizes I got what I came for?

To do so, I need help. I fall to my knees, elbows pressed into that rose-colored comforter, and hands folded in prayer, just like the JPII image that still faces me. With more Italian words springing up from the inner courtyard in a cacophony of unidentifiable voices—*qual'e una buona, mi sento, fradicia*—I cross myself, bow my head, and implore, "Dear kind Egeria. Protector of women and prophesier of victory. Pray for me."

TOWARD THOSE FLAMES

Monday, past noon

Santi Giovanni e Paolo. St. John and St. Paul. Were they eunuchs or Roman soldiers? The answer depends on which source you believe: the secular, perhaps disparaging Wikipedia, or the religious, likely whitewashed story from the Order of Passionist Priests, whose home church, the Church of Santi Giovanni e Paolo, is built over the two saints' graves. Both sources agree John and Paul were in service to the former Emperor Constantine's daughter, Constantia, at the time of their deaths. That's when a henchman for the new Emperor Julian came calling in the middle of the night.

Whether the ensuing confrontation was the result of Paul and John's refusal to serve Julian or to correct Constantia's decision to leave her vast fortune to them, the answer again depends on source. What all agree is that despite Constantine's deathbed conversion to Christianity, Julian reinstalled a mix of philosophy and polytheism as the true way for the Roman Empire. His mentor, Maximus of Ephesus, joined him at the Constantinople palace. That home-of-Artemis connection for his greatest tutor might be one reason that Emperor Julian's most remembered philosophical work is entitled, "To the Mother of the Gods." In it, he extolls, "Who then is the Mother of the Gods? She is the Source of the Intelligible and Creative Powers, which direct the visible ones . . . she exists as a great goddess next to the Great One, and in union with the Great Creator." We all know the lesson. To the victor go the spoils, including the writing of history. Thus, the Passionist Order and all of the Catholic Church, for that matter, call Emperor Julian the Apostate, meaning the transgressor. They also relegate to him the title of last non-Christian emperor. Scholars insist a Christian soldier from Julian's own army stabbed Julian to death on the battlefield. Julian's last words were said to be, *"Nenikekas Galilaie."* "Thou hast conquered, O Galilean."

As for Julian's earlier role in the deaths of John and Paul, none dispute an army officer named Terantianus arrived at the men's Celian Hill estate in the middle of the night and beheaded them for their disobedience. Terantianus likely knew the chance he took. Because John and Paul had been busy sharing Constantia's wealth with the poor, they had become local heroes. So in an attempt to conceal his acts, Terantianus buried both their bodies on the spot.

Terantiantus was right. John and Paul were missed, and their shallow graves were soon discovered. Once lifted from the soil, their bodies were venerated and then buried again. Early Christians made pilgrimages to their graves, one of the few sites of devotion within the Servian Wall, and they mourned en masse.

Sometime in the early fifth century, Roman senator Pammachius acquired Constantia's former estate and built a house church over the graves of John and Paul. The church was first known as the Titulus Pammachii, in honor of the senator, but within a hundred or so years it became known by the name it still carries: the Minor Basilica dei Santi Giovanni e Paolo. Since then, the church has withstood six Roman sackings, two major earthquakes, and one Napoleonic invasion. All this may be why, when I take the time to study the church up close, I'm not overwhelmed by its beauty.

It's not the most attractive of churches. No Michelangelo or Bramante completed its design. Rather, standing in its piazza, my first thought is that it looks like the architectural equivalent of a meal my mother used to make called Stuff. She made it by searching the cupboard and freezer for whatever food remained the three or so days before payday. Usually it was a mix of boiled potatoes, canned green beans, and frozen ground beef. The minor basilica didn't seem very different in complexity.

A boxy, three-story main building dominates the piazza. Attached to it is a nine-columned, covered portico that looks medieval in origin. I half expect the friar from *Romeo and Juliet* to walk across it with a death-feigning tincture in hand. An inscription on the portico's main beam across the columns mentions both Giovanni and Paolo by name, as well as that of Cardinal Conti di Sutri, who must have commissioned the portico's building. The majority of the main church is made from rust-colored bricks with little mortar between their rows and columns. On top of this structure is the arched and columned upper façade originating from the original fifth-century basilica. The arches, which might have once been doors, are filled in with the building's rust-colored brick. It leaves me with the sense that someone is entombed here rather than enshrined. It feels like a grave.

Attached to the main church body are a chapel and rotunda, both built in the 1800s. And in front of that side chapel, just to its right, is a Romanesque bell tower. It dates from the twelfth century and is believed to rest upon the travertine foundations of the original Temple of Claudius.

In a way that makes the church seem even less inviting, a black iron fence encloses the portico. Nevertheless, I walk through. The portico's floored surface is made of long, rectangular tiles set tightly in a pattern of intermingling triangles and arrows. They must be cool to the touch, because a brown tabby cat, with long white whiskers and tufts of white fur growing from her ears, rests upon it. She doesn't flinch when I pass her. I ignore my urge to give her a scratch.

I look for any sign that might tell me what time Mass starts and find it by a set of dark wooden doors; doors that look more like an opening to an arctic entry than to any Roman church. The Italian on the sign is difficult to read. All I can make out are the times 12:00 and 13:30. Are these when Mass is held? If so, this is Plan A. Find Ormechea here.

A few days before leaving for Rome, I had emailed Reese Dunklin, the *Dallas Morning News* reporter mentioned earlier. In 2004 he traveled to Rome to write a story about American priests relocated to Rome and the Vatican in the aftermath of the Church's sex abuse scandal. Bernard Law, the former cardinal for the Archdiocese of Boston, was the city's most famous exile. In addition to Law, Reese attempted to meet with at least six other American clergy accused of or indicted for child sexual abuse. When he arrived at the General Curia to speak to Ormechea, Ormechea refused to come down to see him. He later refused to take Reese's call.

When Reese's four-part series was published and I got wind of it from one of my regular computer searches for Ormechea's name, I called him to thank him for his work. I reminded him of this in my recent email and let him know of my upcoming trip. He replied in less than an hour asking how I intended to contact Ormechea. When I told him I would probably write him a letter and ask him to call me, Reese bluntly asked, "You're traveling all that way, from Alaska to Rome. Why give the guy a chance to ignore you?" It was Reese who suggested I at least try to see if Ormechea might be saying Mass and, if so, to just show up. And here I am, trying to follow that advice.

The only problem is I can't tell what these hours, twelve and one-thirty, mean. If Mass were at noon, I've missed it. If it's going to be at one-thirty, I still have a half hour to go. But that inscrutable Italian sign also mentioned something about *costruzione*. Could it be daily Mass was cancelled because of construction?

When I finally walk through the entryway, cancellation seems the most likely choice. Scaffolding reaches up to the fifth-century ceiling, and the church lights are dimmed to the point of nonexistence. But for a few sconces, votive candles, and whatever amount of sun could make its way through the windows not covered over in brick, the church is as dark as a movie theater.

From what I can see, only two other people, a couple, are in the church with me. They stand halfway up the nave and seem reticent to approach the high altar and the urn said to inter the remains of Saint John and Saint Paul. Perhaps if they knew the thirty-one chandeliers hanging from the ceiling were originally from New York's Waldorf Astoria (a gift from Archbishop Spellman, to spruce up the place) they may have lingered longer. But before I could leave the entry, they made their way back past me and left. Now I'm alone, and I'm afraid I can't move.

Just to my right is an interior door. It opens to a bright, white marble foyer, octagonal in shape. Beyond the foyer is a second open door to a long hallway. Judging by its path, it likely leads to the General Curia. For a moment I think I should go inside and take that path. But then my mind immediately turns to who might walk through that door, to the priest scheduled to cover the potential one-thirty Mass, who might find me, and who might figure out my intended actions, even before I do. Then, still frozen, I picture Karen in the closet.

I met her when I was a legislative aide in Juneau, the same year I met Faris's cousin, Garrett. Karen and I were both in our late twenties and worked for the same state representative, a big barrel of a man who cared more about his chances to become governor than anyone else. Where I had been studious and intent on getting research on proposed legislation correct, Karen was easygoing and funny, charismatic and charming. She could put our boss in his place without him even knowing she had done so. I liked her immediately. Apparently so did the head of the Alaska State Troopers. He regularly visited our office to lobby for additional Department of Public Safety funds. Karen had been our legislator's point person for the department's budget.

Whether the affair began then or ten years later is uncertain. But whenever it started, it didn't end well. Perhaps it was because of the trooper's gubernatorial ambitions. Just as likely, it could have been because he really did love his wife. In any case, in the summer of 2002, he told Karen their affair was over. Despite her pleas for him to reconsider, he was adamant.

On a Friday night, when he and his wife were still out, Karen broke into their home to confront them. She hid in their basement closet for at least an hour, remaining there even after they came home. She was waiting for them to play the two messages she had left on their answering machine. One was to the trooper, telling him she had put off buying a house and a horse because of his promises. The other was to his wife, telling her she had been deceived.

According to the wife, once the messages were listened to, once the husband explained he had been trying to end things with Karen for months and he really just wanted his life back, Karen came out of the closet, .44 caliber magnum blazing. She killed her lover instantly. Then she ran up the stairs to terrorize the wife. The wife said Karen sat next to her on the couch and stroked the gun like it was a puppy. Karen told her to hurry with her prayers and then shot her four times. Miraculously, the woman escaped, locked herself in an upstairs bedroom, and survived. Karen then returned to her lover's body and shot him two more times. She saved her last bullet for herself.

Those who knew Karen were shocked. As vice president of Alaska's Chamber of Commerce, each of her actions was completely against character, unexpected, diseased, and disturbed. That is, except for the standing-in-the-closet part. I could get that. I could be there with her, waiting, playing out the alternatives, wondering if she could convince her boyfriend to love her again, and thinking she could petition the wife to let him go. Maybe Karen even thought for a time that there was an easier way out. She could just wait for the husband and wife to go to sleep and then leave. Until she heard what? Was it the couple laughing or planning their next trip together? What turned her into a murderer?

Standing in the church's entry, waiting for a priest to say or not say Mass, I know one thing about myself. I don't want to be a person without choices. But what, if anything, makes me any different than Karen? At a millisecond's notice, I could close my eyes and see my small brother. I could see Charlie being convinced to place a grown man's penis in his mouth. I could hear the music Kurt had blaring on the car stereo just before he smashed into that tree. And I could feel the walls of denial squeezing Greg even tighter. I inhaled my father's despair and exhaled my mother's delusions.

The sound of jangling keys brings me back. When I look up, a sacristan is opening the gate to the side chapel. I leave the entrance and move in his direction. As I approach, the sacristan, small bodied and dressed in charcoal gray, smiles and then leaves.

The sign at the chapel's entry reads, CAPELLA DI SAN PAOLO DELLA CROCE, FONDATORE DEI RELIGIOSI DELLA PASSION DI GESU CHRISTO. The Chapel of Saint Paul of the Cross, Founder of the Religious Order of the Passion of Jesus Christ.

In the late eighteenth century, a couple of decades before Napoleon's Roman invasion, a pope granted the Church of Santi Giovanni e Paolo to Paolo Francesco Danei. Paolo and his brother, John Baptist, had formed a religious order fully titled the Congregation of Discalced (meaning "shoeless") Clerks of the Most Holy Cross and Passion of Our Lord Jesus Christ—the Passionists for short. According to Paolo the purpose of his order was to teach people how to pray.

I knew him well, Paolo, but under the name of Saint Paul of the Cross. In a stained glass window back at Immaculate Conception Church, he stood with his left arm outstretched, reaching, and looking skyward. A cobalt-blue cloak rested on his shoulders. The white robe beneath it barely covered his ankles, exposing his shoeless feet. A crowned Mary filled the top right frame of the window. She cast a golden ray that swept down from heaven, emblazoning Paul's serene face, and reached to the bottom frame of the window, where the ray of light encircled a globe. I suppose this was to symbolize that the reach of the Passionists was boundless; not a continent on earth would go untouched. Beneath Paul, a modern, young boy in a teal blue suit knelt down, head bowed, fingers uplifted in prayer. He was under Paul's tutorship, but apparently not Mary's. Her golden ray made a wide sweep to avoid him.

As kids, Tim, my sisters, and I often went to the twelve-thirty Sunday Mass parentless either because Dad was at the firehouse or Mom had already pulled communion duty for the nine o'clock service. By habit, we sat in the pew just to the left of Saint Paul's window and six rows from the back-of-the-church confessional where each week's Sunday bulletins were kept for distribution following the closing hymn. We had the timing down. If we made our move just as the ushers walked to the front of the church with collection plates for the offertory, we could make a fast genuflect, open the confessional door, and grab at least one bulletin to serve as proof of our Sunday Mass attendance. In doing so, we cut Mass down by a good thirty minutes, which was time enough for a walk to Oven Fresh Bakery for donuts or to a pond near the Sisters of Resurrection Retirement Center to feed the ducks. In most cases, it was a combination of the two: the ducks loved fresh donuts.

We weren't bad Catholics; we were just well-practiced ones who sometimes deserved a Bavarian Cream. Our memorization of Mass had been flawless. From the opening "In the name of the Father and of the Son and of the Holy Ghost" to the closing "this Mass has ended, now go in peace to love and serve the Lord," we had it down. We knew every verse of "Yahweh, I Know You Are Near," and when to say "Thanks be to God" or when to replace it, with "Praise to you, Lord Jesus Christ." Thanks to daily religion class at our parochial schools, we were well aware that the Eucharist was the transubstantiated body of Christ and that the liturgical calendar flowed from Advent through Christmas, Lent, Triduum, and Easter, with thirty-four weeks of ordinary time filled in between them. Together, they marked our migration from one year to the next.

We also could count on the fact that during homilies Fathers Jerome would be forgetful, Father Keith may have nipped a bit of the sauce, and Father Alan liked to leave the crowd laughing. Thus, on the very rare occasions when we left after the opening processional, we could easily tell our mother, "Guess what Father said today," and never raise her suspicion. Either that or she just took it in stride. Mom was on so many church committees, some Mr. or Mrs. Saint Vincent DePaul Society member could have filled her in. If we were playing games, she might have been doing the same, right back at us.

There was one last thing about that stained glass window at I. C. Between Mary and Saint Paul was the Passionist Order's insignia. It was a heart, outlined in white, with the words *Jesu XPI Passio*, "the Passion of Jesus Christ," written within it. Beneath the words were three nails symbolizing the crucifixion. Above them grew a white cross, which was encircled in a Holy Trinity clover. And, as I enter the rotunda, there it is, in stained glass again, this time shining refracted light from the cupola onto the remains of Saint Paul of the Cross himself.

His corpse is touted as uncorrupted, but nothing about it, displayed like Snow White in a glass coffin, looks as if he's sleeping. Dead people look dead. Besides, there's no way to even see his alleged decaylessness. Every part of his body is covered in either the Passionist's signature black robe or a dark wire mesh. His facemask is Halloween scary, and the more I think of the two of us alone, my breakfast starts to rise.

At the center of the rotunda is a cardinal-red carpet upon which nearly twenty armless chairs are arranged in a semicircle, facing the corpse. The walls and floor are a dark patterned marble. The majority of the paintings in the room present the life of Saint Paul. Above his body, he is a young twenty-something Paul kneeling upon an altar. Two angels and ghostlike women hover over him. Above me, in the interior of the dome, is a painted scene of Paul on his death-bed. He holds his hand to his heart while a standing priest presents a chalice to him. Nine other robed Passionists kneel around his bed. One more Passionist is standing, but he looks away from Paul and raises his hands to his eyes, as if the soon-to-come death is too much for him to face. In another painting, just above the deathbed scene, Paul stands, arms outstretched, as in my old I. C. window, but now he's risen into eternal glory. No less than seven female angels and Mary share the glory of heaven with him. Besides a baby Jesus in Mary's arms, not a man is in sight.

Now that the sacristan with his jangling keys is gone, the church takes on a pre-tornado-sky silence. I half expect a dove to fly down from the dome, but the only noise I hear comes from my own breath and the scratching of my pen against paper. I write: "I feel nervous and frenzied and that my time is limited. I must set the intention. Let today be a day of rest and reflection. Let miracles abound. Let this journey be about my healing."

I pull my pen back when the words come out, shocked, as if someone has stolen my body. What the hell is wrong with me? I was here either to throttle Ormechea or to cajole him into admissions. I was here for Tim, Charlie, Kurt, Greg, and the rest of the boys, even the ones I didn't know. I wasn't here for me. I wasn't here for my healing. I sigh and rub my thumbs against my eyes.

When I look up, I see him. Not Ormechea, not the corpse before me, but the larger-than-life portrait of Jesus kneeling in the garden of Gethsemane. His elbows push into a rock and his bare feet grip against the earth like he's willing himself to stand but can't muster the final move. His chest is open, in a yoga camel pose, and his chin is outstretched, beyond perpendicular to his neck. He doesn't know it, but a beautiful angel stands in front of him. Her right hand is raised, as if she's saying, "Stop." In her left hand, she extends a full cup. In the Gospel according to Mark, at this moment, Jesus is to say, "Father, for you all things are possible; remove this cup from me; yet not what I want, but what you want." The angel appears to be giving the answer. "Take the cup."

"Take the cup." What did this mean in my case? Take the cup of healing my words were unexpectedly wishing for me, or take the cup of representative for the lost boys, as witness, as truth-teller, maybe even revenge-seeker. Which is it?

It's twenty minutes to two. No one-thirty Mass has started. No Father Ormechea has descended. No nothing. I repack my journal and get up to go, but just outside the side chapel is a circular display of votive candles.

I light seven of them in total, one for each of the known victims and one also for me. Once lit, I pray primarily for the men's happiness and their children's one-day success. I pray for the wives, girlfriends, or maybe even the boyfriends who love them. I pray laughter comes easy, and when trouble befalls them, that they always know they'd seen worse. I ask for each of them one miracle. And still, despite my good and best intentions, I pray for one more thing. I pray the flames rise up and burn this place down to the ground.

List them before they fall away. A brief accounting, because, despite this mission, I am not cruel. I understand circumstance, and I know moments matter.

Like my second memory—"'Momma, I can't sleep,' and her cradling me on a toddler's bed until I did. Or driving, age five, on my father's lap down a traffic-free Coventry Lane. Turning around on that same road a year later to see he was no longer holding the seat of my bicycle."

Because nothing occurs in a vacuum. Because the pathway from cause to effect didn't begin with them, but was hundreds of generations in the making. Just ask Priscilla, Chrispina, and Cissa.

"My father's instruction when I lost the role of fairy godmother and was relegated to that which struck twelve, 'Be the best clock you can be.'"

Because some moments did let me know I was safe.

"Like holding my mother's hand while stepping onto a bus, a train, a boat, a plane or sleeping a full summer by her mother's side when *The Exorcist* was in the theaters, and I was afraid to die."

Because, no matter how much I try to limit my life because of that closed door, it didn't happen to me. It didn't. Because, I gather, not delete. Because I have a good memory of good memories. So list them, before they fall away, because they feel like sunshine on my face, like warm rain on my shoulders, and like four messy dogs and one brave cat sleeping soundly by an open fire.

❧

As soon as the prayer left my lips, I know it's best to regret it. That's because I know, better than most, what comes next, after the rubble has cooled, the remains are identified, and arson investigators reach their conclusions. I also know better than most not to joke about fires or to wish them on anyone, unless I really meant it.

❧

The last full day my uncle lived was Tim's nineteenth birthday. Dan's youngest son, Paul, remembered having an early breakfast with him before leaving for high school. Dan reported to Engine Company 7, on Belmont Avenue, to captain Hook and Ladder Truck 58 as he had for the last seven years.

Though his belly and his sideburns had at times grown to sizes even he mocked, at fifty-six and a thirty-two-year Chicago Fire Department veteran, he was still ruggedly handsome. In his twenties, he had a temperament fit for bar brawls, and his body carried the damage to prove it. Upon request, he would collapse his thrice-broke nose. His front teeth tilted slightly inward as if they too were pushed off course by some errant fist to the face.

His laughter shook vases. My sister Julie often told the story of how he made her an accomplice at our parents' twenty-fifth anniversary party. She was just eleven, and he had her go around and ask guests if they would like her to refresh their drinks. If the drink had alcohol in it, she would assure the guest another adult would help her make it. Julie then took an agreeing guest's Styrofoam cup to Uncle Dan who would make the drink and refill the cup, but then poke a hole in the bottom of it. He would show Julie how to carry the cup, just so, until she handed it back to Dan's intended target. When the guest, usually one of Dan's brothers or sisters, got the drink, it would slowly leak all over them. Uncle Dan would stand to the side and laugh until he was spotted. Always more willing to be on his side than against him, that guest would join Dan in the corner while Julie picked out his next target.

For my part, my uncle seemed to understand my serious side. Like no one

else in my blue-collar family, he got the value of a college education and sup-
ported my efforts to one day get one. Every *A* I received got his applause. When
I got a *B*, he was the only one to ask if I could've done better. He also saw my
country mouse tendencies. Any time I asked, he would recount for me in great
detail his 1969 trip to Alaska in a Volkswagen van. He would listen equally
enthralled as I told him about being chased by a moose in Yellowstone or how
Mom had to hold me back from pursuing a black bear and its two cubs.

Although he could be cruel in discipline, I received only his gentility. Perhaps because both of his daughters were stillborn and I was born shortly after
one of them, Catherine, was buried, I like to think he somewhat adopted me
and kept an eye on my progression. Like my father, he called me "Joannie." Like
my grandfather, he had a way of making me feel like the only one in a room. I
loved him fiercely. I was just starting to see his imperfections before he died.
He had a restlessness to him that flared in his temper. He felt stuck. What he
couldn't have for himself, however, he willed to his children. Education was the
road out and up.

That said, he loved being a fireman and led his young team with discipline
and repeated ritualistic training. On the last full day he reported to the fire
station, that team included Michael Talley, Michael Forchione, Billy Karda,
and Sam Lasco; each were no older than thirty. In fact, January 31st had
been Michael Forchione's birthday as well. The chalkboard assigning late-
night watches gave the first to him, birthday boy, and the second to Talley-Ho,
Michael Talley. Each man had been trained to follow Dan's directions, but it
was Michael Talley who paid most attention. He told his wife, to become a
great firefighter, he needed to stay by his captain's side. An African American,
if Michael knew my uncle had voted for George Wallace because of his support
of segregation or how Dan railed against affirmative action whenever taunted
about lost or delayed promotions, maybe he would have reconsidered his own
guidance. But I'm also certain Dan had reconsidered many of his former biases
by the time Michael joined the force, and as for Michael, my uncle considered
him a man without comparison. I might also say he loved him like a son, but I
knew how much Dan loved his three boys. No love could compete with that.

The fire bell rang at 3:47 a.m. on February 1, 1985, likely when someone nick-
named Ricky Lee, per the station's chalkboard, was on third-watch duty. With

the fire station just a mile and a half away from the alarm, Truck 58 was the second apparatus on scene, but I will learn later it should have been the first. The fire had started in a first-floor electronics store. A family of three living in the apartment above it heard a strange noise coming from below them, but they were already trapped in the building by the time they understood its source. Their sole means of escape was to break open a window, jump to an adjoining rooftop, and wait for rescue.

It was a frigid night with temperatures well below zero. Water froze shortly after leaving the fire hoses. Helmets and facemasks were coated in ice. While some have said that as an officer my uncle should have remained on street level to command his crew from below, those who knew Dan best, including my grandfather, claimed that was rarely Dan's way. As Grandpa told the *Chicago Tribune*, "They say he was up on the roof with his company. That was where he belonged." What we won't learn until long after my grandfather's death is that it did not have to be the men in Truck 58. A battalion chief ordered the crew roof-side as punishment for their being late to the scene, an unenviable task even on a night without consequence.

One could also debate whether what happened next was due to the unusually heavy snow that had accumulated on a three-story flat roof or, perhaps, a maintenance crew who forgot to strengthen the rooftop joists before installing a commercial-sized air conditioning unit that previous summer. But neither of these would have been factors if Jang Han Bae hadn't given Suk Joong Kim two videocassette recorders and three thousand dollars to set his own store on fire. The noise the upstairs tenants likely heard was Kim using the keys Bae had given him to open the store. Once there, he spread six bottles of isopropyl alcohol around the remaining inventory—the portion that had not already been relocated to Bae's garage—ignited the fire, and then relocked the store. Kim called Bae about midnight to say that if nothing happened Bae should just return to the store later that morning as usual.

There was no usual. At 4:01 a.m., a woman in an adjacent third-floor apartment building heard one fireman scream, "Oh my God! Get out of here!" It may have been Billy Karda. After being ordered to vent the lower windows on the way up the ladder, Billy was about to step on the roof when it started to give way. His next recollection was of smoke and fire. He leaped off the ladder and landed twenty feet below in a pile of snow.

It was Sam Lasco who recalled Forchione's first cut into the roof. A flame shot through the opening, and he heard a scream. At Bae's first-degree murder trial, he told the jury, "The captain was a big guy. The flame was shooting over his head and engulfed Forchione."

This we do know. When the air conditioning unit broke free, Dan, the two Michaels, and Sam Lasco went down with it. Although engulfed in fire from his hips to knees and face to neck, Sam somehow managed to climb out. Not before, however, witnessing my uncle in flames and Forchione "just gone." He'll recall climbing up a beam that fell into the flames with them, but Billy Karda will tell him that before Karda jumped, he saw. "There was no beam," and it was more like "he walked up the air, or who knows, maybe up the arm of God or something."

As for Dan, Michael Forchione, and Michael Talley, we tell ourselves they died instantly. We say they were knocked unconscious by either the air conditioning unit or the blunt force of the floor hitting their ribs. We try not to think of the fact that Michael Talley's body was found farther away from the others, as if, for a time, he had strength to crawl toward a door. Despite autopsy reports to the contrary, we link no cause of death to the flames that burned their bodies beyond recognition and melted their helmets to their scalps. No fireball consumed their throats. No panic-filled thoughts occupied their minds.

For the first five years after Dan's death, no family member could listen to the Talking Heads's "Burning Down the House" without feeling like running. We couldn't forgive a justice system that let Suk Joong Kim escape to Korea once his confession was thrown out, even though it was likely true Chicago police officers interrogating him refused his requests for an attorney. Despite Jang Bae's lack of intent to kill a single person, even those apartment residents, let alone the firemen, we believed he deserved the natural life sentence he received. And every time February 2, 3, 4, and 5 came around, we remembered wakes and funerals, really bad coffee, Entenmann's Danish, hundreds of mourners, and thousands of prayers. In an instant, we could recollect the three fire trucks that stood waiting outside Holy Name Cathedral to carry three flag-draped coffins to Chicagoland cemeteries. Its ladder raised for the men who hadn't descended it, Truck 58 was parked at the front. We could smell the incensed air and hear the eleven-ring tome announcing, "It's time to return, safe, home." We could do all of this, easily, without forethought because, in some odd way, those memories and triggers kept Dan alive.

After four weeks of intensive care and numerous skin grafts, Sam Lasco was released from the hospital. About a year after the blaze, he was featured in *People* magazine still wearing a plastic mask, filled with antibacterial cream to

protect his face from infection. He told the magazine writer, "As for the arson-
ists who set that fire, I'm still really mad at them. Maybe I could understand it
if they were poor. But if they set that fire out of nothing but greed, I'd like to
do to them what they did to me."

ᐱᗷ

This idea of wishing people on fire is so cruel the desire must always have an
origin. For Sam, it came from seeing the videotapes of the body recovery, and
the funeral. He said they "made me sick to the stomach." When he watched, he
felt like he was "in a room without a door," and he wanted out.

As for Ormechea, my desire to set his church and him on fire likely stemmed
from this recognition. After he molested Tim, countless times, he still chose to
join thirty other priests on Holy Name Cathedral's altar to say the funeral Mass
for my uncle. If Dan could have grabbed that asshole by the throat from the casket, I have no doubt he would have. Part of me now believed that was up to me.

The day Dan died I had a difficult time accepting it was true, even when
WGN News posted his photo on its noon, 5:00, and 9:00 p.m. telecasts. I
thought it could still be a case of mistaken identity. Proof would have to come
in the casket, but we'd been informed there could be no chance of an open one.
Every feature, but two nostril holes, was erased. As a longtime *General Hospital*
fan, all I could think was, "Isn't that convenient?" When the body couldn't
be found, or was perhaps unrecognizable, that was always when the character
returned three years later after escaping a mortal enemy. Until I went to sleep, I
thought my uncle would soon be doing the same.

But in my dream, I was in a back pew of I. C., not far from the Saint Paul
of the Cross window, praying. Just like today, a few sconces lit the church and
glimmered against the crucifix on the altar. Candles in their red votive glass
flickered under Saint Joseph's statue. I said one Hail Mary, then another, then
another, and then started to cry. When I stopped, I looked behind me. I hadn't
heard anyone come in, but three rows back sat a bald man with a scarred face.
Although he looked frightening, I smiled at him. He asked me what I was doing.
I told him I was praying for my uncle. That's when he said, "Do not pray for me.
Pray for your family. As I am."

This was a much more fitting prayer than my fire-inspired idealizations, I
think, while making my way to the front altar of Santi Giovanni e Paolo. With
time for Mass long past, my anxiety of being found out has lessened. If my can-

dles were somehow imbued with isopropyl alcohol, it would make me no better than Jang Han Bae to fail to think of the unintended consequences, like the safety of the key-jangling sacristan or the brown tabby cat resting on the portico. Dan would expect better from me, and he should. But he wouldn't expect perfection. For, if I could warn the sacristan and shoo away the cat, wouldn't he allow me this one failure, to have a temper that could flare and be as forceful as his once had been?

I know Tim expected it just as well. On a recent anniversary of that four-alarm call, Tim wrote on his Facebook page:

> The day after my nineteenth birthday, I was awoken by my crying dad because his brother Dan was murdered in an arson fire on Milwaukee Avenue. He fell through the roof with two other firefighters. All three died and one was badly burned and spent months in the hospital. Years before that day, I remember riding my bike to sit and talk with Uncle Dan at his firehouse near our home. He was easier to talk to than my dad at that time in my life. I had so many problems back then, and he was so strong and caring . . . I never told him who hurt me, because I was certain he would kill for me. When he was killed I remember feeling very scared. . . . I had nobody to help me anymore.

Come on Dan. Let me kill!

A few days after Dan died, my cousin Patrick retrieved his briefcase from the firehouse. It held keys, a wallet, a checkbook, a calculator, and a calendar: the items to bring him home, buy his groceries, pay his bills, and help him plan his year. But somewhere in the pile of the take-for-granted routine was a hand-written poem of Dan's called "The Aria of the Butterfly."

Could it compare to Mary Oliver's "When Death Comes," or Wendell Berry's "The Wish to Be Generous"? No. Not in form or even in metaphor. But in sentiment or message? Yes. Definitely. In the poem's closing lines, in observation of the butterfly, Dan wrote:

> Are those wings a mantle of your soul and life, drawn out from an otherwise repelling insect body?
> That *my* life and *my* soul may, as such, find grace with God's pleasure, despite the repelling stains of my living being.
> That I may be lifted aloft, up—up there, where the Butterflies sing.

I wanted that lifting for him, more than anything. And for a time I was gullible. Every butterfly I saw, I thought of it as a messenger. I greeted them each as my uncle. I wanted more than anything to believe, just like my soap operas characters that returned, that he could come back, even if it had to be in this form.

I still want him here. But in Rome? I don't want a playful, rueful butterfly. I want the man I knew. The one who would be pissed off if someone cut his life short or raped his nephew. I want the insect body that the mantle of soul and life enfolded. I want his help. Because, like Sam Lasco, God help me, I still want someone to burn. And if I can't do it to him myself, if I am no killer, I hope it won't be too much to ask Dan, and maybe my patron saint as well, for a little divine intervention.

My illusion goes like this. I fantasize that on this church's baroquified front altar, under gleaming chandeliers, Ormechea will place his hands under water streaming from an altar boy's glass pitcher and recite the words said to be those of Pontius Pilate, "Lord, wash away my inequities and cleanse me of my sins."

God's answer, however, will be, "No." Then, without one of my hands in its creation, a Queen-of-Heaven golden ray delivered on point will strike, igniting flames around him. Be it Ormechea's death by boiling blood vessels, carbon monoxide poisoning, heat stroke, or shock from the pain, both Dan and Joan of Arc will know what came first. Ormechea would eventually be engulfed, clothes burning, flesh singing, scalp melting. But before his last breath, before his eyes liquefy, his last vision will be of me. He will reach out, beseeching, asking for my help. He will try to speak, but he can't be heard. Why? Because, fires, you see, scream and bang and whistle and pierce the air more than you could ever imagine. They have voices of their own. Voices you cannot control. Only a strong, loud voice can speak over them.

He was hidden in a corner behind the door of the main entrance where I would never expect to find a pew. How long he had been there, I also couldn't say. But once I spot him, I walk by, pretending to go to a side altar to Saint Gemma, twice.

With a long nose, thick eyebrows, and a shadow of bags under each dark eye, he has an old-man Italian face. His skin is grizzled. Each minor fold in his neck is distinguishable. He wears a tattered beige short-sleeve shirt. It's tucked into loose, camel-brown polyester pants. His black sockless loafers peek out from behind him as he kneels. He holds rosary beads in his left hand and cups each one in his right as he softly mumbles a prayer for us sinners, *"Santa Maria, Madre di Dio, prega per noi peccatori."*

Like all those butterflies I once passed, I want desperately to call out "Dan" and to ask him, "What should I do next?" I want him to know I'm here in Rome, in part, even for him. I want to find out whether any hint of self-contempt rose in Ormechea's brain when he dared to pray over his coffin. I want to know if he thought this act might somehow justify his actions. And I want Dan to know I'm scared. Scared of what I might do, just as much as I'm frightened I might not be able to do enough.

I take a step toward the old Italian man—Daniele, should I call him?—readying to say all of this, to this reconfigured-dream miracle, but I stop. Daniele's head is still bowed. His fingers still move from one bead to the next. He recites, *"adesso e nell'ora della nostra morte. Amen."* He gives no sign that he notices me.

I don't interrupt. Up until the moment I open the main door and step onto the red-tiled portico, the one that still holds a sleeping cat, I want no evidence of his singular humanity. I need him to be more than that.

December 13, 2002

"Are you sure?" I sat at my desk pressing a pen cap into a legal pad. To the pad's left was a copy of Illinois State Statute Chapter 38, Section 3-5.

"It's a sucky answer, but I'm sure," Shauna Boliker, the assistant state's attorney assigned to Tim's case, said.

Despite my question, I knew she was right. The criminal statute of limitations had expired three years after the last time Ormechea sexually assaulted Tim. It was why, before turning the wrong end of my pen against the notepad, I had written the year "1985" upon it. Despite the later witnesses to Ormechea's more flagrant behavior, the only way for criminal prosecution to have been possible would have been if Charlie's father and my own had gone to the police when they first confronted their sons.

"I'm frustrated too, Joan." I believed her. There hadn't been a time when she hadn't taken Tim's calls. She was also the person who finally convinced Charlie to come forward without compromising the anonymity he required. "So you're aware," Shauna continued, "both the governor and the state's attorney know the statute of limitations is broken. It's not even close to what Massachusetts had in effect in 1983, let alone today. It's why they've been able to get more of these guys than Illinois has. There's legislation in the state house now to change it. If it passes, the statute won't lapse until a child victim turns thirty-eight."

The proposed law would have fit Tim's situation perfectly. "But it's not retroactive," I said, continuing to suck the air out of the conversation.

"True."

"And no fraud or absence from the State of Illinois would toll the statute under Section 3-7?"

"I can't see any evidence of fraud. If it were to exist, they'd likely be hiding it and it's almost impossible to discover. But tolling the statute might be an option? When did Ormechea leave your parish and move to Kentucky?"

"Not until June 1988." I wrote that year down as well. Next to it, I wrote, FIND V. LESS THAN 18.

I was in the process of adding the initials "G. C." when Shauna said, "That's still not soon enough for our legal case. If it's any consolation, the publicity the church scandals are getting is making it better for any child being victimized today. "

I thought of what Tim had written in his affidavit. "If you do one thing," he said, "stop Ormechea. Get him away from kids!"

I told Shauna, "Actually, it does matter. It's what Tim cares about the most. So where do we go from here?"

"Two things will happen. I'll write a letter to the new provincial, Father Higgins, and let him know, that but for the lapsed statute of limitations, we would have prosecuted. Then I'll talk to Kentucky's Attorney General's Office. Once the press comes out, they may be able to locate a more recent victim down there."

Perhaps Ormechea had come close to getting caught too many times and upon being assigned to a new parish, curtailed his ways, because, in spite of Deputy AG Harry Rothgerber's efforts and the *Louisville Courier*'s running of two stories on Ormechea, no Kentucky victim came forward. However, as the seventh priest within the Archdiocese of Louisville that had been accused of abusing children, its archbishop already knew what he would do. He demanded Ormechea's removal. The Passionist Order transferred him out of Kentucky in less than three days. At the time, it told no one where he was going.

Shortly after complying with the archbishop's demand, Father Higgins wrote to Tim in care of our parents. He let Tim know Ormechea was "dismayed by Tim's allegations," but still "reluctantly agreed" to resign based upon them.

Then Father Higgins suggested Tim meet with him to "give me the opportunity to apologize to you personally and on behalf of our entire community."

At the time I asked Tim, "So, are you gonna to talk to him?" If he sought
my advice, I would have said he shouldn't. The priest's double standard of first
expressing Ormechea's dismay and then offering an apology was a joke.

"He spelled my name wrong, Joan, even though Mom and Dad have been
in the parish, what, thirty years? And why should he think I care Ormechea is
dismayed by the allegations?"

"Exactly."

"What's the point of that comment other than to get in another dig? They
don't believe me. No, they want me to think they don't believe me. The part
about the apology? I don't buy it, either. You know a lawyer looked at this letter
before he sent it. There's nothing real in it."

I didn't disagree with Tim then, and now, nine and a half years later, still
couldn't. I also couldn't recall when Father Higgins first admitted Ormechea
had been sent to Rome, but he didn't deny it when Reese Dunklin called him
for a comment in 2004. He told Reese his province removed Ormechea to
Rome, with the approval of the General Curia, because the order had no US
facility that could be considered appropriately distant from children. "I want
him in a place where it's very clear we're taking all the precautions necessary,"
Father Higgins said.

❧

Late Monday afternoon

The sign reads PARCHO GIOCHI. Park of Play? No. Playground. Once I left
the church, I knew my next move had to be exactly what I told Vivian it would
be last night. I needed to write Ormechea a letter. For him to agree to meet with
me, it had to be a good one.

A short walk from the church, down the Viale Cardinale Francesco Spellman,
named for the chandelier guy, the expansive grass fields of Celimontana looked
to be a restful place for writing. Before its Renaissance gardens entertained
the Borghese's and Orsini's, Celimontana was a vineyard. And before it was a
vineyard, legend has it that might also have been the site where Numa met his
beloved Egeria. If this were true, I could use her help. The park was pretty enough
to be. Garden pathways opened up to grotto settings filled with palm trees
whose fronds grew up and out in fanlike symmetry. Beneath them, manicured

bushes blended into hand-built, stone walls. Rusted piping, from what looked to be the remains of an outbuilding, irrigated ponds filled with goldfish. I was certain flowers erupted at their edges during the height of summer.

Celimontana is a local's park. Even my *Rome 2012* guidebook failed to make mention of it. A travel website says "only few tourists find their way here," and when they do, it's primarily to look for one of the eight Egyptian obelisks scattered throughout the city.

The obelisk is located down a side garden path. It's the only obelisk in Rome that had been owned by a private citizen. His name was Ciriaco Mattei. The Roman government gifted the surviving 2.68 meters of the obelisk to Ciriaco, because of his patronage of the arts; and, as the former owner of Celimontana, Ciriaco installed it there in 1582.

The obelisk had been one of two taken from the Temple of Ra in Heliopolis, Egypt shortly after Mark Antony's and Cleopatra's defeat. A rumor says the metal globe at its top contains Emperor Augustus's ashes. The base upon which the obelisk sits is said to contain the architectural vestiges of the Basilica Hilariana, a place of worship once dedicated to Cybele, the Mother of the Gods.

Again, I seemed to be in good company. I was ready to start writing my letter, next to the obelisk, but soon after my arrival, a group of high school students in matching navy blue sweaters descended. I looked to my watch. It was only two thirty. I considered asking a couple of the kids, separated from the mass, in my makeshift Italian-Spanish, *"no escola?"* But, I changed my mind even before speaking. The boy of the pair, who just a moment before looked so sweet, gave me a "go away" look. He then turned his attention back to the girl at his side and brushed her hair behind her ear. *Perhaps she should consider braids,* I know I thought.

The "Go away" looks are why I'm standing under the Parco Giochi wood sign. The playground it indicates differs in distinctive ways from its American equivalent. Rather than being surrounded by a soft-surface rubber, park officials still trusted the dry, clay-colored dirt to cushion a child's fall off the swings or slide. Where a chain-link fence might surround it back in the States, here a wood-slab fence that went to midsection height encloses the play area. Within it, there's a see-saw, a toddler's swing, an older child's swing, a rope net, a fort, and a bright orange, spiral plastic slide. Also enclosed are two wooden benches. A thirty-something mother sits with her toddler son on one end of the see-saw while her older child, a girl of about nine, in white shoes and white pants, goes high into the air. When she's up there, the bell tower from the Basilica of Giovanni e Paolo's is in easy view, I'd say no more than a three-minute walk away.

"Buster, Buster, Buster Brown, what will you give me if I let you down?" Tim used to ask me when I sat high on the see-saw in Olympia Park.

"A puppy?"

"Nah."

A baseball mitt?

"No."

"A football?"

"Not that either."

I could tell. I was going to be up there for a while.

While I've mentioned the frequency—many times, over a period of three years—and given you clues about that ever-tiny twin bed, I haven't recounted the full scope of Ormechea's assaults against Tim. It's mainly because the details don't matter. The adult survivor of childhood sexual assault will tell you it's not the physical act itself that matters, but what came with it. The degradation. The fear. The anxiety. The abandonment. The powerlessness.

Leslie Lothstein, director of psychology at the Institute of Living in Hartford, Connecticut, adds that sexual abuse by a Catholic priest has its own "unique dynamic," because "Catholics see their priests as having a direct link to God—as possessing God-like powers." Many of her patients talk to her about "soul murder." That is, they "felt as if something had been taken deeply inside of them in which the body wasn't hurt as much as the soul." Another therapist, Laurie Pearlman, says one of her clients told her, "It was like having sex with Jesus."

The first time I tried to write in essay form about what Ormechea did to Tim, I took a lyric approach. Although my narrator was omnipotent, she refused to share her full observations. She spoke of a closed door that should have been opened and of a face inside she never saw. She—what am I saying?—I was distant for one reason only. I couldn't write about it. Until I finally did. At first, perhaps still, I faltered. I claimed I couldn't tell the story because I didn't own the story. I was the standing-in-the-hallway sister, not the fly-on-the-wall witness. I could tell a potential reader one million things about that hallway. How, from its vantage point, I could see out both the front window and the back door. How its wallpaper was pulling away from the crown molding. That in 1981 it had light blue carpet, but in 2002 it was covered in a cherry wood veneer. I could stay in that hallway, standing there not just for minutes, but for years.

If the key emergency responses to stress are flight or fight, mine is freeze. When I tried to write, again, at Tim's request, my fingers froze above the keyboard. The same reaction chilled my throat. Air got stuck, and my brain immobilized. I was the snowshoe hare that stood motionless not sure of how to move. Because of that, I was going nowhere. That is, until I started to fill in the small things that Tim's affidavit didn't include. I could start with only a few, like the click his doorknob made when turned all the way to the right, or how his door opened inward and brushed against his blue carpet's tip-sheared edge. How at five foot ten and about two-hundred and twenty pounds, Ormechea's figure must have filled the doorframe. If Tim's bedroom light were out, I also knew the hallway's candle-shaped lighting pendant, before the door closed, would have caused Ormechea's bald spot to shine. It very likely also reflected the excitement in his eyes.

Through knowledge of Tim's ten-by-twenty room, I knew his options were few. Beyond hiding in the bedroom closet that held our mother's evening gowns and the wardrobe case where Cha was once found in that moving van long ago, Tim's only real option was to feign sleep. And I knew, through speaking to him, he tried this many, many times. His football-emblazoned comforter would be tight around him. His knees were almost always to his chest. He would face his bedroom closet and the framed picture of a guardian angel looking over a little boy and his sister crossing a decaying bridge with a raging river below. He would make fake snore and yawn sounds. He always hoped some night it would be enough. He always wanted to be fine because, as Mom told him, "God always looked out for children."

What he still can't tell me was how he felt when the left bottom corner of his mattress sunk under the weight of Ormechea's body or what he thought as he felt the man inch closer and closer, buttock cheek by buttock cheek, to Tim's midsection.

He remembered the kisses. How at first, while lingering, they never left Tim's forehead or the top of his nose. But over time, they changed. With hot, moist breath, sometimes smelling like beer, Ormechea hovered over Tim's mouth, breathing in, breathing out. He lifted Tim's chin. Breathing in, breathing out. As only prey can know, like that frozen snowshoe hare, Tim knew his efforts at turning away would be useless. Once J. B.'s breath stopped, once his lips touched Tim's, once J. B. squealed and his tongue darted, Tim knew all he could do was count. One, one-thousand. Two . . .

Tim would tell me that when the abuse was in full throes the room grew quiet. Sometimes he could hear the television in the kitchen playing some sit-com theme song. At other times, it was the mumbled voices of Mom and Dad in the front room or a fire truck or ambulance blaring down Harlem Avenue. But most of the time, it was just the sound of J. B.'s breath, breathing in, breathing out, quick and excited, then thick and sticky. The smell of it would linger in the room, tied to the comforter, until Tim would bring it outside the following day to air it out on the clothesline for reasons Mom didn't understand.

I know this common space bedroom. There was only enough room for J. B.'s legs to dangle off one side of the mattress, in the direction of the bedroom door, before he bent from the waist, grabbed Tim at the shoulder, and turned the boy from his side to his back.

J. B. must have had his rules, because he rarely deviated. While kissing him, stroking him, first on the cheek, with the brush of fingernail, then on the soft space just above the breast bone, the place of baptismal anointing. Next on to the boy's bare left nipple. Ormechea would tell Tim, "This is natural and what God intended," and "I need a special boy in special ways." "This was just what Jesus did with the Apostles."

When Tim's body reacted ever so slightly to the touch, betraying him really, that's when Ormechea would lie down and turn him over.

It's best to stop, isn't it? To let the separation of time give us the benefit of distance from raw emotion. Otherwise, how are any of us to survive? We can ignore how Ormechea's eyes rolled back in ecstasy. And why fill our heads with the moans and groans?—"He sounded like he was biting into a good piece of steak," Tim will say—Why picture a disdainful man dicing and slicing a little boy as he reached his hands into and beneath the elastic waistband of one small pair of tighty whiteys.

Let's not think, not even once, of the grasp being so complete Tim wasn't able to breathe. And let's not turn our minds from J. B.'s hardened penis pressing into the back and into buttocks, against the stomach and the thighs of one small child. And don't, for one second, imagine what Tim may still not have the ability to say. That after twenty-two years, "It scares me J. B. could've done more than I recounted." End with this. Finally, sometimes an hour later, Ormechea's groans would cease and be replaced by one last kiss, tender and soft on the forehead, just like a mother's. His parting wish was more a curse.

"Good night, Timmie. Sweet dreams."

The little girl is still high in the air. I'm certain she giggles. Her baby brother pauses; his feet ready to replace hers, high in the air after that final push-off.

"I know what you want, Tim. An answer to your question." I hit the ground faster than I can say, "Are the children of Italy safe?"

Sitting on one of the two enclosed benches, I watch the brother and sister play. While doing so, I nod to the mother who next sifts through her purse. By that nod, I mean to say, "Be not afraid, at least not of me." Then, I look down and write:

> Dear Father J. B.,
>
> I must admit, it remains difficult, near impossible, to use this title. I haven't called you "father" in years. But I write for you to receive this message in the great hope that peace will follow. Thus I begin this letter with the words of Saint Julie Billiart, founder of my aunt's religious order: "Ask, hope, and expect everything from God's infinite goodness."
>
> This is Joan Nockels writing you. Presently, I sit in Celimontana, not far from your home. I came to Rome not as a pilgrim but as a woman on a quest for answers, many of which you hold; others of which lie in me for further discovery, whether or not we speak.
>
> On a day not very different than this day, now ten years ago, I was working in my office when the phone rang. It was Tim. He was calling me from the Blue Line, on his way home from work. He told me, "Joan, what happened to those boys in Boston happened to me."
>
> I didn't have to guess who hurt him. I knew immediately it was you. And so from that day on, I can say all of our lives changed, yours included.
>
> I wonder if you have any idea how much I love my brother. From the day of my first memory, my world was about him, protecting him, loving him. But covered

in that innate sense of purpose was this understanding. Use your power to make his life a blessing.

I have come to terms with my own limitations. A child myself, it was not my job to open his bedroom door when you were behind it. But for his sake, as well as my own, it is my quest to open it now: to open it wide.

So I write to you in the names of these men:

Tim Nockels

Charlie Tierney

Kurt Wilowski

Greg Conrad

And I write in the names of these parents:

Mary and Walter Nockels

And I write in the name of someone else whose life has been greatly altered by your chosen actions:

Joan Nockels Wilson

To say, we are here, and you have impacted us.

Despite my anger, I know there's another person whose life has greatly changed. Despite your beautiful surroundings and today's birds, now in endless song around me, I know you are in exile, no longer with a home. I know your name is stained and the mark of child abuser and raper is indelible. I know you can't hide from what you have done. And I can only believe that you must ask God for forgiveness and wonder, even with your learning, if it will ever come. I have to believe there are some things even God can't forgive. I also wonder whether you look back on your life, especially in these senior years, and see how it may have been different if you yourself were stronger and more whole.

Is it time, Father? Is it time for you to ask for our forgiveness. Are you ready? Have you thought of your words, especially now when you're free of criminal statute of limitations and civil lawsuits? What would you say to us? How would you tell us that you have changed?

I'm here to listen. I'm here to take your words and bring them to your victims, one of whom, my father, is quite ill. You were his friend, weren't you? Or was it a guise to get to my brother? With this letter I include my father's transcribed words. Let me bring home to him the peace solely your acknowledgment of his pain can bring.

Talk to me. Let me listen. Ask for our forgiveness. I may not be able to give it, but it cannot come without the request. I'm here through Saturday morning at the Hotel Lancelot. I enclose a card as a way to reach me.

I'm weary, Father. I'm so tired of fighting the demons of failure that plague me for not protecting my brother from you. I'm weakened by his continuing struggles and how he now protects his sons even from my own parents. I want him to shine. I want his other life, the one he would have had if you and he never met. I know that is not possible, but I grieve for his lost days and missed successes. Part of me knows, like Don Quixote, I'm battling windmills. But part of me hopes that, just as Saint Julie says, you can't have what you need, unless you ask for it first. And so I say in closing. "Ask, hope, and expect everything from God's infinite goodness."

❧

There's another sign at the playground. It's handwritten in green marker on a weathered and cracked whiteboard. It says:

> *Ai bambini del parco. Questi giochi sono stati realizati del comune per voi ed a voi ora sono affidati. E' anche compito vostro difenderli per continuare a giocare nel vostro parco. Buon Divertimento. L'asserore ai guardini del Comune di Roma.*

The Google translate program on my iPhone, which I forgot to use back at the church, is of some help. Even though it doesn't recognize all the words, I believe the sign reads:

> Dear Children of the Park,
>   These games were built by the town for you and you are now assigned to it. To continue playing in the park, it's your job to defend it. Have Fun!
>   The Park's Superintendent.

If I had a green marker, I would rewrite:

> Dear Children of the Park,
>   Congratulations! You're doing a nice job. The playground is spotless. Not one sign of graffiti or untended-to garbage is in place. But, please, while you're playing here, do me one favor. Look up! Not far from you, at the bell tower of the church, La Chiesa del Santi Giovanni e Paolo, is a man who harms children. From them, he takes both body and soul. From the sisters that love them, he leaves venom.
>   He was sent from America to Rome, we were told, because there are no children here. So don't let him sit on your park's benches. Don't you dare let him giggle at you. Never let him follow you. I wish I could have done more, and I'm so sorry our predicament has led to yours. But believe me, children, I love you. My brother loves you. Our hearts cry with and for you. So don't forget. I'm counting on this. Please, for all our sakes, look up!

BOILING BLOOD

Late Monday afternoon

The second-century Mithraeum became the foundation for the fourth-century Basilica of San Clemente. The fourth-century basilica did the same for the eleventh-century one. The Claudium holds up Giovanni e Paolo's bell tower. The Colosseum was built only after draining Emperor Nero's manmade lake that once surrounded his Golden Palace. Abandoning the Colosseum to attend to the Basilica of Saint John the Lateran? Yes. The area between Rome's Oppian and Celian Hills is all about rebuilding. What was a community of erasure became a metropolis of accretion. It could keep going, converting rooftop to future basement floor, blocking stairwells, filling labyrinths, until what is present has no past and what is future can always look forward to a better view.

The problem, of course, is not the builder in this paradigm, but the one who keeps digging. The historian who unearths the secret passages until she's thirty feet below sea level peering into Nero's secret garden. Does it serve a value to keep going down when others go up? Ask Janyce, Abbie's maternal birth grandmother. She witnessed the deaths of her husband, both of her parents, and her eldest daughter, Abbie's mother, in less than four years. It's why she queries, ringing her hands and speaking indirectly yet pointedly to me, "Why keep digging for answers? Why can't people just get over the past?"

And what of folklore that became historic fact or historic fact that converted back to folklore? These between-hill lands carry this as well. Just steps from the Hotel Lancelot, at the intersection of Via dei Querceti and Via dei Santi Quattro, is a tiny oratory, no bigger than a front hall closet. It encases an image of the Madonna and Child, but don't be fooled. The shrine is to the ninth-century Pope Joan who, en route from the Vatican to the Lateran Palace, is said to have been stoned to death on this spot, that is, right after giving birth to her son. Official Church doctrine calls her the stuff of legend. Her defenders respond, "Sure. There may be no contemporary record of her, but neither is there any such record for any ninth-century pope. Why not believe a smart and capable woman could fool the masses. They do all the time." Even absent direct proof, modern-day pilgrims still push flowers and prayers through the shrine's iron grill. She is as real for them as any pope gets.

❧

After leaving my letter for Ormechea back in my room and telling Faris I won't return for dinner, it's time for another quest. Walking by a motorcycle shop on Capo d'Africa, an old, bald man wearing a dark gray suit and light tan shoes carries a lilac paper bag. Rather than the bag itself, he holds tight to whatever's inside of it. His platinum-blonde wife points to something on the ground that might be in his way, perhaps a sewer grate. As I pass, she mumbles. He sighs. Next, along Via dei Santi Quattro, a young woman in black boots whose four-inch heels hit the cobblestone in stiletto points kicks a deflated silver soccer ball (the victim of her heels?) for her golden lab. He takes off after it, dragging his left hind leg a bit like Cletus does.

Graffiti on a garage door reads either *"Pisso Malo"* or *"Pieso Malo,"* but whatever is "bad" doesn't translate easily. On Via Terme de Tito, a black-and-white illustration of a woman intrigues me. She looks like the portrait of Teresa Montessori hanging in Abbie's school. But for her eyes, she's formed completely out of intersecting vertical and horizontal lines. The drawing is signed, "Sten-Lex," the combined names, I later find out, of a pair of well-known Italian street artists. Umbrella pine trees block the sun. The smell of still fresh pastries fill the air. People click and shuffle through intersections. At one, the intersection of Vias Labicana and Merulana, three red-striped officers in black boots crowd around one motorcycle. The decal across its front panel reads *CARABINIERI.* The police.

Dear Officers,

Let me confess. Every statement in my letter to Ormechea is true, but for one. Under the version of Illinois State Statute Chapter 38, Section 3-7 governing Ormechea's crimes, the period "within which a prosecution must be commenced does not include any period in which (a) The defendant is not usually and publicly a resident within the State." You see. A few trips home to officiate weddings or baptisms made Ormechea no more an Illinois resident after 1988 than I was. Therefore, the statute of lim-

itations hasn't lapsed for one victim: one whose abuse could be substantiated with witnesses, most of them still living.

Greg Conrad was just sixteen when Father MacDonald removed Ormechea from I. C. and shipped him out of state. Assuming Ormechea's abuse of the boy had continued at least until that separation, no period of the governing three-year statute of limitations for aggravated abuse of a minor had expired. And even if the contact between the two ended once it was witnessed by Patricia Sprague and Loretta Finger the year before, two years are still left to prosecute. Two glorious years. But there was a problem. In 1987, when Mary Lou Murphy and Patricia Heidkamp identified Greg by name to Father MacDonald, and, in 1988, when Joan Troka did the same to her attorney, Greg twice denied Father Ormechea had ever touched him, let alone hurt him. Historic fact or folklore? Let us be the judge.

For his part, Greg's brother, Cory, expressed how he was still "uncomfortable" when Ormechea was around. Ormechea remained a close family friend and, at his mother's request, even baptized Cory's own child. Ormechea was even closer to the brothers' father, Kevin, a retired Skokie Police Department property crimes detective. Once, when my father tried to ask Mr. Conrad about Ormechea, he shooed him away saying, "all allegations against the priest, including Tim's, were lies". In *Immaculate Conception Parish 1904 to 2004, A Century of Grace*, the unnamed author wrote of Ormechea: "One can only regret that many of the things that happen in a century ever happened at all." It was Kevin Conrad alone who raised the priest's name within that book in any positive light. On the page mentioning the parish's contributors to the One Hundred Dollar Club, Kevin made a contribution in Ormechea's name. By comparison, the new pastor of I. C., Father Eric Meyer, did so in the name of my parents.

We had hoped, by 2002, events in Greg's life might make him more approachable. We thought we could ask him about the van, the kiss, the videotaped wrestling matches, the gifted stereos and television sets, the weekends alone. There was only one problem. Greg still denied being abused, first to his brother, Cory, then to Tim, and then, finally, to me.

Our phone call was short. Greg had relocated to Miami, so I mentioned what it was like to be a relocated Chicagoan. There might've even been a few questions about Alaska. But when it came time to speak substantively, Greg said he couldn't help me.

"Can't or won't?"

"Does it matter? My family's still so close to him. My mother even visited him recently. Besides, I have nothing to say. Nothing happened."

I was blunt. "Greg, at least try not to lie to me. You and I both know there were witnesses."

"I'm not sure what you mean."

I wanted to ask him how he could think, for even one second, of protecting Ormechea. I wanted to know if he was in love with the guy. Is that what this denial was about? Most of all, I wanted to say, this wasn't about him anymore. It was about Tim, and Kurt, and Charlie, and what I needed to do was to put the asshole away. But instead, I wished Greg luck. Then I told him that if he changed his mind, to call me, any time, day or night. "As long as he's out of the country, we can still make this happen. We can still make this right," I said, right before he hung up the phone.

There are two potential explanations for Greg's response. In one, it is possible Ormechea never abused him. That everyone was mistaken or overly judgmental. That the kisses Loretta Finger witnessed were, as Ormechea described, just an up-close counseling session for a boy who was having a difficult time at home. And that all Patricia Sprague witnessed was a close conversation in that van's front seat. Surely Greg's father, a police detective, wouldn't be the priest's biggest defender if the man had done wrong.

But the more plausible explanation, at least to me, is that facts don't lie, modus operandi don't change, and just because Greg refused to talk didn't mean it never happened. Women like Patricia Sprague berated themselves for never protecting Greg. Although he had never asked for my protection, I decided long ago I wasn't leaving him either. The words I had written to myself, "find v. less than 18," "G.C." had become indelible.

I'll have to admit it. To keep an eye on Greg and determine if there were ever a good time to help change his mind, I stalked Greg online, just as I had done for Ormechea. Via a simple Google search for "Greg Conrad, Chicago," I was able to confirm his career choice. Greg had become a cameraman. While living in Chicago, he freelanced for *The Steve Harvey Show* and had some role in filming John Hughes's *Flubber*. He worked on other major motion pictures, including *Life As we Know It, 101 Dalmatians*, and *Now You See Me*, and, ironically, he filmed a reality television series called *Should the Guilty Go Free?*

These were all the signature accomplishments making his parents proud; the gleaming cocktail moments, when Kevin and Vicky could preen.

But there is a more surreptitious side to Greg's business that even he doesn't hide. In fact, he seems to brag about it. His business, Miami Productions Limited, has a website. In addition to describing Greg's experience both pre- and post-production, there are links to some of his works, including a YouTube video that begins with one woman pulling the G-string of another and smacking her on the butt. It's a "documentary" for the Free Speech Coalition, the lobbying arm of the adult entertainment industry. Between takes of women with triple-D breasts either showing cleavage to the camera or gyrating and bending over on stripper poles or mechanical bulls, the Free Speech Coalition's executive director, Diana Duke, clad in a turtleneck and blazer, speaks of all the benefits the porn industry brings to business owners and consumers alike. They're protecting America's freedom.

The next link on Greg's website is to a movie trailer. The opening shot is set to the music of The Carpenters's "Close to You," and words projected across the screen state, "On September 13, 2009, seven friends broke into an abandoned sex club." The film is entitled, *The Devil.* Its main character is a reclusive man, who hasn't been seen much since being teased in high school by those seven carefree and sexed-up girls. And in the minute and thirty-two second trailer that follows, the women, all dressed in either skin-tight or ripped negligees, are tied to crosses, rotating torture chambers, or mattress-less bed frames. One woman wears a devil's horn; another carries a black rose. Both look terrified when the man they once tormented, dressed in a black mask and cape, rapes them at knifepoint.

It doesn't end there. A link on Greg's IMDb page in turn links to a webpage for a porn film called *It's All For The Fun.* In its available trailer, the pool is filled with about seven women (again) to every one long-dicked guy. And Greg's Twitter feed is no different. One tweet reads, "My porn star's hotter than your porn star." It links to a photo of a naked woman's torso. Rods pierce each of her nipples and her belly button is tattooed like the sun. Another tweet, responding to @somepornqueen, says, "I've been taking Extenze and wondered if I could . . . Click, tick tick." And yet another, "Waiting on a Pornstar. I guess life could be worse."

While Cory and Greg's sister have married, he has not. Rather, as his meetin.org profile states, he's interested in partaking in a wide sampling of women. Since recently moving from Miami to San Diego, he's joined nineteen meet-up groups. To date, he's a member of Crazy Cooking (while his apartment is likely too small to host a dinner, he's willing to try); Cheap Movie Night in La Jolla; Art Gallery Parties in San Diego; Swimming Pools, Movie Stars; Networking for the Film Industry, the Miramar College of Republicans ("From Chicago and recently moved to San Diego via Miami, I'm a Republican living in a Democratic world"); New (Or Not) to La Jolla; the La Jolla Salsa Meetin Group (he doesn't know how, but would like to try); the Torrey Pines Volleyball Group for Beginners (the same); the Torrey Pines Singles Group; the Smart, No-Plus Ones; Let's Go Clubbing ("Nothing good can come from this. I'm in."); Laid Back People Making Friends; Just for Grins; and Tits and Gore. Based upon his answers to posed questions, I know he will do anything but skydive, and he doesn't like chick flicks, but he'll go, "If the chick's good looking enough." If he had only five dollars left and had to spend it on someone else, he would buy that person a joint, "because, if you buy someone a joint, there is a pretty good chance they are gonna smoke it with you." If he had one more day to live, he would, in turn, "do as many of you [laid back] people as I can." After all, he just wants to enjoy life, have good friends, and fun times. And, if he could produce a tits and gore movie, preferably with more tits than gore, that would be the proverbial cherry on top. He's also in the process of making one, by the way. His new production company, GCP, LLC, promises potential investors, "The return of your capital investments with a one hundred percent insurance guarantee. "

On one of his new meet-up group's webpage, Greg's posted a photo of himself. When placed against his eighth-grade image, the forty-four-year-old leaves me much more decided than confused. He was abused. I still can't figure out his eyes. The flash used for the picture reflects in his left pupil, but he also looks dazed, as if he might have shared one of those before-mentioned joints with the blonde in a blue plaid flannel shirt that he's cropped from view. His brown eyebrows extend long past his eyes to the far sides of his face, and a mustache and goatee frame his stained, but straightened teeth open smile. His hair, though still light, is greased back and pulled into a ponytail, further evidencing a receding, squared hairline. He's relatively thin and apparently tall. But he wears a burnt-orange sweater with a V-neck, long brown leather jacket over it. Frankly, he looks smarmy. He looks like a porn producer.

"Can I protect this?" I've found myself asking. I have to, I knew to answer, because he's also my only hope.

❧

The policy reasons in favor of statutes of limitations go back to ancient Greece. According to Danielle S. Allen in *The World of Prometheus: The Politics of Punishing in Democratic Athens*, the only appropriate time to seek public redress for a wrong was when a citizen was still in the throes of anger, and the only appropriate time to be angry was immediately after the event that caused the harm. Orators before Athenian courts faulted litigants for waiting too long to state their claims and implied from their delay the claims were either not truthful or not important enough to the claimant to be prosecuted. "Delay evidenced a crucial lack of 'hot blood,'" which, in turn, subverted Athens's means of managing conflict. To accommodate a trial schedule in which any one of the city-state's thirty thousand free citizens could seek redress, trials could take no longer than one day to complete. To bring a public interest claim, proponents had no more than three hours. A jury of two hundred free citizens rendered their verdicts immediately on an up or down vote. Without "hot blood" and quick action, the democracy's justice system would have easily collapsed.

American jurisprudence allows a bit more leeway. As Tyler T. Ochoa and Judge Andrew Wistrich, the authors of a law review article entitled "The Puzzling Purposes of Statutes of Limitation", explain, the primary purpose and effect of these statutes is to protect defendants, not plaintiffs, from uncertainty in their lives. Eventually, all defendants earn the right to stop looking in the rearview mirror. Our past wrongs, even if we were to admit them, can remain there and go unpunished. We can breathe a little easier, get on with the present, and plan for the future.

Statutes of limitation also serve the purpose of preventing claims going forward based on evidence that might have grown inferior. Moreover, they avoid retroactive implementation of contemporary standards. A plaintiff, including a prosecuting state authority, is, therefore, encouraged to exhibit the Athenian's "hot blood" by pursuing all causes with reasonable diligence, and implementing, in turn, our British forbearer's belief that "long dormant claims have more of cruelty than justice in them."

All these rationales are defensible means for the management of disputes in a civil society, but they don't explain why statute of limitations increase in length based upon the seriousness of a defendant's crime. One would assume the more serious the violation, the more hot-blooded the claimant should be. So, under all these rationales, shouldn't the most serious of crimes deserve the shortest statute of limitations and not the longest?

In American jurisprudence, the answer appears to be no, not because the claimant should have acted sooner, but because there is some conduct that should never escape punishment. Murder of the physical body? In nearly every civil jurisdiction, including long-ago Athens, no statutes of limitations governed or governs this crime. The perpetrator will need to look in the rearview mirror pretty much forever. But, the statute of limitations for murder of the soul? Absent tolling, it has the same protection owed a stolen wallet.

List them before they fall away. The states of emotion, mind, and memory, not subject to statutes of limitation. The flight, fight, or freeze of the lizard brain. The disgust for the pageantry, the show. The hypocrisy of calling him Father. The emotional-triggering event and the response mechanism. The superhighway neural pathways that take you right back because, in your mind, it did, it did happen yesterday. The impossibility of "just get over it" when the "it" has made you. Because hot blood can and does boil again. At the slightest trigger. Don't forget grief's new forms. Like the text my sister, a Chicago cop, sent just moments ago: "If I were there, I'd kill him." The groovy girls Greg would really like to do. The single malt, make that a double, Charlie is ordering. Tim's refusal to return any of my texts. The mission, the quest, the drive, for answers, maybe even—what is happening to me?—for revenge.

Around about 313, Constantine gifted the home of his second wife, Fausta, to then Pope Miltadiades to build the first sanctioned Christian Church in Rome. Located in the land of erasure and accretion between the Celian and Oppian Hills, that church eventually became the Basilica of Saint John the Lateran. Its accompanying residence, the Lateran Palace, served as the Holy See for nearly one thousand years, until 1309, when the papacy moved to Avignon, France. By the time the popes returned to the eternal city, about eighty years later, the Lateran Palace was a shell of its former self. It was Sixtus V (by the way, the same pope who issued the papal bull outlawing contraception) who ordered the old palace to be leveled and replaced. He hired the architect Domenica Fontana for the task. Fontana was best known for his lack of flair, which, in turn, may be why he completed the construction of the new papal home under budget. With use of the excess funds, he built a boring, three-story building just kitty-corner to the palace. It now houses two features from the original residence. The one I've come to see is La Scala Sancta, the "Holy Stairs."

The twenty-eight marble stairs are purported to be the ones Jesus climbed to meet Pontius Pilate before being sentenced to death. Bloodstains from his many open wounds are supposed to be there too. Even more than Pope Joan could ever be, the likelihood the Scala Sancta is a fake is overwhelming. True, its proponents assert Constantine's mother, Helena, brought them from Jerusalem to Rome in 326 on her relics-collecting expedition. In addition to the stairwell, she's said to have netted a segment of Jesus's cross, a spike from the crown of thorns, a broken nail that pierced Jesus's feet, a scourging pillar, and the finger Saint Thomas once poked into Jesus's side. Critics, however, overwhelmingly point not only to the lack of historical record of Helena's return voyage with such a heavy load, but to the reality that no one would've been able to locate the stairwell in the first place. Why? Pilate had no permanent residence in Jerusalem. He stayed at one of Herod's many residences at different times, and which one was of use on that fateful Good Friday still remains unknown.

Just as my Bible's introductory text at least implies Paul wasn't alive to write the epistles to Timothy, so too does the placard to the right of the Holy Stairs leave room to doubt their authenticity. It reads:

> Abstracting from any critical evaluation of the origins of the Scala Sancta stairway, the fact remains that the Scala Sancta has always been, and still is in our day, an authentic expression of the popular religiosity, which uses symbols to express its faith.

I get it. It doesn't matter if it's real, so long as we believe it is.

One more thing. On the Scala Sancta, no feet allowed. Anyone ascending its twenty-eight steps must do so on his or her knees, which is no easy trek in a dress ending lower thigh and made even more difficult by the hard, unforgiving walnut wood covering each rise. Nevertheless, for three euros, I buy the English-language card listing the prayer for each step and kneel.

Step one. "O My Jesus! By the anguish of heart Thou didst experience, on separating from Thy most holy mother, to go to Thy death, have mercy on me!" The card says add a Hail Mary and an invocation to your patron saint before proceeding forward. Instead, I pray, "I don't understand. I'm not a violent person. Even after twenty years of living in Alaska, I still ask Richard to remember each moose he may shoot during hunting season has a mother and maybe even a child. I teach my daughter gentleness and respect, even for insects. Yet, here in Rome, in the seat of Christianity, I ask my uncle to burn a church down. I quip about finding a .22—but really still think it's a great idea, even after writing that peace-inducing letter to Ormechea. Why? Here's what's present just as much now as when Ormechea committed his acts of violence. I see the half-lives of Greg, Charlie, and Tim, the no-life of Kurt, and I want someone to pay. Still. Statute of limitations or no! Jesus, have mercy on my murder-dreaming, moose-saving soul."

At step two, my script says, "O My Jesus! By the confusion Thou didst feel and that caused Thee to sweat blood in the Garden of Olives, have mercy on me!" But I take from this text just the same thing I understood when looking at the Gethsemane portrait at Santi Giovanni e Paolo. *Even you, Jesus, asked for the lifting of burden.* Here is what burdens me: At this moment, I can see them all. Tim on the trading floor, ignoring my texts; Charlie with a scotch; Greg, waiting on a porn star; Kurt in a grave. But for Kurt, we spin on this planet, going about our days and weeks of new ordinary. I know we've grown. I know we are all more than our pasts. But for me, especially here in Rome, the idea mounts. We are still Ormechea's pawns. Why do I think this? Is this the cost of remembrance and gathering? "Jesus, have mercy on my memory-collecting soul."

Did I say how painful this surface is? I thought the knee-to-wood contact would be difficult, especially with a hard wood like walnut, but I didn't expect the surface to be so uneven. I'm balancing my weight on less than ten percent of my knee bone, turning left, then right, to expand the contact, leaning forward then back, to relieve the pressure. At step three, I lean forward, almost into a handstand, and reach for the small glass opening. It's supposed to show me Jesus's blood, but there is no *there* there. I say the third prayer quickly. "O My Jesus! By the intense grief that filled Thy heart on seeing Thyself betrayed by the perfidious Judas, have mercy on me!" I don't pause to entreat Saint Joan or offer a Hail Mary, but I wonder if "deceitful" or "untrustworthy" might be more understandable to the praying pilgrims than "perfidious."

Through constant leaning or quick prayer, I make it to step eight and then remember what the placard said below. If I complete this thing, I'll get an indulgence; since this is my first time doing it, it will be a plenary one. What is that again? If a pilgrim cannot kneel and instead climbs one of the two sets of stairs that surround this one, she'll get a partial plenary indulgence. In either case, this must be good. The only problem is, I can't remember what an indulgence is. So I just pray an improvised offering, on this patella-piercing parade,

"O My Jesus! By the silence Thou didst observe in the presence of those who bore false witness against Thee, and of the iniquitous Pilate, whose steps these may or may not be, have mercy on me, because I am friggin' confused."

It was somewhere on these steps, five hundred years ago, that Martin Luther was rumored to say, "Who knows whether it is so?" He left the stairs mid-ascent. He later explained to his son that his remark was of the Holy Spirit's prompting, which, in turn, led him to devise his *sola fide* doctrine. That doctrine holds that it's through faith alone we are saved. Acts, plenary indulgences such as this, I now remember, are not necessary.

Even before Luther stood up, he had it a little easier than me. He didn't have to deal with this awful wood. It hadn't been installed in 1510. In addition, his tunic at least covered his knees. But I can't help it, I think. I believe in acts. This silly one, for example, of me at stair fourteen—the halfway mark—is an indication of my faith in something even when I many times think, there is no proof of anything. A man reading some innocuous page in the Bible or an old man in a church who may or may not be a ghost of my uncle can only go so far. I need the provocation from the outside to motivate action in me.

When I was a teenager, even while in Catholic school, I became an atheist. A God with the time to care for each of us, at that time four billion (compared to our now seven billion) people on earth, made no sense. We were in this alone, might as well recognize it and get on with the business of making the world a better place. For a girl with many more books than friends, the choice of atheism was a lonely one. It separated me from my parents, from my Aunt Lorraine, and everything that had been familiar. When I was nineteen, there was one thing that changed my mind. I'd been taking a humanities class at college, and the professor assigned a portion of the New Testament so we could study the structure of Roman society. Although I don't recall the passage I was reading, I do recall the setting. It was late May, three months after my uncle's death. I was reading outside on a green hill overlooking Lake Michigan. With the sun warm on my skin and a light breeze coming in from the water, I closed my eyes. Whether I actually fell asleep I couldn't say, but when I looked up, a monarch butterfly was fanning its wings on the open page of my Bible. As long as I refused myself movement, it stayed put. When I reached for it, it did as all smart bugs do. It left. Was it Uncle Dan? I know I believed this at the time. But then, based on that outward sign, I made an action choice as well. I closed the Bible, picked up my things, and went to the Sheil Catholic Center on campus to pray.

Though I relied on a little butterfly to make a significant choice, and despite significant reasons to doubt that I very much respect, I really haven't left God since. More important, it wasn't the butterfly that mattered so much to me. It was taking the action, in this case, walking inside the church and praying, that evidenced the faith. So, unlike Luther, and even though he had ample good reason to walk away on these Holy Stairs, I can't give up. I have to finish the marathon, not just start it. I have to reach step twenty-eight.

Step eighteen. "O My Jesus! By the excessive weariness that overcame Thee, while bearing the burden of the cross on Thy shoulders, have mercy on me!" *Uh-oh.* Here we go again, the odyssey that is Joan. The closer I get to the end, I begin to waver. Now, my words at step fourteen, "I have to," are coming back to haunt me. They've been my cross for what seems like my entire existence. I have to get the best grades, jobs, Boston Marathon qualifying time, figure out how to skate ski, get married, be the best mother, save a dog, write Tim's story, trick Ormechea, better yet, be the end of him. I would say I'm cursed, but, through therapy, I know this isn't exactly true. The only person responsible for the burden is the one who assigned it: me. Say it! *Who knows whether it is so,* and just get up. Tell your taskmaster to just leave you alone. You've done your time. You've done enough!

Another glass opening is before me. I peer through it for a better view, but again, there is no blood. Nor is there gleaming white marble in bright contrast to it. It's just a surface that looks like a dirty sidewalk. Maybe it's me? I'm so nearsighted that Richard has said he's come to the conclusion there are things I just can't see, even with my contacts in or glasses on, like toothpaste in the sink or peanut butter on a cabinet handle.

There was a time I really had no idea how poor my vision was. Despite the early clues, like having to sit as close to the screen as possible to make out the words coming from an overhead projector in the back of class, it wasn't until sixth grade I was pegged as needing glasses. Only then did my mother bring me to an optometrist. When the doctor put my glasses on me for the first time, it was also the first time I ever saw myself as others saw me. My hair was oily, dirty, and stuck to my scalp in patches. I hadn't been a fan of daily baths, and, since no one forced them on me, I could go at least a week without one. The problem was, despite the teasing, I had no idea how sorry I had looked. Until the day I saw clearly. Leaving the optometrist's office, I took my glasses off again, went home, and immediately washed my hair in the bathroom sink. After combing it, I went outside. Standing on the front porch, with clean hair, I put my glasses back on and saw from a distance something else I had never seen before. Distinguishable leaves. I guess it's looking through this glass window and trying to see blood (me) or gleam (leaves) that's reminded me of it. Weak and now with savaged knees, I try to forget. Step twenty. "O My Jesus! By the agony Thou didst endure, when Thy garments were roughly torn from Thee—like me, from my vision—have mercy on me."

In a northwest suburb, in a three-bedroom bungalow he could easily afford, with perhaps light music—Rachmaninoff? Mozart?—playing, my brother slept. Is this why I envision him resting peacefully? That despite me being the butt of many school yard jokes, Tim never joined in. Granted, he didn't offer what would have been a helpful suggestion, like, "Get out of the woods, country mouse, and take a bath," but he didn't scorn me for not doing so either. In doing so, he kept my loyalty, the "I'm not leaving this war-ravaged barrack without you" kind. The kind that's led me here, to the twenty-something-eth step, praying for a way to make him whole.

It's funny. When I think of Tim, who he really is, rather than what was done to him, the anger vanishes. Like when he told me, a decade ago, that he forgave our parents, many years before, for letting Ormechea lay waste to him. I felt a resonance in him. It filled the room he was in, the phone line that brought his words to me, and my law office as well. It filled me too. I could breathe easier, because he had. But something's changed. He's more frightened now. With the economic downturn, he will probably lose that house. And with fear for his children's well-being, what comes next? A staged accident so they can collect life insurance? I'm scared.

It's step twenty-six. I pray, "O My Jesus! By the great love for me with which Thy Divine Heart was inflamed, on breathing forth Thy last sigh, have mercy on me." I even add, "Hail Mary full of grace. The Lord is with thee. Blessed art thou amongst women, and blessed is the fruit of thy womb, Jesus," and "Saint Joan, have pity on me," but I'm not done. I take out my journal to remember a line I had jotted on its back pages, "Speak the truth, even if your voice shakes." Even if you're really, really scared.

At this point, finishing the Scala Sancta is a foregone conclusion. Atop the twenty-eighth step, I say the final prayer. "I desire to venerate with deep respect the bloodstained traces of Your Divine feet, and I humbly beg You, by the merits of Your Passion, to grant, that I may one day ascend to the throne of Glory, where You live and reign with the Father and the Holy Ghost forever and ever. Amen." But I don't want that prayer, I want this one. *Dear Jesus, if this trip can make a difference, let it. If my words can have any power, let them. Don't let my brother go. Remove from him the darkness, because I can't. No matter how much I vainly try.*

When I finally rise and set myself in a pew in the second remnant of the first Lateran Palace, the Sancta Sanctorum, the chapel of the Holy of Holies, I take a photograph of my knees, for remembrance. They're as I expected. Red and swollen. A long-ago scar across the right knee cap juts out white in contrast. Capillaries have burst on the left one. The outer skin layers crease and, as if sunburned, look ready to peel.

A quick check of the Scala Sancta website tells me that as a plenary indulgence, I've earned nine years off purgatory for every step I ascended! So, I'm 252 years ahead. Luther's right. *That* doesn't make sense. But like walking into that Sheil Center church long ago, I still believe it's the action that matters. I climbed these stairs, faithless and doubting. Even though it was fleeting, somewhere along the way and directly through the pain, a remembrance of belief emerged, a belief in me. As for wishing Ormechea to fall into a fire-filled pit? I can't say I'm done with these thoughts either. For the time being, I remain "hot blooded," ready for revenge. But I'll try to take what follows as a clue, an outward sign even that will require my further commitment, because when I enter the bookstore at the top of the Scala Sancta to buy myself a wooden rosary, just like the kind my grandfather bought for me long ago, I read something there I never knew. In 1853, the Scala Sancta was placed under the protection of an order of religious nuns. They were called the Passionist Sisters and were founded at the direction of Saint Paul of the Cross. When one of its members—I can't make out her nametag—hands me my change and says *"Dio sia con voi,"*—"God be with you"—I know enough Italian to reply, *"É!"*

He already is.

Monday, before dusk

La Linea A. La Linea Rossa. La prossima fermata è di Spagna. L'uscita a la sinistra.

By the time I board my second subway in Rome, the Red Line from Saint John the Lateran to Spagna, to see Audry Hepburn's Spanish Steps, I feel like a Metro pro. Rush hour here is no different than Chicago's. A train car stops, doors open, a rush of people push out, a rush of people push in. That's about it. Together we smell like human sweat, car exhaust, and some day-shift chef's cooking oil. Despite the crowds, it's okay to be one of the last to board. I'm not going to find a seat anyway, and if I did, it would only give the pickpockets extended time to figure out where my money is. For my part, everything I own that's worth stealing is pressed against my bare skin, except my journal and one book, which can be accessed only by opening two clips and two zippers. If someone wants to take my bag completely, they'll need to wrestle it out of both my hands.

Those standing with me in the center vestibule don't seem to mind the additional personal space I take by keeping both elbows bent and slightly away from my body. A local woman in a long blue sweater tied at the waist takes a similar pose, but rather than holding her bag in front of her, she leans it against the subway wall to prevent anyone from reaching in. I want to point out our tricks to the young Japanese girl in a red slicker who wears her backpack on, of all places, her back. But the odds look like they're still with her. She makes it to her exit at Barberini just fine.

I've come to see the Spanish Steps for Abbie. This is a place she and I will one day visit together. To make good on my promise, I have to find our best place for gelato. So too, it appears, do the hundreds of tourists already here. Even though the Scala Sancta took much longer than I originally thought—climbing on your knees can do that—when I arrive about seven and at least an hour before sunset. A crowd, five people thick, surrounds Bernini's Sinking Boat Fountain. If John Keats were suddenly transported to 2012, there would be no possible way he would have heard its waters from his deathbed in the pink apartment building to its right. His epitaph, HERE LIES ONE WHOSE NAME WAS WRIT IN WATER, made partly in tribute to the fountain might have instead read, in homage to the fashion-minded on Via Condotti, "Can I get that in a bigger size?"

Crowds of teenagers fill two-thirds of the Spanish Steps. Where the five hundred pots filled with magenta-colored azaleas stand, the line to move up the stairs turns to single file. Moreover, Italians haven't outlawed smoking on the steps or teenagers erupting into a song that goes something like *way, way, way, la da, la, la da di, la la way.* Fresh from whatever happened on those Holy Stairs, I'm just not in the mood to sing along. Besides, I still can't figure out when to vocalize that second *la.*

It's okay. My Faris-given map shows some green space ahead, so I turn left at the Roman obelisk and the church of Trinità dei Monti and make my way to the broad and quiet Borghese Gardens. This is how ill prepared I am when it comes to taking this trip as solely a tourist. The only things I've read about the Villa Borghese were in Elizabeth Gilbert's *Eat, Pray, Love*. Specific to this text, I know there's a fountain she really liked here where a woman and her faun fight over their baby faun. On another night, she looked out at the evening sky from the Piazza Napoleone and got really depressed.

Despite everything, I still know I'm not that. I know depression; it made it almost impossible for me to lift my head to see Tim's face on New Year's Eve heading into 2001. And most especially, it was what gripped me not long after that when I wondered how difficult or easy it might be to make a hard right off the Glenn Highway into the Eagle River sixty feet below. That was the moment I stopped being too proud to take Zoloft. With medication, my dog Cletus, travels to Spain, parties for Russell Crowe, and advice from my father—to remember I'm a Nockels—I made my way, over the next two years, to the other side.

Because I know that tomorrow I'll need to find Ormechea, there are other words than depressed to describe my mental and emotional states this evening. Like Anxious. Like Weary. Like Afraid. Still the Villa Borghese did its best to dispel all of them. As it did for Gilbert, the view from the Piazza Napoleone of the soon-to-be-setting sun showered Saint Peter's Basilica and the domes of at least four other cathedrals in gold. Electrified violin strains from a street musician playing "Con Te Partiro" in the Piazza del Popolo below serenaded us all. The wide promenades of Viale di Villa Medici and Via dei Bambini feature happy children, tourists on rickshaws, old men arguing, a lady reading, and an old couple with matching jackets trying to find their way to something shown on a park map. Calliope music plays from the merry-go-round, filled not with horses but a range of vehicles, including an ambulance and Volkswagen bug. Along the shaded walkways, Italian pines stand over palm trees, which in turn shade cypresses, which then cover magnolias, over and over again, until we get to the smallest of grass blades.

With some time to reference my guidebook, I'll learn this park began its manicured life under Cardinal Scipione Borghese's ownership and was converted to public use about two hundred years later, after Napoleon's invasion. Despite the fall of Napoleon's empire and a few more political uprisings to follow, the Villa Borghese has never lost its public character. My book declares its nineteen acres in the heart of the city the equivalent of New York's Central Park.

Even with stiff competition from the faun statue and the statue of Moses's mother beating her breast as she is about to send her little boy adrift down the Nile, it's the hall-of-fame busts of notable Italians that almost gets me to forget what keeps me angry and afraid. More than two hundred stone casts of Italian greats are spread out along pathways in the Parco Pincio portion of the Villa. Some have seen their share of abuse. Machiavelli is missing his nose. Blue cat ears have been added to the sun crest on Saint Thomas Aquinas's chest. Someone has given Leonardo Da Vinci one blue eye. Pliny the Elder looks blinded. Still, the who-might-be-next walk, especially down La Viale di Villa Medici, feels like a pop quiz. And as I walk from statue to statue, I remember my mother at the kitchen sink flipping through my self-made flashcards to quiz me.

So here we go. Saint Thomas Aquinas. Proponent of natural law and author of *Summa Theologica*. Score. The two years I spent at Berkeley studying jurisprudence hadn't gone to waste, even if it didn't even net a master's. And to his left, Pythagoras. $A^2 + B^2 = C^2$. Hello sophomore-year geometry. I should have taken more math in college, but I thought that becoming an engineer meant driving a train. Across from him, Zeuxis, no idea, and next to him Scipio Africanus. Man, you got me. But, I'm back on board at Cicero, Julius Caesar, and Horace.

And so the next half hour, walking down Viales Orologio, Bambini, and Ippocastani, I pop quiz my way to a C minus. I love the little surprise feeling in my chest every time I get an answer right, but I still question my inadequate education and memory nearly every time I don't. I did cut myself slack and grade on a curve for not knowing one iota about famous Italian physicians, dukes, or patriots. There's only so much one brain could hold. But that's the thing, isn't it? Is mine already too full?

By the time I end my test, the sky is starting to turn dusk blue and park crowds are dissipating. I'm back again at the statue of one blue-eyed Leonardo. I sit down on a green bench under green trees. Across the way, a couple and their teenage son stand next to a little kiosk with the sign above it reading Pesca & Vinci. It looks like the Italian rendition of the Claw. The son is maneuvering a joystick and he must be doing well, because midway through, his dad takes out his video camera to film. Because he holds the camera away from his face, I can easily see his smile broadening with each consecutive look his son's way.

I search my mind hoping to recall the times Tim and Dad had these moments. Beyond the fire extinguisher in the car incident and Dad's exploding laughter, there are a few additional times I can remember and nearly none after Tim reached the age of twelve. Father Ormechea took a young boy. After that, the young boy put up the do-not-disturb sign to his own father.

The thought of Tim makes me check my texts. My last to him told him I had arrived in Rome and asked if I should call him. Still, there's no response.

I wonder if I should just ignore his silence and call anyway. But after a quick calculation I realize it's the middle of his workday, not the best time for a substantive talk.

It's been a month since we really spoke. As usual, he called me during his commute home, which that day was on a Metra train. By then, my airplane tickets were purchased and hotel reservations at the Lancelot had been made. Rome was not just a pipe dream. It was an eventuality. I was already on CD five of my *Drivetime Italian* series of disks, trying to learn about conjugating irregular verbs. Tim brought up the subject of his going with me, but immediately dispelled it. Not because of cash flow, but because of what he might do if he ever saw Ormechea again.

"I wouldn't be able to control myself, Joan," he said. "He'd be a dead man."

I believed him. I thought of his forensic psychologist's findings at the time of the lawsuit that "Nockels's fear of his own rage should be taken seriously," and told him he should listen to himself. After all, the most important reasons he had for not going were the two boys he was on his way home to see. Back before these great images of Ormechea burning filled my own brain, I also told him my going in his place would keep everyone safe. I think I added, "Who am I going to harm?"

It was during that phone conversation when I suggested what seemed the oddest thing to both of us. "Imagine the phone call we have one day when we don't talk about him." We both laughed. From that first Blue Line call, we had filled ten years of his Chicago commutes with, at some point, a discussion of Ormechea. It was first the attempted criminal prosecution, then the lawsuit, and then what to do with proceeds. Should it be put in funds for both of his sons? And what if he needed it when the economy turned south? Was there enough money to think about going back to school and trying a career change? Would the Church pay for therapy? Did he even want to call them again to ask?

"I'd like that, you know," he said.

"What?"

"Talking about other things." I heard the signal of the railroad crossing gates his train had passed.

"What would we talk about?"

"Hmmm... the Cubs."

I let out a snort. After the Cubs blew a two-game lead over the San Diego Padres and lost the 1984 pennant race, I lost Tim to the damn White Sox.

"What could you even say about them?"

"They're still losers."

"You know, Julie has a better name for them. She calls them her bad boyfriends because they look all nice in their Cubbie Blues, only to go on and throw daggers at our hearts."

"It's time to convert. Ozzy," a reference to the White Sox manager, "is calling."

"I'm too loyal. I can't leave the Cubs."

"Don't you think I know that by now?"

And back we went, to unfulfilled promises and finally a way, maybe, to complete them.

It was during this phone call I also suggested Tim write a letter to Ormechea and I pick it up from him during my ten-hour layover in Chicago. It was then that he also agreed. He said he would have something ready. And because I do one thing very well, which is push especially when I shouldn't, I next asked about Charlie. "Do you think we should call him too and see if he has anything to say?"

"Not on your life." I didn't know it yet, but I should have guessed from the millisecond it took him to respond. I had hit Tim's anger switch; the one the forensic psychologist said not to ignore.

"Why do you say that?" I asked.

"I've done enough to Charlie. It's time to leave him alone!" I could tell he was growing furious.

"Tim," I said, equally strident, "you did nothing to Charlie. It was all Ormechea! Don't blame yourself for what Charlie's become."

We didn't have too much to go on, but what we heard wasn't good. After speaking to the prosecutor, Charlie agreed to sue along with Tim. He even hired the same lawyers. What Ormechea's insurance company and the Archdiocese of Chicago offered, Charlie took, all the way, we had heard, to bars and liquor stores. His marriage, if not completely over, was soon on its way. He rarely saw his daughter.

"You're wrong," Tim said, getting even louder. I wondered if he was sitting alone, because surely he could be overheard. "So tell me this," he commanded. "Let's say Charlie and I were in Vietnam together and while there we napalmed entire villages. Then let's say, after we came home, I went to Charlie's house every day and reminded him how many children we burned. How we watched their running bodies engulfed in flames still reaching for their mothers. You're telling me that any fallout Charlie would have from that wouldn't be my fault? That's bullshit, Joan! What I did to him? Convincing him to come forward when he wanted to forget and lock those awful thoughts and feelings away? That's on me! Not Ormechea!"

A wiser person would've understood and apologized profusely for even bringing up Charlie's name, but Tim kept attacking the one person my rescuer was bent on saving. And so I kept going. "You can't take credit for Charlie's drinking. It was there even before we found him. And it was there for the one reason you know. He tried, but it's impossible. You can't just forget something as awful as what Ormechea did. Your body won't let you. Your mind will spin and spin and crash until you reach the root, expose the truth, and say, this was not my fault. This was not my doing. Charlie didn't have the ability to do that. Maybe with a phone call from you, he can do that now. But don't ever, ever blame yourself again for what Ormechea caused!"

If we hadn't been through so much together, he would've hung up on me. Instead, I heard everything he did before speaking again. He gathered his belongings, walked off the train and over to his car. There he unlocked his door, sat, and started his engine. I knew he didn't have his seatbelt on yet, because his car's alert started to ring. Then he gave a deep breath and cried. I listened to each gasp, each choke, each whimper, and said nothing. But I knew this as well. He knew I was there, listening.

Then I asked this. "Tim, what you think you're doing to Charlie, do you also think I'm doing that to you?"

He couldn't answer, so I asked again. "Should I cancel this trip and just turn away? Would that make things better for you?"

It was the last thing he said before he composed himself enough to drive and hang up that got me. He said, "No Joan, there's no way I could do that to you."

A few hours after that phone call I went to my counseling appointment with Marsha. We were supposed to be talking about what she called my tool chest, which included not only the little reminders I would bring to Rome to keep me square in the present and ready for my confrontation, but a list of skill sets we had developed in the last six months of therapy. Earlier in the day, I packed one thing I intended to show her. It was a recently acquired used copy of *Jonathan Livingston Seagull*. We had spoken of the book in our last session and thought it could be a welcome addition to my tool chest, but we got to none of it. I arrived in her office ready to tear into Tim for blaming himself for Charlie's life. I repeated myself, arguing, if Charlie had been willing to confront his demons and do the heavy lifting I was doing in therapy confronting my managers, figuring out their fears, and then allaying them, his life wouldn't be so screwed up. And I reiterated that if it was anyone's fault for what has gone wrong with him, it was Ormechea's.

That was when she proved herself the expert in mental health counseling and me the dabbler. She said that while Tim was not responsible for his own abuse, he did need to recognize and acknowledge his role in Charlie's disintegration. And that for a person who had no control over a major trauma in his life, the last thing I should try to do was take responsibility for Charlie's downfall away from Tim.

Immediately after my appointment, I called Tim to apologize, but could only leave a voicemail. I said I was sorry, and I was wrong. I didn't repeat my offer of canceling this trip, because Tim was right. I couldn't do that to me, especially when I believed the answers I needed and the keys to going forward were only in going back. Collecting the fragments from Ormechea, whatever he had to give.

There was also something else I couldn't tell Tim, which even as I write this, I'm nearly too embarrassed to admit. The thing is, for Tim's sake, I'm happy there was a Charlie, and a Greg, and a Kurt (although I would will him alive). This sounds awful to say, but the worst thing a prosecutor can have, absent an admission, is the lack of corroborating evidence. I remember how my colleagues and I in the Violent Unit at the prosecutor's office would be absolutely thrilled to see photos of ligature marks across a victim's neck from the time her low-down boyfriend tried to strangle her. Because, come trial time, she'll have already made up with him and testify the event just didn't go down the way she told the cops. We needed those incident photos so they could tell the truth, especially when victims could not.

Just the same, Charlie's story showed modus operandi. Charlie's story showed opportunity. Along with the stories of victims lucky enough to have brothers, Charlie's story showed Tim told the truth. That what happened to him was not a mere allegation that dismayed the priest. It happened. It happened to Charlie and to Tim.

❧

Here, on my green bench under green trees, I feel myself shaking, and as if

Marsha were here, I think quickly of the tools in my tool chest. I pull out *Jonathan Living Seagull*, which had been locked away in my bag, along with my journal. On page 113, I had written, "Remember your own weariness." This wasn't a call to do something about it, but just to acknowledge its presence. "You, Joan, are weary."

Then, I take stock, and breathe in. The air is starting to cool. It's time to put on my jacket. It's getting dark out too. No matter if I could be a badass on subway trains, as a woman traveling alone, there are safer places to be in a city than in an empty park. Even if the air still smells like lemons, it's time to go. And the leaves on the trees? I see them just as I had the first day I put on my eyeglasses. They can be my universe, cloaking me in a rhapsody of presence. It's then a couple walks past with scooped gelato in hand. I see they got it from the garden café they just left. "I found it, Abbie," I think. "It'll be a long walk to the Spanish Steps, but we'll get our ice cream here."

Maybe it's the acknowledgment of my own purpose for being here. Or maybe just seeing the ice cream, but once I stand and collect myself, once I'm ready to descend to the Piazza del Popolo below, my phone buzzes. I have a text, and it's from Tim. He apologizes for not meeting me in Chicago. He says he needed time to wrap his head around everything that might happen. He says it had him up for nights. He tried to write a letter a couple of times, but when it came down to it, he just had a few things to say, all of which could fit in another text he's about to write.

When the second text arrives, I stop again, this time on the Piazza del Popolo to write his words down, just in case something or someone, say a Metro pickpocket, might happen to take my phone. Then I text Tim, letting him know his message was received. And as to my commitment for its delivery, whether or not I see Ormechea, I write: "To Tim, I promise. It will be done".

Tuesday morning

One thing about closing arguments. I'm pretty good at them. As a prosecutor, I could take assemblages of facts, apply them to the law, and draw up at least one convincing argument for a guilty verdict. I followed, however, another rule a grizzled civil litigator named Dave Oesting taught me years before. He used to say, "Nockels, never believe your own bullshit!" The problem is, it's difficult not to do. By the time you deliver your closing, by necessity to be believable, you have to become your number-one believer. So next you play a game with yourself. Before delivery, you break the facts down to their essential parts and peer at them. You look for any element of untruth or for a factor that can be interpreted another way. Then, until you've explained away the inconsistencies, you reconstruct over and over again. Like the Mithraeum, like the Claudium, like the Colosseum. For the jury's sake, as well as yours, you must remove all unreasonable doubt.

By way of example.

Imagine, if you will, that my letter works and Ormechea agrees to meet with me. Now assume something happens to him less divinely attended to than a burning at the stake. Say a paring knife went missing from the Lancelot's dining room, or somewhere along Via Selci I met someone who knew someone with that sought-after .22. Even if I could make a quick exit through an open service gate at the General Curia and somehow get absorbed into the crowd of locals at Celimontana, I'm still a walking and talking case of premeditation. Purchasing the plane tickets and making the hotel reservations would get a prosecutor more than halfway to me. While the chances are nil that a prosecutor would call a three-year-old to the stand, Abbie might certainly tell her I went to Rome to find the bad man. In any case, with every Google search analyzed, a forensic audit of my computer would be my undoing. As for motive? Every word of mine could be found in a computer file called The Book of Timothy.

Now even with this evidence, what would a prosecutor need to explain? She'd have to start with the psychological makeup of the defendant, me, because despite everything, there's one simple fact. When it comes to it, no matter how much I might wish the opposite, I can't imagine committing murder. Despite the enhanced desire, I'm the pause before contemplated play, the thought before action. Back to you, prosecutor, find your way through. Find me. How about this. Can a switch flip? If, for example, any asshole even thought of touching Abbie, would there be any doubt a manager would rise up in me and take the lead? The angry teenager? The pissed-off rescuer? Surely, at least one would come forward and the result would not be pretty. So if I were acting to stop a present danger, what if my mind were trapped in a past danger? Say a small child is locked behind a closed door. Or there is this. What if the danger is still present? What if the children of Parco Giochi are still unsafe? Is it so implausible to believe I might act? Wouldn't I expect this of me?

❧

October 2002

1:00 p.m., his time, 10:00 p.m., mine.

This is the latest Tim has ever called.

"He knows," his voice rose.

"Who knows what?"

"Ormechea! He knows it's us." Tim had already gone to see Shauna Boliker and she, in turn, had already contacted Father Higgins.

"What makes you believe that he knows?

"Ormechea called me."

I couldn't speak.

"I've gotten four calls from a Louisville area code on my home phone this week. Besides him, I don't know anyone down there."

"Does he say anything?"

"Each call is a hang-up. My answering machine recorded three of them. The fourth time, I picked up, heard someone breathe, and then I heard a click."

"You should call the state's attorney."

"I already did. She's getting my phone records and tracing the number."

"Tim?"

"Yeah, Joan?"

"I like that he knows. He sounds afraid."

That was just how I wanted him. I wanted him to feel stalked and targeted. I wanted him breathless and confused. I wanted him to feel like running, but then I wanted him to wonder where the hell he could go to get away from this. I wanted him to wonder who was talking and who was listening. I wanted him to think about the note he sent Charlie's father and then lose sleep over what exactly he wrote in it. Was it, "I understand I have betrayed your trust and am asking for your forgiveness?" Or was it, "I am sorry you feel it must come to this, and I will respect your wishes." The first, he would realize, was an admission; the second, he could try to explain away.

"And what about that phone call from Mrs. Bauer to the rectory?" He must have known the secretary he tried to fire would have said something about it. I wanted him to cower and then jump at every sound that was just a little off. When a doorknob turned, I wanted him to believe someone was coming for him. When a floorboard creaked, I wanted him to look out the window in search of the patrol car. I wanted to keep him guessing. Keep him terrified and afraid.

❧

Like me, last night sleeping at my hotel and in my dream. I was locked in a room. Outside it, J. B. yelled at my mother for not addressing him as Father. Reese Dunklin, the *Dallas Morning News* reporter, suddenly showed up and said he was running for provincial superior. Then the scene changed. Next, Tim took me up a freight elevator at the Passionist monastery. The elevator stopped on the third floor. Tim lifted the bar to open its door and walked me to a small office. The 1980s era Ormechea sat at a desk. He wore a Roman collar and peered over some papers. He looked up and smiled at us. Tim left and I approached. As I did, I felt fear take my voice. I began to say, "How could you hurt the children?" But the first words were stuck. All I yelled was, "HURT THE CHILDREN." When I woke within the dream saying those stuck words out loud, Richard grabbed my hand.

It wasn't until today, Tuesday morning, that I realized Richard wasn't with me and hadn't grabbed my hand. It's 9:05 a.m., and I'm decidedly alone. I've slept through breakfast. That's a good thing. It'll help me avoid Barbara's perpetual pointed-nose stares. Despite the sun streaming in from the window, I'm not much for a run either. Today, without doubt, is "Mission: Contact Ormechea Day."

As Reese Dunklin suggested, I thought of finding someone who speaks Italian, maybe Faris or Lorena, who could call the Curia for me and find out if and when Ormechea says Mass. But I don't want to pull them into this. I think the plan I thought of last night is better. I get online and complete a Google search for "Passionist parishes, United States." I come up with one that should work, St. Anne's Basilica in Scranton, Pennsylvania. Its pastor is Father Francis Landry.

Following the phone's instructions for calling local numbers, I dial 34, wait to hear the connection, and dial 067711. The phone rings five times.

"*Pronto.*" A man answers.

"*Buon giorno. Parla Inglese?*" I say, already in terror, as if my soon-to-come deception has automatically translated over the phone lines.

"*No, no, un momento, per favore.*" I hear the phone fall against something hard, perhaps a desk, and then hear voices. A woman next comes to the line.

"Hello. May I help you?" she says correctly but haltingly with an Italian accent.

"Thank you." I thought up a name before calling, a combination of Abbie's and my Irish grandmother's. "My name is Abigail Sheehan. I'm visiting from a

Passionist parish in Scranton, Pennsylvania, in the United States. It's called St. Anne's Cathedral." Or was it Basilica? I've already forgotten. "Anyway, I'm visiting Rome and of course grew up being taught by wonderful Passionists priests like Father Landry. I would love to visit your church, um, Santi Giovanni e Paolo, but I wonder if you might have any English speakers there who can take me for a tour. I would so appreciate it. The Passionists shaped me into who I am."

This is not a lie, and I don't seem to be able to stop. I tell this woman about a school I never attended and my husband Steven and me making our first trip to Rome. I even let her know how much I love Saint Paul of the Cross and, "very much want to visit his burial chapel." I want to go further, but somehow this Abigail eventually knows when to hold back.

"Yes, yes, we do have an English speaker," she says. "We have a priest from the Estati Unido. Father John Baptist is here. He can show you."

"An American priest?" I make her repeat herself.

"Yes. An American priest."

"Named Father John Baptist?"

"Yes."

"Nice name, like Saint Paul's brother?"

"Very good you know this."

"That's what happens when the Passionists teach you. You know these things. And he is here, this Father John Baptist? Right now?"

"Yes."

If this were Skype, she would see me hold my breath, as if her "yes" were the most insane word she could ever utter. *Ormechea was here!* He wasn't on vacation in Florence or Venice. I wouldn't just be finding out where he got his coffee or his kiddie porn. I would be finding him.

"Hello?" My pause may have been too long.

"Hello."

"Yes. Thank you. That is wonderful. To have a Passionist priest himself attend to me? That will be very nice."

"I am happy we can help you."

"Just one more question. How do I find him?"

"This will not be a problem for you. He works at the *portera* at three this afternoon."

"The *portera*? What is that?"

"How do you say? Here. He works here, in reception."

"Where you are?"

"Yes."

"Answering the phone?"

"Yes."

"Do I need a special appointment?"

"No. Just show up here at the front by the main door, number thirteen on San Paulo della Croce. We will tell him to expect you."

"At three?" I keep repeating.

"At three."

"Thank you. *Multo grazie.*"

"*Sei il benvenuto. Arrivederci.*"

"Until later. Yes. Until later. Goodbye."

To continue. After talking to Patricia Sprague, when she said she had a hard time even doing that, I looked up the root meaning of the word. It's from the Old English *continuen*, the Old French *continuer*, and the Latin *continuare*. Its original meaning is "to hold together." Its alternates are "to carry onward and to extend" and "to remain in the same state, capacity, or place."

After all these years, I think, I've continued to do what I must. Record his actions, tell their effect, and never forget. Thanks to Tim's words to me just weeks ago, I've realized my own vigilance has extended Ormechea's brutality. Still, I continue. I continue "to remain in this state, this capacity, this place," where someone must keep watch for the simple reason that so many before never did.

And now it's happened. I've found him. I'm five hours away from Abigail Sheehan meeting him. What should I do with that, taskmaster? Chalk it up as yet another accomplished goal? Please tell me there is more. Please tell me I'm making a difference for people who matter. Please tell me this meeting, which I now believe is inevitable, will not extend the brutality.

What do you do when a goal is almost accomplished? How do you handle life when it's almost time to let go? What comes next? A long-ago conversation comes to mind.

It was August 30, 2009. The daughter I didn't know I would have had just turned one. I called Joan Troka because I felt lost. On the fifth ring, just like the receptionist at the General Curia, she picked up.

"Hello?"

"Mrs. Troka?"

"Yes."

"This is Joan Nockels. Do you remember me?" It had been seven years since we spoke."

"Of course I do. How are you, dear?"

I told her the truth. "Deep in the abyss," I said. "I'm having a hard time. You would think this happened to me instead of Tim."

"It happened to *all* of us dear," she replied. She filled me in on her life. It had been a rough year. Her only boy, Jimmy, had just died. More than twenty-five hundred people came to his wake at Smith-Corcoran Funeral Home. All the people at his employer, Walgreens, loved him. Her boyfriend of ten years, a retired judge, had also just passed away. And she had had a second open heart surgery. I think she said she needed oxygen, but she still got around. She enjoyed her time with her daughters and grandchildren. She watched the Ted Kennedy funeral the day before our call, as I had.

"Tell me, are you married?" she asked.

"Yeah, I'm married to a good guy, going on eight years. We live in the mountains outside Anchorage. I have four dogs, two cats, and one chicken, but no children."

"No children? Why?"

Another difficult thing to explain to the older generation. I thought about using my regular line, "I just forgot to have one," but kept it simpler. "I, I just don't think I'll have any. It's better this way. But my dogs and my little one-chicken farm keep me happy. Alaska is my peace on quiet days."

"And your career?" she asked.

"I'm a prosecutor. "

"That seems fitting," She next asked after Tim.

"He's happy," I said, believing and hoping I was right. "He has two beautiful boys and a kind wife. You would like her."

She asked more questions, and my answers went something like, "Vernon Hills." "He still works downtown, but I'm not sure how long. The board is perilous these days." "No, he doesn't go to church. Why would he?" We guessed how many times my mother must have baptized his boys in her kitchen sink.

"And the settlement," she asked. "Did Tim get 'em good?"

"It was okay, not great. When Tim's father-in-law was diagnosed with stage-four pancreatic cancer, Tim decided the family didn't need two battles. He settled for an annuity. He put it in his sons' names, not his. He didn't want them to do without. That's what he told me."

"That's just like your brother, always thinking of other people," she said like she knew. Then she explained. Her former son-in-law was a manager of a pit at the Board of Trade. Her granddaughter worked for him as a runner. One day, just the year before, her granddaughter got sick and wanted to leave work early, but she couldn't leave until her dad approved. "It wasn't much before quitting time that she made for the El and waited on a train."

At some point, her granddaughter passed out and fell to the floor at the Jackson Avenue El station. A man came and picked her up. He sat her on the bench and revived her with a light shake. When she refused medical assistance—she just wanted to go home—he waited with her for the train to arrive. He got on the train and rode with her, on the Blue Line, all the way to her Harlem Avenue stop. He continued on his way only when she assured him that she was safe.

"Why are you telling me this, Mrs. Troka?" I asked.

"Well, when my granddaughter got off at Harlem, the man told her his name and also said this used to be his stop when he was a boy." Her granddaughter asked her if she knew a family named Nockels. "Yes," Joan Troka said she had told her granddaughter, "They had a nice boy named Tim."

Can I say my life hadn't gone on since that phone call with Joan Troka? Could I ever assert I hadn't found some way to make peace or that, for a time, I did forget? A sixteen-month-old-toddler who loved whipped cream and Mozart and who fell into Richard's and my life as unexpectedly as a Hail Mary pass results in only one obvious answer. Yes, for a time, between feedings, infected ears, colds, smiles, the first two words put together, diaper changes, court hearings, visits to prison to meet her birth father, visits to drug treatment centers to see her birth mother, bad dreams, cold fingers, walks in the woods, play in summer pools, and finally realizing the tune to the ABCs and "Twinkle, Twinkle Little Star" were identical, Abbie helped me forget. She gave me a regular life and a plan for the future in much the same way, I suspect, that Cody and Hunter did for Tim. But for me, even with Abbie, it would still always come down to this. Tim was a nice boy; the kind who waited with a stranger for a train to come and wouldn't leave her until he was assured she was safe. Despite my intense love for Abbie, I wasn't leaving Tim until I could be assured of the same thing for him just as well.

❧

The next five hours—from phone call to leaving my room to meet Oremechea—would be divided as follows.

Hour one: reread and rewrite my letter. Once complete, I chose to place it, three yellow pages thick, within a blank card with a photo of the Chugach Mountains in early morning light on the front. Inside the card I wrote the words of a poem I found on poemhunter.com called "In Courage." It went like this:

In courage-you find
no fear
and in courage-no weakness
does appear.
In courage-steps toward
danger taken
and in courage-strengths
within awaken.
In courage-a hero
takes shape
and in courage-the villain
can't escape
In courage-there is a call
to duty
and in courage-out of ugliness
comes beauty

A relatively unknown poet named Dorsey Baker had written it. It was overly obvious, but I hope it conveyed what I felt both Ormechea and I needed. Then, I added the words of a spiritualist named Mark Nepo. His advice seemed fitting as well, when he wrote in *The Book of Awakening*:

So faith, it seems, can be defined as the effort to believe in light when we're covered by clouds, and though it feels like the sun will never come again, the truth is it never stopped burning its light. In fact, its heat and warmth is burning steadily, right now, on the far side of whatever cloud we are under.

Looking at these scribblings, I could tell my offering was little better than a Hallmark card, but they don't make one for this. "On meeting a predator priest." I knew I was trying desperately to convince Ormechea I was simply a poetry-reading and faith-pleading lawyer and couldn't be all that bad. Of course, there would be no tricks up my sleeves.

But what part of these messages, I asked my simpler self, did I also believe? The answer was all of them. When it came down to it, I was no more complex than a Folgers Coffee commercial. I wanted to be that little girl who discovered her brother just home from college making morning coffee for Mom and Dad. I wanted the world safe and perfect. Who the hell was I going to fool?

Hour two: I journaled. I wrote: "It is 11:48. T minus three. What am I feeling? Part scared. Part blessed like I'm manifesting my intentions. What is my intention? To ask to speak. To look for peace through speaking."

There it was again. That word! Peace. Why, when I started to write, did it keep showing up? Did I have any intent to forgive? I cannot. It would betray my brother. But if Ormechea's story comes from a place of truthfulness, perhaps it is to understand.

What can he give me that I don't already have? That is also a good question. I next wrote, "I think my voice will shake." I answered, "It will." I wrote again, "I think I feel alone." I responded in third person. "You, my darling, are not. You are here to be seen, but I already see you. Your quest is just. You have every right to seek it." Then the dialogue continued. I hoped that the "present self," who Marsha prepared me to be, was indeed the one answering.

"Will God be with me?"

"Joan, ask God to be with you."

And so for the remainder of hours two and three, I did. It wasn't a simple "Help me, God" prayer, but a down-on-your-knees litany-of-saints version of prayer. Joan of Arc, Francis of Assisi, Mary Magdalene, even Saint Timothy and Egeria got the call. So too did every Nockels, Sheehan, Blackburn, and Westermeyer who had ever been related to me. Then came the dead dogs. Then the cats. If I remembered the birds, they would have been there too. But after them all, I added a more modern rendition of the Our Father, which I had found in Kate Braestrup's book *Beginner's Grace*. I prayed, even further doctoring the words to an even more sexless greater being.

"Love of all loves, your name is holy above all names and will be worshipped above all names as it will be and is by your child of grace. May I love and act to make your name holy in the sight of all. May you, love, be my life's center, the principle point of my focus. Let you be to me a state of grace and a state of glory, now and forever. Let self-service depart from me. Let love's holy and gracious will direct me here on earth as it is in heaven. Give me what I need for health and peace. Fix my heart on you and not on the temporal. Give me love for my continuance. Forgive me my failures. Help me to love my enemies and pray for those who mistreat and persecute me. Mindful of my frailty, keep me from getting lost and from evil. For you alone are all that matters, now and forever. Amen."

❧

I think it's in moments like these, when it's you against forces you cannot understand or decipher, that you find out what you believe in. My belief was simple and complex all at the same time: I am not alone and, despite the negatives, good still guides the world. Good, however, didn't remove fear. Nothing could do that. Like Dad said, you pick direction, even if it takes you to the basement and away from breathable air. And like it or not, that was what I would be doing in a mere couple of hours. Stay the course of the direction I picked, whether it brought me down or up.

❧

Hours four and five: housemaids knocked, and I turned them away. Lorena called my room and asked if I might need room service. I told her it could wait. Beatrice and Thomas, fresh from a morning tour of some work of art, got into a big fight behind too-thin walls over something as simple as going to dinner. I decided Thomas was a jerk. For diversion, I watched children playing in an apartment across the courtyard and the most recent version of *General Hospital* available on YouTube. In the wake of Robin's death, Patrick had become addicted to medication used to combat ADHD. He was very sad. So was I. I napped. I cried. I showered twice.

And then, remarkably, considering my mental state, I dressed. First in my easy-to-wash-in-the-sink salmon-colored panties and black sports bra, and next in bike shorts and gray Vibrams, my dressy Mary-Jane-styled pair. To symbolize passion, I wore its color in a purple dress and placed a gray cardigan sweater with embroidered flowers along the shoulder line over it.

❧

"You need a bear stick."

"What, honey?"

"A bear stick!" Abbie had said, while I was packing my bag. She wore a Rapunzel dress and her Sleeping Beauty crown. In her hand, she held out one of the sticks from the pile we kept by our front door. "No sticks in the house!" had been our command to Cletus, but he couldn't help but bring them as close as possible to the interior. He dropped them in place right as the front door opened.

"A what?" I was still confused and couldn't close the bag's zipper no matter how I tried. It was time to remove a few books.

"A bear stick for the bad man."

I turned to look at her. She looked as if she gave me the most obvious of answers. I tussled her hair. "Why do you think I need that, sweetie?"

"You told me the bad man had claws, like a bear. That's how he ripped Uncle Tim open on his tummy, right? That's what you said yesterday." I shook. Would I always be the mother who said too much?

"Yes, sweetie. That's what I said. A bear stick is a pretty good idea, but I think we should leave this one for you and Clete. I bet I can find one in a park in Rome."

"Okay. But it has to be big."

❧

"Ask, hope, and expect everything from God's infinite goodness," I tell myself while picking up my bear stick. Abbie didn't know it, but she had made it for me out of green pipe cleaner and orange tissue paper. I poke the stem of my fake poppy through the left side lapel of my sweater, just over my heart.

It's ten minutes to three. Before I reach for my letter kept within a clean white envelope with the words *Father John Baptist Ormechea* written in cursive upon it, I grab one more thing. It's a small metal object. I turn it over twice in the palm of my hand. Its weightlessness surprises me. It's even small enough to fit in the single zippered pocket in the back of my bike shorts, right at the base of my spine. Once zipped in, I pat it twice and walk out the door.

SOLA FIDE

Ladies and Gentlemen of the Jury,

[Pause, look each of them in the eye, and then say it again, with an emphasis on jury]

Ladies and Gentlemen of the Jury,
   The walk to number thirteen of Via San Paolo della Croce didn't go as expected. I wouldn't say it was easier than I had contemplated. That's not a proper word when you notice everything in your sight. Rather, my progress lingered, as if every moment should be properly remembered and then recorded; such as this. When I turned my room key into the front desk, my hand shook and the smile I gave to the front desk clerk, who looked like Antonio but wasn't, and who smelled like Grey Flannel cologne, but not quite exactly, felt fake, as if it were just for show. The "grazie" I uttered, with a little extra flair at the "gra" proved my point. I was nothing more than a con, which, come to think of it, was who I needed to be. In less than ten minutes I needed one man to believe I was either less than or greater than I presented.
   As for the front door to the hotel, it felt too heavy to push open, and for a time, I wanted to linger in the Lancelot's outer courtyard. Through its open parlor window, I could see Mrs. Khan, Helen, sitting down on her gold-brocaded couch. She was speaking with her friend, the one who joined her for dinner on Monday. Helen held both her hands folded in her lap. Her eyes were heavy with thick lids and even thicker charcoal-colored eye shadow. She nodded her head in agreement to her friend's unheard statement and then flicked her right hand out, as if she

were swatting away a fly. She didn't see me. For that, I was grateful. I didn't want to give another fake smile or a runner's friendly nod.

I took one last look around the courtyard before leaving, recording the Before *of this* Before-and-After *Blue Line sequel moment. The hotel's ivy-covered walls reminded me of Wrigley Field. The potted anthurium, with its shiny red blossom, took me to Hawaii. The light scent of citrus muted the smell of tobacco rising from a still burning cigarette in an outdoor ashtray. The cobblestone patio glistened from an afternoon watering.*

A couple came through the gate as I left. Yet again with a quick guess of heritage, I must have had American written all over me, they greeted me with a hello.

I wasn't aware of this before, but the sidewalk on the left side of Via Capo d'Africa curves up on both sides. In a rainstorm, I suspected the walking public hugged either the wall or the curb to stay dry. But maybe that was what those stiletto heels were for in the first place: flood control. As for people walking toward me at seven minutes to three on Tuesday afternoon, I wondered where they might be going. The three-hour lunch break had hit its end. Pharmacies, banks, and beauty salons were just reopening. When a woman my age—midforties, in a universal Italian outfit of black pants, a form-fitting top, stiletto black boots, and a matching handbag with gold insets—passed me, I turned back to see she had met up with a friend of hers at the corner of Vias Ostilla and Capo d'Africa. She gave her the friend the hug I wanted. It seemed strong and compassionate.

The air was thick. The motorcycle horns were loud, and not a stitch of blue sky shone through the clouds. At the park across the street, on Via Claudia, no less than three people walked their little dogs, which included a terrier mix, a Pomeranian, and a basenji. The last one barked at its owner to throw a tennis ball, even though, when he did, the pup could run no farther than his retractable leash would extend.

On Via Claudia, just a block from the dogs, the Roman police have their Celian Hill headquarters. An iron gate, with the word Carabinieri *painted in gold on top of it, opened to let a police cruiser through. I wouldn't be lying to you* [look at any one juror and smile, closed mouth] *when I say I wondered at that moment what it would be like to be in that cruiser heading into police headquarters to make a statement, or, perhaps to be brought to the military hospital just beyond it for a mental health assessment. I also wondered how difficult or easy it would be to get off this Celian Hill and onto a plane, and back to a place still covered, even in late April, in three feet of snow. What would happen, now, in less than five minutes, would decide my course. Was I lawbreaker or its biggest defender?*

You see, here's the thing about evidence. No matter how it amasses, how gather-

able plane or hotel reservations might be, no matter how many lies you tell, aliases you have, or internet searches you conduct, evidence can't be used against you if you don't actually commit a crime.

Perhaps this is an overstatement. Even a second-year law student knows the rules of evidence apply in both a criminal and civil context. An example. When Tim swore in an affidavit that "with his lips pressed against my neck, he sounded like he was biting into a good piece of steak," *his statement could equally establish sexual abuse of a minor, an unclassified felony, just as it could a civil breach of the priest's fiduciary duty to tend to Tim's spiritual care, to keep him safe, and to prepare him for a better world. But in addition to the state of mind* [to bolster your expertise, consider also saying, "or mens rea, as we lawyers like to call it"] *that any potential offender must have, she still needs the guilty* act [consider also saying, for consistency, "the actus reaus"] *to commit the crime. Here is another example. Although I may have wanted to kill Ormechea and could think of twenty ways of doing so,* "wanting to" *is not the crime. Definitively acting on the want is.*

Let's talk more about evidence, because, after eighteen years of legal practice, it intrigues me that we still leave it to the lawyers. If we take evidence out of the legal environment altogether, it's everywhere. It's visible in Egeria's love for King Numa, Saint Timothy's hate for Artemis, Pope John Paul II's ambivalence toward sex offenders, and my fondest wish that no matter what I did my primary intent was always to make a loved one whole.

Please understand the following. This singular moment on Tuesday, April 24, 2012, wasn't the time for asking how this encounter with Ormechea might actually make loved ones whole. Frankly, at that moment, or rather, in those moments, when I walked thin-shoed step by thin-shoed step and felt every cobblestone on Via Claudia, determining "how this will work" *was an impossibility. The superhighway neural pathway of rescue-dom was fully engaged. No frontal lobe capacity was accessible for reason. Instead, I was thinking about a child's giggle and how he smelled of honey-made graham crackers.*

I was thinking about Charlie too. How, for example, did twelve-year-old Charlie feel when the "good" [use that word sardonically, consider sneering] *Father held the boy's head to his lap in the front seat of a powder-blue Chevrolet Cavalier? Think of Charlie's palms braced against the sweaty vinyl seats as he willed himself to lift his teeth, braces and all, up and down the priest's bulging penis. Believe me, I know it's not easy to do, but try to imagine the thoughts going through Charlie's mind in those seemingly unending moments. Did he think of his own father, who was just steps away, watching a football game in his living room on Heart's End?*

Did Charlie feel alone, like no other boy on the planet had any idea what he was going through, especially when one, Tim, was just blocks away? Did he wish he was dead and did he have that wish forty years later when his relief came in a bottle? And what of this? Was Tim right? Was my remembrance of the root cause more of a problem than the root cause itself?

Let's turn to Kurt. He didn't have the words to explain what was happening to his body on the priest's likely visits to his bedroom. So instead, he wrapped his dad's car around a sixty-year-old oak tree off Bryn Mawr Avenue. As for porn-producing Greg, despite my mounting dislike of him, I thought of him too, just as I did of the still-unknown 1981 to 1986 abused plaintiff. I also thought of those who came close, Robert, Cory, Freddy, and the schoolteacher's son.

What would you do for them? [Address another juror personally; choose one who you know, through voir dire, has both siblings and children.] *Most especially, what would you do for your first-memory brother? The person by whom and with whom you would always see the world. Would you kill for him? Would you let him know that when he finally spoke up, he had a voice that mattered, that he made a difference? After all this, it's fair, isn't it? Justified even. To take just one life, when Ormechea has taken so many.*

One small thing. Despite all these revenge-minded thoughts I had while walking to the Curia, I still knew I was five minutes away from tourism central at the Colosseum. There, I could picture a man, let's call him Giuseppe, dressed as a gladiator and happy to pose with me for a photo. "*Un euro, per favore, Americana,*" he would have said, and the pretend Joan, the *turista,* freewheeling, carefree Joan would have pushed her hair behind her ear and shook her head no in laughter. Or who knows? Maybe she, I mean I, would have said yes, adding up in my mind all the kitschy reminders of Rome I could create for some empty shelf or wall space back home. Add to this photo, one of me in a toga, a snow globe of Saint Peter's, and a bobblehead of Pope Benedict.

But instead of *that* Joan, I got to stand behind a brick post at the intersection of Viale Spellman and Via della San Paolo della Croce. I hid there for five minutes and stared at the open gate marked with the number thirteen. And now, when I think about it, I realize I stood just as Saint Paul of the Cross did, even still does, in that stained glass window back at I. C., arms outstretched, looking skyward. Saint Paul of the Cross said he came to proclaim "the passion of Christ" and "a love that compels."

I wanted him to know, just as I want you to know, that I too knew something about compelling love, for it alone had brought me there, to that wide-open, wrought-iron gate.

Through it was an unexpectedly newly poured ten-step cement stairway. It led to an equally surprising black pavement ramp. I was surprised because I thought everything in Rome should be more ancient. The ramp ended with a two-step rise to a walnut door, big enough for two giants to walk through, which, in turn, was surrounded in white paving stone. Behind that closed door, in the reception area, I was told, was an American priest who had been living on these General Curia grounds for ten years. It wasn't the only closed door he had been behind.

"Why ten years?" I had asked the nice Italian woman on the phone at the Curia, but she failed to answer. Maybe she didn't understand the question. Maybe she thought the answer was of no consequence or none of my business.

I would be lying to you if I told you I didn't visualize the Amanda Knox–like headline in the next day's *La Repubblica*. What would be my nickname? Although a Nockels, at forty-seven, Foxy Nocksy certainly didn't fit. Perhaps *la procuratore* for prosecutor or *la sorella* for sister. No. I thought something more to the point would've been best. Once translated, it would've read: AMERICAN LAWYER AVENGES HER BROTHER: HUNTS DOWN AND KILLS PREDATOR PRIEST. You see despite my desired intention "to do no harm" and to make it home safely to Abbie, I very much wanted the headline. I even thought, if murder is something I could do, with you as my judges, I could also talk my way out of any potential punishment.

Here is how I might say it.

There is the occasion [no invoking the Fifth after a decade, hell thirty years, of silence] *that homicide is justified* [purposely use that innocuous term—homicide—not murder, assassination, gutting, slaying, your regular burning at the stake], *that breathing should simply cease when death is long deserved.*

As to the motives for my actions? They're easy enough to understand. The priest raped my brother. Sure, we could quibble about whether a penis entered any orifice, that's what we lawyers do well, but there is no doubt that bastard, that bad bear, as my daughter would call him, clawed into Tim what the professionals call the "life-long scars of childhood sexual abuse." [Emphasize this point.] *The life-long scars. No one* "gets over it." *Hell, even look at Oprah, who said, long ago, she forgave. Who said forgiveness is* "giving up the hope that the past could be any different." *The fact she spends her entire life seeking approval and love from every American? This shows she's damaged goods. This shows she didn't get over it. Neither did Tim. And even though I am no one's direct victim, neither did I.*

Will you forgive me for my choice? [Look to one juror.] *Should you?* [Then another.] *Would you, yourself, have done any differently?*

❧

What happened next occurred more quickly than my earlier timidity exhibited. I commanded my right leg into action, just as surely as I reached my left hand toward the object I had zipped into my back pocket. I willed it to be my guidance and took sustenance from its presence up and through the gate to number thirteen and along every step up that new stairway.

Step one. Sunglasses still on, I lowered my gaze, wondering what remote camera might signal my identity before I wanted it to be realized. I was right to do so. Later, he'll tell me that my gait walking up those long stairs seemed familiar and that my height caused him to wonder if he knew me.

Step two. You must know I was frightened, but by then, I had no choice.

Steps three and four. The stairs were short in width and moved so quickly. Though I could physically turn around, I was *that* fireman, marching into the basement. I had, you see, committed.

Steps five and six. A silent one-word prayer came to mind. It went like this. *Help.*

Steps seven through ten. *Help. Help. Help. Help.*

At the black pavement that ramped its way up for forty feet, almost all the way to the open door, I raised my chin and rolled my shoulders back. The air felt warm against my cheek. Letter in hand, I reached again for my back pocket and gripped what remained inside for as long as possible.

❧

One last rise, ladies and gentlemen, my friends. I call you that now. With one push against one half of the giant-sized door, I was inside.

❧

The entry was dark. So too was the tile and the ceiling another eight feet overhead. But light came through the plate glass window to my left, and, like a mosquito, I immediately turned toward it. Beyond it, a seated man had already pressed the security buzzer that opened a second door. Did I push it or did it automatically spring open? That, I can't tell you, because my head was still turned toward that man behind the plate glass. His face was looking at a computer monitor; his right side was in profile. He wore wireless glasses. He was thicker than I recalled; even thicker than his passionistsglobalnetwork.org photo.

Forgive, forgive, forgive, forgive. The only words I remembered from his wedding day homily to me sprang to mind. *No, no, no, no,* was my immediate answer. But still . . . With two full steps and one turn to my left, I faced him fully. That's when he stood. Vertical file cabinets were behind him. So was another desk and another person. Two large windows lit the room. A round wall clock told the time. It was 3:08 p.m. I was just fashionably late for my basilica tour.

The man spoke first. "Are you the woman from Pennsylvania?" he asked, hastily, not looking directly to my face. Rather, he looked beyond it, as if a small bird had entered the building with me.

"No, Father, I'm not," I said. My voice sounded small. For dramatic effect, I took off my sunglasses, perhaps like a movie star might, and flipped my head back to my left. I spoke again. "I'm the woman from Chicago," I said.

I looked directly at him, waiting for him to recognize me. While doing so, I wondered how much he knew, through newspaper articles or conversations with his attorneys, of the role I played in forcing his removal? How long would he let me stand there?

I next saw what looked like weakened knees when he began to fall forward, but he quickly braced himself with extended fingers against his metal desk. As if to further stabilize himself, he widened his stance, crossed his arms, and then uncrossed them again. He wore a light, short-sleeved shirt tucked into a mustard-brown belt and matching slacks. The hair on his arms stood out darkly.

For five long seconds—one Mississippi, two Mississippi, three . . . he didn't seem to know where he was. His next fearful glance was back at my face, but what had he also seen? The way I kept my left hand behind me? What did he remember?

Blinking and rubbing his eyes, he uttered, "Oh my God!" His still-high tenor voice, devoid of accent, creaked out the way a seventy-four-year-old's might, a little bit ancient, but still spry. Then he asked, "Julie?"

Close enough, I thought. Recalling my sister helped me know that he had the right family. "No, Father." I had already used that word twice more than desired or expected. "It's Joan. Joan Nockels."

"Joannie!" I let him familiarize himself and greet me as my father always had. The Joannie of *Joannie Loves Chachie*. The harmless, innocuous, never-had-an-evil-thought-in-her-brain Joannie.

"Yes, Joannie. It's me." I smiled.

What did I look like to him at that moment? Only he could tell you what stood out. I couldn't say whether the slight tailwind I had encountered walking up Via Claudia had blown my hair off its part or whether my dress had curled up against my right thigh from too much sweat. But I did will myself to stand as tall as possible and to move closer toward him like a force that could only be stopped by good manners. He smiled a weak smile and brushed a large hand over his remaining hair. Then he grabbed the desk again and looked around himself. Although they weren't my focus, I could next count two people in our presence, both of them men. One passed behind me on the way out the security door. The other stood attentive, as if witnessing an airport reunion.

And as for all of this, ladies and gentlemen of the jury [say it again, slowly, quietly], *ladies and gentlemen of the jury, my friends, here was the moment when all fantasies had to end and all final decisions had to be made, not out of fear, but out of a determined commitment.*

You see. This is the thing about evidence. No matter what you've done, no matter what trails you've left or state of mind you might hold, no matter if the violence you know you're capable of inflicting might indeed be great, no matter if you came to these General Curia grounds under an angel's guidance or the devil's, no evidence—not one delectable bit of it—can be used against you unless you give it a reason, the *actus reus,* to be used against you.

ᐧᐧ

And for me, my next action was the use of my best asset.

Do you think you can do that, Joan? Speak over a fire?

Speech. I took my left hand out (empty, just as it was supposed to be), from behind my back and raised both hands, palms up, skyward, the way a priest does during a Eucharist's consecration.

"Don't be afraid, Father," I said to the still-shrinking man before me. "I've come in peace."

঎

And there it is, an encounter ten years and twenty-eights days in the making begins in peace, not in violence, and the person most shocked at the offering is me. I wish I could say it's part of my elaborate con, but it's not. When I see Ormechea shrink in my presence, I know for a fact that I am no boyfriend-killing Karen. He looks just like every foster dog I've brought into my home: pathetic. Compassion? The last thing I expect to offer is, unfortunately, the first thing I give.

> Dear Joan,
>
> Please, after all these years in which, let me add, it's been YOU that's kept this curse going, please don't tell me you're feeling sorry for him. This isn't supposed to be easy for him. Get it together! If you can't kill, stay on task. By the way, I'm sorry you couldn't go through with it, but I knew you never had it in you. So get your admission. I'm fatiguing here, sister. Not one more false step.
>
> Tim

Thankfully, when I lift my palms upward, the note in my right hand falls to the floor. I bend down quickly to get it. When I pick it up, I drop it purposefully a little farther away a second time. I need a chance to turn this around.

> Dear Tim,
>
> It's time to remember the long game.
>
> Joan

Count to one. The travertine marble floor is cool against my fingertips. Now two. Sweep the back pocket and hold tight to what's inside it. When I rise, I smile, but this smile is intended, and with premeditation. I see Ormechea's gaze move up and down my body, not in a sensual manner, more as if he's taking stock. How has she aged? Do her shoulders round? Can she get rid of those elevens on her forehead or has her worry made them permanent? Maybe, perhaps, if I'm lucky, is she armed?

He points to the computer monitor on the desk, confirming what I suspected. There is a camera. "When I saw you walk up, I thought, 'she's a tall one,' but something about your gait seemed so familiar." He's right. When I didn't watch myself or follow a physical therapy and massage routine, I drag my left leg a bit, like Dad had done before me. It has something to do with the out-of-alignment Nockels' hips.

"I'm glad you remember me," I say softly. I smile again and run a finger along my hairline, pushing any strand that's fallen out of place behind an ear, which, come to think of it, may have been one of things he saw me do incessantly on my wedding day. Although my hair was in an up-do and half a bottle of hairspray had been unleashed to keep it in place, Chicago humidity had its own plan for it. A small section had fallen out right before my walk down the aisle. I constantly adjusted it back to its should-have-been-shellacked place.

"Of course, I do, Joannie." It's as if he's flipped a switch too. His voice sounds energized, memorable, and unaltered. And then he says the one thing that I register, even at this moment, can make him mine. He says, "It's wonderful to see you!"

My face must not show the shock. Wonderful to see me? Me? The woman who's still trying to land him in jail? Who has fixated on you and has stalked you incessantly? What's wonderful about that? Part of this I even think of saying, but instead, gazing at him, mouth certainly agape, I ask an unfiltered, "Why?"

As if he's a schoolboy readying for reading in front of the class, he straightens his polo shirt and adjusts his belt buckle. He fiddles with a pile of paper in front of him, leaving it just so, and looks to me again.

"Why?" he repeats my question with a laugh, as if it were silly to ask, as if the answer should be obvious. "Because you're a face from home," he says. And I, like the porcupines I've seen with raised and bristled haunches back home, feel like I'm about to puncture him.

A face from home? Belatedly, I realize my presence might be bringing the one thing I never intended: a gift. It doesn't matter who I've become, what purpose I might hold, or if there were a direct correlation between the words "Joan" and "vengeance." To him, I'm his heyday. I'm young boys in in light blue shirts and black slacks playing touch football on the I. C. playground. I'm meeting the Wilowskis at Sally's Restaurant for its famous apple pancakes or the Conrads at Dino's for a slice of cheese and sausage. I'm endless cups of coffee brewed in parish ladies' percolators. *Come by any time, Father.* I'm warm summer evenings in a place where everyone speaks English and where long-ago friends never deserted him. As for his series of crimes? Well *snip, snip, gone away with you, my friends.* Extraction, it appears, is not simply my mother's skill.

As I first noticed when I saw him in profile, he looks healthier than I desire. True, he has fewer and grayer hairs than before, but he's smart to wear it short instead of in his former comb-over. I imagine some skilled Italian barber named Francesco tending to him, because his face doesn't have a whisker on it either. He looks polished. His skin is Southern California brown, and except for a couple of lines from his nose to his chin that make him look like a marionette any time he frowns, his face is surprisingly wrinkle-free. He has a natural tendency to cross his arms across his stomach when there's a lull in our conversation, but it doesn't appear to be an effort to close off dialogue. Rather, it's more as if he has to hold himself in place just to see what might come next.

Everything I know about Ormechea, narcissistic qualities most included, tells me he would be highly embarrassed by me finding him in his current occupation of part-time receptionist. Joan Troka would love this, I think. Is he forbidden to open the mail, as she was, and who holds a tight rein to him making sure he doesn't arrive to work not thirty seconds late? But I need to be polite, and to defer, appropriately so, to his earned title, his "last profession," no matter his current assignment.

"Did you kick him in the shins?" Richard will ask when I call him while I'm standing on the Clivo di Scauro, not ten minutes after leaving the General Curia. He'll have me on speakerphone. "Or hit him with the bear stick?" Abbie will add in the slurred speech of a toddler's tongue that should not, in any way, understand the question.

"No, I didn't do either of those." My voice will sound resigned, and they'll both seem disappointed. For Richard's part, he'll say I owed Ormechea the shin kick for the damage he'd done to our marriage.

"You can't blame him," I'll respond, surprisingly giving the priest cover. "How I let him influence me, and then us, that's been all my doing."

"Well, if you didn't kick him," he'll ask, "what did you say?"

❧

The words come out in soliloquy. I say, "Father Ormechea," I'll end up calling him Father at least ten times, "I'm not here to shock you, although this must be a shock. I've come from Anchorage to Rome not to see the sights, but to see you. After ten long years, Father, I'm weary, and I need some answers. I don't know if you're willing to speak with me, and I think you'll need time to figure out the answer to that question, so I've written you a letter further explaining the reason for my presence and asking you to meet with me again. Perhaps you could read it and just think about talking to me in a few days. I'm in Rome until Saturday and staying close by. My hotel information and phone numbers are in the note as well. "

"Oh," he says, just, "oh," standing in place, not moving toward me or shrinking back. I take a couple of steps closer and hand him the envelope marked by my grade-school cursive. He reaches out a hand and grabs the letter from me. His eyes blink a few times, and he raises his hand to another man, tall, with black hair and a large build for an Italian, who just came in the door behind me.

"There's a letter from my father in the envelope as well," I continue. "You may know from calls back to the States, he's ill and certain you have no desire to talk to me. But if you do, you might be making a difference for Dad as well." I start to get, not weepy, but effusive, adding every trick I can think of to will our future conversation into a one-day existence. My ailing father is first. Next comes my faithful mother. "And my mother, she's never given up hope of reconciliation." Then this, "I can only imagine how life-altering all this has been for you."

Dear Joan,
   It's me again, Tim. Please confirm you're acting.
   T.

"One day you were a pastor at Saint Agnes, the next gone, and now you're here, away from family and friends. I'd like to hear your story."

Dear Tim,
   I think so, but I'm playing it a little too well. Dave would say I'm believing my own bullshit. There is this, however. To get to him to speak with me, I first have to convince

him it's a good idea.
   J.

Before answering, Ormechea fiddles with the letter in his hand, turning it sealed side up and then down. He looks to the man behind me and seems to grant him approval to leave. The other airport-reunion-observing guy behind him is still watching. Ormechea asks, as if he didn't understand me the first time, "You came all the way here, from Alaska, just to see me?"

"Yes, Father. Not the Trevi Fountain or Saint Peter's Basilica." I smile. "Just you."

"Me," he repeats, but this time not as a question. His hands loosen, and his chest is out. Is it possible he's puffing like a peacock?

I nod my head in accord, and now he smiles. Based on that smile and his "it's wonderful to see you" comment, I take one more chance.

See, Tim. I'm on top of this.

Why give him the opportunity to think his way out of a future meeting?

"Father, in my note, I suggest you call me if you're willing to speak. But, if it's not too much trouble, could we just agree right now to meet again? You can always change your mind. I'll respect that."

"You're here through Saturday?" he asks. He's been listening.

"Yes, but come to think of it, I leave early that day, so we would need to meet before then."

"And you have no other set plans?"

"No, Father." I laugh and hold both arms out toward him. "It's all about you."

There is an awkward moment of silence as he considers his options, perhaps wondering if he should talk to his superiors first, but, with a nod of his head in the affirmative direction, I see he's made a choice. "How about Thursday morning, say ten o'clock?" he says, "You can meet me here."

It's rarely the prosecutor that gets to eke out the confession from their unwilling subject. Generally the detectives get to have that fun. Thus, even if my tenure at the Anchorage DA's office had been longer, it wouldn't have prepared me for any second meeting with Ormechea. Neither would the countless number of depositions I conducted in the civil arena, because rarely do we get a smoking gun moment, despite what reruns of *Law & Order* might telecast. Why? At deposition, the deponent is well schooled in deposition etiquette. Only answer the question asked. If the question calls for a yes or no response, that is what you give. "Yes" or "No," never an explanation. And so instructions to deponents go. Make sure you understand the question; if you don't, seek clarification. Pause before speaking; give the lawyer time to object to the form or for some other matter. When she's done, know what you intend to say before you even open your mouth. And finally, when things get rough and you don't want to answer, don't worry, let your lawyer find another reason to object. That will slow the pace and offer the opportunity to regroup.

Instead real truth seeking comes in smaller, less courtroom-like measures, like the time I was trying to prove that the former owners of a company who said they complied with all environmental regulations hadn't. I spent a day interviewing ten current employees in a makeshift office at one of the company's more remote sites. Like depositions, the interviews were largely unhelpful. It wasn't until I sat down to have coffee with a guy named Todd that he casually asked me if I'd seen the video tape they keep by the breakroom TV. In it, company workers filled the containment pits with water to overflow, easily letting any excess diesel and contaminated soil spill into a nearby creek, a source for drinking water, not twenty feet from the site. That had me convinced, truth came out casually, unexpectedly, and usually over a cup of coffee. So, when Richard asked why I didn't kick Ormechea in the shins or my imagined Tim expressed disappointment in my tactics, I had this to rely on. Wait, please, for that first cup of Folgers. Then be my judge.

In case Ormechea is watching on camera when I leave the General Curia, I turn around one last time and wave goodbye. I reserve reaction until I'm well down Clivo di Scauro. Since his shift has just started and he has all this free time Abigail Sheehan was once expected to fill, I wonder how long it will take him to open my letter. Would he do it right away or wait until he's alone in his room? Whenever he does, I hope he starts with the poems. I hope he sees himself as Dorsey Baker's courageous hero taking shape and that our next meeting will let that long shaded sun shine through.

I do know this. Despite my attempts to entice, my letter still has pointed accusations, and if anything were discernible from my father's words, there is an undoubted link between the Devil and the wayward priest. If Ormechea is offended, he needs to be convinced that speaking with me will right these derisions and an improved reputation will be his prize. He has to have confidence in the outcome. That's why I know, the one thing I couldn't give him, not yet, were Tim's words. Those had to wait for delivery until later.

❧

To say I wander for the next couple of hours is an understatement. From the Clivo di Scauro to Celimontana again, I make some phone calls, first to Richard, as I said, and then to my mother. I text Tim to say, "Got him." A bit premature, I admit, but I want to feel good about this. I eventually even make my way to Giuseppe, at tourism central. When he asks, "*Un euro, per favore, Americana?*" unfortunately no carefree, *turista* Joan appears. I'm not in the mood. I decline politely, I hope, and walk to the back, less-populated side of the Colosseum. It's there I get my new gig: picture taker.

I'm sitting on a small hill. Behind me, the Colosseum, il Colosseo, looks almost rural in setting. Green grass predominates. No busy streets are in view. This must be why three couples, in quick succession, approach me to take their photos with the human-made monolith behind them. Now, the sky's turned a rich and dark orange, and the sun's reflection on the ruins must make me think, *this* is what it means to survive. Even if this ancient structure no longer provides a venue to entertain the Gladiator-enthralled masses, at least it still stands.

When each couple returns home, wherever and whenever that might be, my silent hope is that each of my photos will find their respective living room wall on which to hang. I hope the couples will notice how I framed each of them in the bottom right corner of the viewfinder and how I tried to find the correct angle so that the setting sun would reflect against their glowing skin just as richly as it did the Colosseum's stone foundation. I hope that whenever they are broken, this photo whispers them, "Whatever you do, darlings, just keep standing, and let the sun glorify you."

❧

Oh! I wish there were more fun-loving, quixotic characters I could add to this evening, because I can see I'm growing morose. My photographed couples disappeared like once-used flashcubes. I have nothing more of them to report. Wouldn't it be nice if Lorena would deliver me a half carafe of red wine? Or how about my preening Barbara, oblivious Matthew, and playing-with-his-chest-hair Douglas trio? Shouldn't the love triangle make an appearance as well, to tell me about their tour to Saint Peter in Chains and the Mamertine Prison and how they found the keys? They would surely add to what's been my solo-voyage evening. But that's the thing I have to remember, isn't it? I'm exactly alone.

I take the object out of my back pocket and hold it, flipping it from hand to hand, over and over again. It's the size of a walnut husk and it's painted red. Along with a bronze mermaid statue Abbie named Jesus, she found it in a Homer Alaska gift shop and asked me to buy it for her. She slipped that little heart into my backpack without my noticing the same time she tried to give me Cletus's bear stick. When I found it during my layover in Chicago, I called to thank her. She said she left it for me so I wouldn't forget she loved me. I held it many times on the flight to Madrid and then Rome. At some point, perhaps when I considered kissing the tarmac at Fiumicino, the little charm had morphed from Abbie's heart to Tim's. It had become my talisman to keep me brave and my lucky charm to bring success.

I still have to admit that when the little heart rested against my spine on my walk to the General Curia, when my fingers brushed against it, albeit behind smooth fabric, and when I, at times, clung to it while meeting Ormechea, I nearly convinced myself it was my dreamed-of .22, the weapon that would lead to Ormechea's undoing. But the more I think about it, here on my Colosseum gazing hill, I realize this is exactly what Tim's heart is. From the first moment he was willing to share his story, Tim became Ormechea's undoing. I was here, in Rome, just for the last unfastening.

I once had a chicken named Kate. It wasn't the smartest decision to have her, because I didn't know much about keeping chickens in a place named Bear Valley. I had Kate long before we installed an electric fence around her coop, to keep the bear and lynx away, and a mesh roof over her run, to protect her from hawks and owls. She was a black Sex Link and the epitome of one tough bird. She was also a bit of a bitch. As the top hen pecker, she killed two of her flock mates. She kept one hen in her company, and it might have stayed that way if a friend's dog hadn't torn her comrade to pieces.

For almost three years she was alone and for half that time, thinking she might be miserable, I wondered if I should off her. It was only after a Derick Burleson's poetry class on Tennyson's *Ulysses* and the dramatic monologue, in which the author takes on the character of someone else, that Kate, through my own hand, wrote herself into continued existence. Her poem was entitled "Black Chicken," and she had this to say.

Thanks to Kaya, I'm alone.

The mongrel dog took the hen I pecked and plucked her feathers skullduggery style.

As usual, you didn't even ask to see the carcass; your mate consistently makes death disappear for you right before your eyes.

This solitude of a chicken you say? So against flock mentality and the wants I'm supposed to have.

True, sometimes I cackle and await the answer that doesn't come. I dust my feathers and feel no one's heat, but the sun's.

And so you look at me, in what? Sympathy? Intrusion?

You, who never raised a hatchet, except to chop kindling, think longingly of my neck on the block!

Know this, my considering executioner,

The night is wild, and I roost in sumac.

The earth is moist, and I inhale its dwellers.

The forest makes calls, and I cry, like an eagle, in return.

I can be myself.

A tribe of one, at rest in isolation.

So listen closely, wayward friend.

Put that ax down!

There is no use for it or for you either.

Funny. It seemed once I wrote Kate into survival, our dynamic changed. Whenever I opened the front door in the morning or came home from work at night, she ran to me, with her wings outstretched and chortling a hen's mix of greetings and complaints. It wasn't just for food. That chicken followed me for walks in the woods, had a fondness for jumping on Cletus's back, and chose a good IPA over a sip of water every time.

What predators she might encounter while I was away, I couldn't predict each day, but she had the decided ability to outmaneuver all of them. My neighbor Allison once watched her outsmart a black bear in pursuit. That same summer, a lynx silently waited out a litter of feral rabbits living under our shed, just steps from Kate's coop. Yet each morning and night Kate was there to greet me. Until, that is, she wasn't.

It was the start of winter in 2010. By then we had moved her heated and lit coop, a monstrosity Richard had made for me the prior Christmas, to its permanent site. We surrounded it with a six-foot fence. Although we knew it would be difficult, we even contemplated introducing Kate to a new set of pullets. Then came the first day, then the second, and then the third, when we couldn't find her. I thought the worst when I found a bear print on the coop's window. While our fence was up, we hadn't yet hooked up the electrified wire, and without it, the fence was no real barrier for any predator. It was, however, for a chicken. By containing Kate, she must've run out of escape options.

I had just about given up on finding her when I remembered to check around the old doghouse, then dismantled that had once served as Kate's first coop. I found her there, nestled in a corner, in old straw, and gathered her up to return her to roost. That's when I noticed her sagging comb and her beak half open. She was struggling to breathe.

If there ever were a chicken I would consider taking to a vet, it was Kate. But usually by the time you notice an infection or ailment in a hen, it's already too late. I took her in the garage that night. I tried to give her her favorite local beer, the Fairweather brand, and the bananas she used to gulp up like amusement park offerings. She would have none of it. All she would take were the eyedropper offerings of water I positioned over her beak, and even that she did reluctantly.

Can a chicken feel love? That's certainly too much to ask from a direct descendant of the dinosaur, but I believe this. With me, that night, she felt unthreatened, and I think she knew her putative executioner had become her biggest protector.

I mention Kate not simply because she was one great chicken (yes, the two words can go together without the word *fried* between them), but because the moment before she took her last breath, she raised her head, flapped her wings—with the ferocity of a wild trumpeter swan, I should add—and then fell back into my arms, dead.

Let me testify, though you needn't agree, when she offered herself up in that manner, head high, wings untamed, I had little doubt some force in her was flying away. Where did she go? My Christian faith tells me it's not heaven for heaven is solely for the forgiven human soul. Other religions might be of assistance. Zen Buddhists, for example, will tell me Kate's purpose was to teach me a lesson and, once taught, her life force was again free to leave. I get that, but I also highly doubt Kate's life was solely for my benefit. Therefore, my belief in something more universal takes refuge in this. Any force any of us might call the Father, Yahweh, Creator, or even Mother of the Gods is much greater than anything we can comprehend. That Kate should just perish? I don't think so.

Or that Kate existed only for me? No to that as well. That Kate still thrives somewhere, not for my benefit, but as a tribe of one. This gives me sustenance, because that little chicken didn't go anywhere she didn't want to be.

ঽ৵

Wednesday morning

Which brings me to my purpose, one day before my second meeting with Ormechea, of exploring what it means to have faith, whether it be faith that even a chicken's spirit might go on or, more on-point, that, if I really try to observe, every step I'm taking in this millennia-ravaged Rome is not alone.

We, for I cannot be alone . . .

Last night, this amateur photographer made it back to the Hotel Lancelot in time for our collective dinner. Perhaps out of fatigue, but more likely out of a renewed sense of openness, I felt freer to speak. Over roasted asparagus and skirt steak, Barbara looked at me slack jawed when I explained the day's developments.

"I guess you didn't need Matthew," she said, somewhat sadly.

I next let Vivian know how much help Abbie's little heart gave me. And on a later, Matthew-directed moonlight tour around the Basilica of Saint John the Lateran, Father Stephan and I had time to discuss his midlife choice of religious calling. He said he had been a wandering soul, a vagabond in spirit up until then, but with his parishioners he thought he was the calm one, the one whose ear I knew sweet-singing Beatrice would have, and the one who might prod Thomas back to gentle husbandry. Which brings me again to my question. Although our conversation never turned directly to the subject of faith, to me, he's a walking example of what I think is most important about it.

The age-old debate between Martin Luther and the criminally and ethically flawed Renaissance papacy was whether justification by *sola fide*, that is, by faith alone, was enough to save the human soul. For the man who believed that with God all things are possible, Luther's answer—my Wisconsin Synod husband often reminds me—was a simple yes, born, perhaps, upon the steps of La Scala Sancta when he pondered, "Who knows whether it is so?"

As for Luther's opponents then, Catholic course correctors will assert faith *plus acts* are necessary for a sinner's redemption. "Faith, if it not have works, is dead," pronounced the sixteenth-century Council of Trent. And, as described in the New Advent online Catholic Encyclopedia, faith must be attended with repentance, penance, love of God, charity, and virtue for the kingdom of God to ever be at hand. My friend studying to become a Catholic deacon will add that even modern-day Lutherans believe faith alone is not enough to achieve justification, but I can think of at least one modern-day Lutheran, my husband, who would still disagree.

As for me, my Catholic religion's guidance on the subject would be less objectionable if the Renaissance system of bought indulgences didn't pollute what was charitable and virtuous. And Martin Luther's guidance might also have sway if it did not theoretically permit the serial murderer, with Jesus in his heart, to be justified.

I understand faith a bit differently now and have come to believe that faith is an act or decision whose benefit has nothing to do with justification. That is, if, in the case of Father Stephan, faith's sole purpose is to bring him contentment, then no end game of salvation, or even flying to wherever Kate might be, is necessary. Heaven, it would seem, is right here on earth.

Two Loyola University freshmen recently met with my aunt and penned what they titled, *The Memoir of Sister Ann Carolyn Blackburn*. In it, my aunt described as gifts the times in her life when it was especially difficult for her to connect with God. She said these moments enriched her faith, rather than lessened it. So when a debilitating disease caused her unbearable pain, she thanked God for teaching her how to suffer, and when she fell shortly after a hip replacement, she further thanked God for the little things she could still do, like pray. The acts themselves of suffering and of prayer were building blocks of her faith because she didn't ever believe she was going through them alone. With the appearance, yet again, of the Book of Timothy, my Alaska connection to the Khan family, and finally finding Ormechea so easily, neither did I.

Last summer, my friend Pamela and I went to see Bill Maher in concert. We loved Bill, especially when he lampooned Alaska's ex-half-term, Putin-imagining governor, but we both got quiet when he started to go on about the foolishness of believing in God. Like Pamela and me, he had been raised Catholic. Nevertheless, he called the belief in any higher power, be it Jesus, Buddha, or New Age spiritualism, "a purposeful suspension of critical thinking." He asked if God exists, why didn't he or she speak to us directly, and he concluded the only purpose of believing in a greater power is to allay our collective fear of death.

I liked Bill Maher, and no singular part of me can say he's not potentially correct. Beyond my own experiences, I have no need or desire to press my beliefs on others. If they are happy to consider them, I'm happy to offer them, and to listen to criticisms of them, no obligation required. But, halfway through Maher's critique of the Holy Trinity, Pamela leaned over to me and said, "He sounds so Catholic."

She was right. His argument seemed Ignatian in presentation. Present the thesis and prove it in three parts, the Father, Son, and Holy Spirit of it all. I still have to disagree with Bill. From my singular human existence, I've come to believe faith is not the suspension of critical thinking; rather, it's what steps in when critical thinking can't provide an answer any more believable than the one critical thinking offers. An example. Judging by the number of pages in a typical Bible, there was a one in seventeen hundred chance that the man across the aisle on the plane would be reading from the Book of Timothy. So what are the odds that, at pivotal moments in my life, I would encounter these epistles a second time and then, you will soon find out, even a third? Is a threefold coincidence any more believable than the idea that a loving force might be finding a way to reach me through the best means possible? Perhaps, to Bill Maher, coincidence is the only plausible explanation, but I suspended no more critical thinking otherwise than he. Critical does not mean hopeless.

As to whether God speaks directly to humankind, I can think of numerous times, at least for me, that something greater than me got my attention. From seeing a dog reach her eleventh year when all doctors said she would die at six months of age, to my answered prayer on the Camino de Santiago, to a daughter falling into my life when I had given up on even the possibility of her, God whispered, "hello." And if I were to take my aunt's guidance, even moments of suffering are moments of conversation.

Maher's last point? That a belief in God allays the fear of death? It does. As much as any Christian, I want to believe the Book of John's pronouncement that God's house has many dwelling places and my savior has gone to prepare a place for me. If he had me in mind, my dwelling place would have one awesome patio at the corners of Pocahontas Trail and Hiawatha Drive. There, the Cubs game would be on the radio, and they would be winning. My uncle would be laughing the laugh that shakes vases, and my grandfather would be dressed head to toe in yellow, looking like one big banana. I also want to believe what my aunt has witnessed tending to sisters who are dying. She's said she's seen a spiritual aura around them when they pass on, and it gives her courage to face death. But the thing is, even with a belief in God, we still fear what is, in no uncertain terms, an end of an earthly existence. Whether an energy that cannot be destroyed follows or doesn't follow, fear doesn't vanish. A belief in God is no more its undoing than a belief against God. No, as my father told me, never expect to live, or in this case die, without fear, but don't withhold making a choice because of it.

From my aunt's memoir: "I remember when I was twenty years old, and now I'm eighty-three. My mother said you live and learn. That's what living is: learning." If there's one thing I've learned, especially here in Rome, it is that a loving God does not abandon, and when I'm awake and alive, rarely the day will go by that I don't feel this is so. Is this Christian enough? Do I still get to carry the Jesus card? The pope might disagree, but I've made my peace. And as to whether I might be wrong? Yes, Bill Maher, that is a decided possibility. But, in my critical thinking, I choose God.

Late Wednesday morning

I don't realize Wednesday is a national holiday until I see the Via dei Fori Imperiali, from the Colosseum to Vittorio Emmanuel Monument, is free of all the crazy, maniacal Italian drivers I witnessed upon my arrival and open solely to pedestrians. It's *Festa della Liberazione,* a day commemorating the end of World War II in Italy. Although I still need to prepare my list of questions for Ormechea and develop the best strategy for asking them, it feels like my liberation day too, the day to simply be a tourist.

Last night I came up with a plan. My first stop would be the top of the Emmanuel Vittorio Monument. Then I would walk to the Pantheon, and finally spend an afternoon lazing about the Piazza Navona, *Return to Me*–style. Before leaving the hotel for the day, I ran it by Robert, the Ghanian diplomat. He did his best not to question my overtly tourist track steps, but I could still see his smile turn into a scowl, which I think implied, "Why not go see the real Rome? San Lorenzo or Trastevere?" He was off to look at the last of two apartments on the outskirts of town. We left together, me making a left at the hotel's gate and he a right.

"Jo-ann," he spoke my name the way the Spanish do, "be sure to have some fun!" he said, straightening his tie one last time. Even going to look at apartments, he was still the best dressed among us.

Fun. The last time I remember having fun ended with me making out with a cab driver on my "red shoes, no knickers" night out with my friend Jenny in London. Come to think of it, he wasn't the cab driver. He was a passenger in a private cab we commandeered after the bars closed, and I believe he worked crew on some billionaire's yacht then parked down on the Thames. Good thing I had Jenny to get us out of there, or I may have been found at the bottom of the river the next morning. Still, for my last memory of fun to be more than eleven years ago, something had to be done about that, just not today. With tomorrow's fare still to come, fun seems so out of the question. But relaxing, inquisitive, and potentially stressless? These are possible. And how about sarcastic? *Nessun problema.*

I take comfort that Romans almost to a person lampoon the Vittorio Emmanuel Monument, *il Vittoriano*, as an eyesore, giving it nicknames like the Wedding Cake, the Typewriter, and False Teeth. One website remarks that the best thing about riding the elevator to the top of the monument is taking panoramic photos of the city that don't include it. One downside? Taking too many photos of its chariot ladies will eventually lead to me being too late to see inside the Pantheon before its noon closure. But that's okay. My photo of a municipal cop in a heated conversation with a gladiator wearing brown leather shoes and leg warmers and holding a tiara makes up for any missed frame of the Pantheon's oculus or Raphael's Latin epigram, *Timuet quo sospite vinci, Rerum magna parens / et moriente mori.* "Living, great Nature fear'd he might outvie / Her works; and dying, fears herself might die."

If anything were to die for in this city, it would have to be the *tonnarelli cacio provola di bufala affumicata grigliata* (the grilled, smoked buffalo cheese with zucchini, anchovies, and chili pepper) offered at a small al fresco café off the Piazza San Salvatore in Lauro. But don't ask me how to find it again. I thought I was following the signs to the Piazza Navona. Then I went a little right down Via dei Giovanni Vecchio, left on Via Banchim, and right again on some unknown street before I ended up three piazzas away. Even though I was starving, I was cautious before requesting a table at the Ristorante Sangallo Ai Coronari. The servers looked uppity in their white linen suits and pink ties and so did the primarily Italian patrons. Then I thought, if they'd let a French poodle stay (one still sits under a table just to my left), they could hardly complain about an American with euros.

I write in my journal. "There is no dispute. I'm going to eat this entire bowl of macaroni. I don't know how to explain it. Fresh noodles, thick cheese, lightly cooked bacon, and then the pepper." I must be falling in love. Because after the first course and second glass of rosa (there will be four), I look at the snooty patrons with newly found admiration. "Even the old are fashionable," I write. "Beautiful sunglasses, good skin, but I know by their looks they won't fare well in my home. I keep picturing the woman wearing a pink sweater in this seventy-five degree heat freezing. But back to the pasta and the *secondi piatti* that tastes like fried cheese dipped in oil. Kill me now."

If it weren't for the pasta and fried cheese with a second serving of grease, I'd have to admit I'm drinking enough wine this afternoon to put Roman cab drivers in trouble. Okay, I'll also have to admit, London was not my first go-around with cabbies, which might be why I still think of the yachtsman as one. And perhaps that's why I also don't suspect that my walk along the Tiber River, just a block from my new favorite restaurant in the whole wide world, will lead me to the place I have no desire to go on the day of Pope Benedict's papal greeting: the friggin' Vatican.

It was Vivian who told me at dinner last night that her group was going back there today. Matthew had secured tickets for the pope's Wednesday audience. They'd leave early, at 6:00 a.m., to try to get the best seats. I had no interest in going. As for Pope Benedict, he would always remain to me Joseph Cardinal Ratzinger, John Paul II's Rottweiler, and Prefect of the Congregation for the Doctrine of the Faith, who like his predecessor pope, ignored the clergy sex abuse crisis in the United States until press coverage wouldn't allow it. Add to this the *New York Times*'s Maureen Dowd March 27, 2010, critique:

> He has started two investigations of American nuns to check on their "quality of life"—code for seeing if they've grown too independent. As a cardinal he wrote a Vatican document urging women to be submissive partners and not take on adversarial roles toward men.

Like many before him, there's no doubt this man-crowned man has little to offer me.

But Antonio Raggi, Lazzaro Morelli, Paolo Naldini, Cosimo Fancelli, Girolamo Lucenti, Ercole Ferrata, and Domenico Guidi? Each of them do. Each of their sculpted angels—angel with the thorn crown, angel with the column, angel with the cross, sponge, whip, lance, veil—pull me across Il Ponte Sant'Angelo just like I'm a sixteenth-century pilgrim. And once I turn left on Via della Conciliazione, I don't have a choice. Saint Peter's Basilica and the saint himself, it seems, are calling me home.

❧

Which brings me to the last person who did so. It was the spring of 2010, and, after nine years of our one-on-one meetings, I had come to say goodbye.

"Miss Joan, come, come sit down," he said. Although eighty-two years old, I could swear he leaped over a small coffee table to clear a pile of books from an office chair to make it ready for me. From it, I could see out his window. Pickup trucks and Subaru station wagons in a nearby parking lot were slush-brown and circles of earth around birch and spruce trees were starting to show. Spring break-up was under way. The books I replaced, titles including *Arise from Darkness, Faith and Revelation,* and *Collected Works of Bernard Lonergan: Philosophical and Theological Papers, 1965–1980,* joined yet another pile of weathered titles, like *Paying Attention to God, The Discernment of Spirit,* and *A Pilgrim's Journey,* on the floor near some still empty boxes. I couldn't tell if they were staying or going with him on his move to Tacoma. But I was happy to see not everything had been packed away. He still had the quilt hanging that a parishioner had made for him showing the years of his journey from son of a grocer to his time in Anchorage directing the Holy Spirit Retreat Center. He also kept on his wall a map of Alaska with pins marking the villages and towns he and Father Armand Nigro had visited to codirect Ignatian retreats.

Despite both him and Father Nigro, the Society of Jesus had decimated western Alaska. For over fifty years, its Northwest Province, based out of Portland, Oregon, shipped pedophile priests and missionaries from seven Jesuit provinces and even other countries to remote villages on the shores of the Bering Sea and Yukon and Kuskokwim Rivers, leaving child victims in ruins. The Order's more than $160 million settlement with scores of Yupik and Athabascan victims was the primary reason the Jesuits were closing their Alaska operations. Just two months from the day I came to see him, Vincent Beuzer, S.J., would be the last Jesuit to leave.

However, take the image of a pedophile priest, say Father Ormechea or the long list of western Alaska criminals, replace it with a kind, thoughtful, compassionate servant of God, and the best person to fill that mold was Father Beuzer. Because he never stopped teaching, like the former Gonzaga University professor of theology he had been, I took a pen and paper to each of his Sunday homilies, recording all of his offerings over the years. February 24 of some unmarked year: "God's dream is to fashion a human family into God's own image and likeness." August 3: "The biggest need people have is to feel the personal presence of God. To have a good heart is not good enough. Rather to have a good heart in which the Holy Spirit loves and lives is the goal." May 20: "Give what you have to give to God. Don't worry that it's not enough." June 2: "If you already think you know, you will never grow in knowing." July 16: "The Holy Spirit is at work, whenever there is work of the spirit in us. Fear not, Jesus said, I am with you." August 10: "'Come to the water' is an invitation to allow God to be operative in our lives. The call is always made. The question is, are we listening and are we ready to respond in the way God has planned for us?" Never, not once, did his homilies touch the subjects archdiocesan priests now seemed compelled to address, like abortion, homosexuality, or upcoming national elections. Instead, all Vincent Beuzer offered up was a God who wanted to know us and love us as individuals.

It was Linda, again, my Chicago Catholic compatriot, who suggested I see him for one-on-one spiritual counseling, even after Zoloft had evened out the lows of the clinical depression that followed my separation and divorce. Though I could get to work, run again, and start recharting my five-year plan, I was tremendously still in a blame-game state of mind. I wrote a twenty-page statement in support of my marriage's annulment entitled, "The Piercing." As the title suggests, it cast my ex-husband as the evilest among evils and me as the perfect spouse who deserved not one wrong sent her way. Father B., as I and most called him, read this Gospel according to Saint Joan. After doing so, he just remarked, "Jesus is showing you his cross." But over the course of nine years of regular spiritual counseling, some times more frequently than others, he gradually lifted me from the darkness neither Zoloft nor Marsha could banish. "Joan," he would say, smile wrinkling, eyes so energized and ready, I would think, to shake me, "What makes you think you are doing this alone?"

By the time of his retirement and the Jesuit's exodus from the Last Frontier, Father B. was a white-haired old man with a receding hairline, who was still the size of a linebacker, although he played basketball in high school. He had gray-green eyes and a nose that leaned to the left. "Too many bar fights, like Uncle Dan?" I wondered. His smile looked like he was the only one in on an inside joke. And, like me, elevens were well-creased into his forehead from too much thinking. This, for example, list of questions he levied at his former theology professor and twentieth-century equivalent of Thomas Aquinas, Father Benard Lonergan, in the above-mentioned treatise: "How can you justify starting methodology with cognitional theory?" "Could you explain authentic subjectivity?" "In doctrines, do you get a statement about God in which you have no understanding of the meaning of it?"

He had used so much brain power in his academic career I could easily forgive him for losing his way mid-Mass, which he had been doing with greater frequency, though he was the first to laugh at his own failings, to carry his own cross. Father B. never judged why I married Richard so quickly or chastened me on my inability to forgive. He believed humans had to start where they were and if they had little faith, then they had to take little steps. When Abbie came around, he treated her like the miracle she was.

As for Ormechea, over the years, I told Father B. all about him and how I struggled remaining in a Church that kept him as a priest, just a mile from the Vatican. I am certain I went on more than once about the inequality the Church afforded to women and that if and when I tithed it would be by turning over my donations to my brother. But when it came to me remaining Catholic, he always said the same thing, over and over, even on the last day of our meeting in his book-piled office. "Joan," he said, "we need your righteousness. You can leave the Catholic Church when Jesus does."

On that last day, he smiled after saying it, giving me his "gotcha" laugh. His voice was calm and inquisitive, but stained with a gravel that filled his throat. I thanked him for everything he had done for me, including bringing a belief in possibility back to my life. I let him know that when I was broken, he healed me. I told him I would miss his homilies and those tiniest of reminders he would offer in sayings like, "Remember, often we focus on Peter's failure, but at least he got out of the boat." Or, "This is what you need to believe and trust. We are all part of God's salvation story." And finally, my favorite, "There are two dogs in this life, one represents good, the other evil. Which one wins depends on which one you feed."

I said everything I wanted to say. I'm still grateful for that. And before leaving that day, he gave me the hug that I'd become used to only from him. Since in his philosophy, the Holy Spirit resided in the human heart, he pressed my back firmly where my heart would be. As if God the spirit were there, I felt Father B.'s love and care from the center out.

His retirement didn't last as long as we had hoped. He died on a Sunday, just months before my visit to Rome. And when he did, it felt like Jesus had left the Catholic Church alongside him.

I think that's why I don't expect the view of Saint Peter's from Via della Conciliazione to entrance me. God had already left the building. But when I see it, I walk west, unbidden, unstoppable, a lamb to the slaughter, a lover to her beloved. Even the African street salesmen selling knockoffs of designer handbags and sunglasses can't pull me off course with their propositioning *"Veinte euros, senora"* and *"una bolsa,* very nice." I can't stop until I rest, surrounded by Bernini's colonnades and saints, against the footing of Saint Peter's Square's central obelisk.

Tongalese, Italian, German, French, Spanish, Japanese, and English. I can hear each language offered up at the same time, like a Pentecostal babble. Despite the obelisk as sundial, the bells of St. Peter's still ring to mark the hour, just like the long-ago clock I once played. *Bong. Bong. Bong. Bong.* It's 4:00 p.m. A cast of pigeons takes flight at the sound. A young Italian girl, five years old, maybe six, in a bubblegum-pink sweater eats chips that look like Pringles out of a paper cylinder. A Rubik's cube is on the ground to her right. She and her family, I think this is who these people are, wear bright yellow ribbons that look like age-group awards for a 5K. Her grandfather, I think that's who he is, has a bandaged hand and a red face. He calls to the little girl, "Francesca!" She drops her potato chips beside the discarded game and runs to him, smiling.

As for the Germans, they look like a pack of teenagers. They lay in the late afternoon's hot sun. Boy, girl, girl, boy, girl. Their leader wears a Panama hat and carries a red umbrella. It seems like overkill. When he stands, the others rise. The leader yells; the pack responds. The leader yells again; again the pack responds. I trust they'll be making their way to the Spanish Steps soon.

My sister Joycie, what would I do without her? She sends me another text. "Good luk tmrow–don't get arrested please."

I text back, "Won't happen, sure I want to go home."

And she quickly replies, "K–good 2 hear. Will be thinking of u. gonna be hard. Won't be surprised if he hides from u but hope he doesn't." Because of her, I decide it's best to pen my second letter to Ormechea, the just-in-case-he-won't-meet-with-me one. I write,

Dear Father,

 Sitting here by the obelisk in Saint Peter's Square, I'm writing to you once again. I had hoped to deliver Tim's message to you and give you necessary perspective to receive it. But in case you change your mind and don't meet with me, I still need to fulfill my promise to Tim. So here you have it. The letter is enclosed. For my part, I thank you for the greeting you provided me on Tuesday. It was greatly unexpected.

As a closing, I try out, "Journeying toward peace." Hmmm. The German leader yells out something forceful. The Italian grandpa with the bandage yells back something that shuts the boy up. I consider rewriting my letter. That damn word *peace* showed up again. Peace was never on my wish list. Revenge was. Answers still are. And "Why," the old argument between critic and taskmaster starts in my head, "Why, again, is this *my* fucking journey?"

"Stop swearing, especially here."

"Okay. Why, again, is this *my* journey?"

"Because it is *your* journey."

"What?"

"I've told you before, Joan." Even his voice in my head held his cadence, both deliberate and half amused. "Righteousness is a misunderstood virtue, especially when the word *self* is too often affiliated with it. Again, what is righteousness?" Father B. was in college-professor mode.

"The quality of being morally right or justifiable."

"And where does it reside?"

"'Ontological' or 'real righteousness' is the quality that adheres to the soul when one does righteous acts."

"And who bestows righteousness?"

I quote his source. "In Augustine's view, God bestows justifying righteousness upon the sinner in such a way that it becomes part of his or her person."

"Maybe that had something to do with *you* becoming a lawyer?"

"Perhaps so."

"What was that answer?" He's smiling.

"Yes, Father."

"And, maybe, this is why this is your quest and no one else's?"

I'm reluctant to answer, even him; so he tries again. "If I can tell you anything, Joan, it's to learn not to be dismissive of who you are. When you do that, you're dismissing the righteousness God bestowed. So, do me this favor. 'Learn not to be afraid.'"

"Be Awake and Alive." It was a reminder Marsha gave me when I went to her office last December, just after learning of Father B.'s death. It was her Kundalini yoga teaching talking, much more than her cognitive behavioral training, because what she was telling me was Father B. wasn't done with me yet. If he had more to teach, he would find a way to reach me, even if it had to be through my embedded memory of him.

❧

My Germans are leaving. Little Francesca already has. Oddly, the Square seems small without them, and even the pope seems like one tiny man I can handle. I can't help myself. I search the colonnades for any presence of woman. While I know fifteen percent of Bernini's statues depict females, it's difficult to find their curves and femininity under their billowing marble robes, especially at a distance. Only Mary herself stands out, and not in the statues. Coined the *Mater Ecclesiae* and a gift of Opus Dei to John Paul II, her mosaic fills a corner square of the papal palace, just to the far right and a couple levels below Pope Benedict's bedroom. It's a young Mary. She holds her toddler son, who, even at this age, raises his right hand, index and middle finger extended, in the form of a blessing to the multitude. The crowned Mary, Mother of the Church, looks queenly. Not a hint of sentiment floods her dark brown eyes, but her blue hooded robe still symbolizes just what it had for illiterate pilgrims centuries before. She is purity herself, and her mission is sacred.

According to Catholic teaching, I know I'm supposed to love her as a daughter does her mother, but if I do, it's the love of a teenage daughter pissed off at her mom. Her humanity and loss of a child, I can embrace, but her seeming deification and revirginization? Never. To me, this image, created in the hands of men, is a hierarchical afterthought that separates her from her sisterhood. But today, at this moment, she's all I have.

When John Paul II had her mosaic installed, he expressed his wish "that all who come to St. Peter's Square may raise their eyes to Mary and greet her with filial trust and prayer." So here goes, Mary, "If there is an ounce of real woman in you, help a daughter out."

❧

Combine these theoretical questions from Father B.—"How do we discern God's unique desires for us, individually, and how do we respond?"—with the following from the Second Vatican Council's teaching on faith—"[It] is a supernatural virtue by which we, with the inspiration and assistance of God's grace, believe those things to be true which He has revealed"—and you get my answer. The answer to all of my questions, the tonic for all of my fears, the courage not to be afraid might be found in the singular example a chicken named Kate once showed: "Wherever you might be going, raise your head. Believe you can, and then you will, fly."

Wednesday evening
And so I have it. My day of tourism is nearly coming to an end. True, earlier in the evening after leaving Saint Peter's Square, I'll have eventually found the Piazza Navona and laughed as an old man lip-synched Elvis tunes for the evening crowds. I'll also have bought wooden toys for Abbie in a Pinocchio shop and experimented at a gelateria with two flavors of gelato, lavender and chocolate cranberry. Afterward I will wind my way home to the Lancelot, getting lost at least three times before I find its evergreen gate. Every moment of the way, however, I will relish in another night's soft warm air and feel just a hint of my bare-shouldered childhood returning.

"Did you have fun?" Robert might have asked.

"I've become too serious to have fun. But I do have this," I would have said. "I do have joy."

And, thus, perhaps I shouldn't be surprised, when I've grown so nostalgic, that I find him once again, set free, like Kate, when I'm back in my room. I search YouTube for his name: "Father Vincent Beuzer, S.J." Though posted in 2009, almost exactly two years before his death, I've never seen this video nor known it to exist.

In the video, Father B. is much younger than I ever saw him. Black-haired with graying sideburns and clad in a Roman collar, he stands behind a classroom podium. Written on the chalkboard behind him is the date, "Wednesday,

April 5th." I look online through old calendars for a year that might match the weekday. Perhaps this is 1989. The intended subject of his lecture, "Coping with Stress . . ." is also written on the board. Then, he starts speaking. In a voice sounding younger and gravel-free but still familiar, he sets up this parable:

> A person comes to a priest. He has serious problems. The priest listens to him and says, "You know what I'd recommend is that . . . I recommend that you see this person because he *really* is a good clinical psychologist or good psychiatrist." And so the *priest* refers him to a psychologist or a professional therapist or someone in the healing services. Isn't that what takes place? When you see people who have deep serious problems, when there is real serious suffering, interior suffering, what you do is you say, "Well I really think you should see a doctor. You should see someone who's really trained to deal with these things."

Then, he summarizes what's wrong with this scenario:

> Usually we send them to everyone, [he pauses and gives that Father B. smile] but we never pray for them. Priests don't pray for them. Mothers and fathers don't pray for their children. Husbands don't pray for their wives. Wives don't pray for their husbands. You say, "Sure I believe in the God who heals, Father. God can do anything." And I say that is not the proof of the pudding. The proof of the pudding is to take a look at your own actions, for priests to take a look at their own actions, for bishops to take a look at their own actions, for people within families to take a look at their own actions, and if you are not praying for specific graces of healing, then you do not have faith in this area.

His smile lingers when he says the last phrase, "then you do not have faith in this area." He concludes:

> You have God in your pocket, but he is not a God who is so near to you, you would call upon him with familiarity and ask him for anything you want. You don't have the kind of faith that the leper has who says, "Jesus, son of David, have mercy on me. I want to be able to go back to my family. I don't want to be on the outside of the city all alone." And Jesus asks him, "Do you really want to be healed?" Now, that *same* Jesus Christ? Do we believe that he is so near and that he still has the power of the Holy Spirit that he will cure when we ask. *That's the question.* Our actions will reveal our faith or lack of faith. Our inner expectations will reveal our hope or lack or lack of hope.

After at least three viewings, I have to ask myself. Is his theory one of faith alone? *Sola fide?* No, for him faith depends on works, even if the works are solely of the interior variety: like the *choice* to believe. So then, is his theory one of justification through both faith and works? No, never at any point does Father B. discuss heavenly reward. All of his stories are occurring down here on earth. They exemplify the question, *How should we live? Not, how shall we die?*

For Father B., the answer appears to be, *We truly live only when our earthly actions demonstrate a faith in a God who heals. In such a case,* he might even add, *faith is neither a lie nor a suspension of critical thinking; it's just a way of being, exhibited, as always, through daily choice.*

I want to say more, to add to his teaching this final thesis: "Actions, Father, even internal choices, are the building blocks for faith, the components that make it stronger. They're why faith, without any connection to justification, can and will be enough to feel an affinity with a loving God every single day." And here I find myself saying out loud, mimicking his wise, wry countenance, "Perhaps I'm more your student than I know. For let me tell you what I've learned, because this is what living is: learning. In the beginning was the Word, Father, and the Word was just this, *sola. Fide.*"

HOW THEY KILL MONKEYS

Ingredients:
2¼ cups personal desire to get some answers
1 teaspoon chicken shit
1 teaspoon "It's not too late; grab Faris's paring knife."
1 cup prosecutor mode, softened to room temperature
¾ cup preparation
¾ cup "Don't sleep, prep again."
1 teaspoon vanilla extract, add more to taste, only if necessary
2 large ovaries
2 cups, the whole package, of acting

Preheat subject with peace-inducing letter. Place chicken shit and "It's not too late" in emotional-overload containers and set aside. Beat softened prosecutor mode, preparation, personal desire, and "Don't sleep, prep again" together until smooth. Add ovaries, one at a time, beating mixture well after each addition. Stir in acting, lots of acting, as well as the vanilla, until he can do just one thing: believe you're genuine. Make sure the vanilla isn't so thick you believe it too. If altogether possible, get rid of the chicken shit. Use "It's not too late" only in your fantasies. Even if it's just there, you're going to need it.

Thursday morning

It's 8:00 a.m. I woke up later than expected and missed breakfast with the Brits. They've already left for Assisi, and I'm sad to have missed them, especially, oddly enough, Barbara. I can judge by first impression so quickly and neglect to realize until she's gone that among her group she was the first to smile, wel-come me to sit, and open up all topics of conversation, not just of Matthew and his Vatican library supply of Roman trivia. Last night, I could see how her kids were being tough on her. When Melissa's purse was pickpocketed en route to the Trevi Fountain, she came back to the hotel and somehow managed to blame her mother for not warning her against carrying it. Mothers. They're the easiest target, aren't they? Whether the blessed Mary ever virgin or the Mary of Erasure, we can focus the laser gun of disappointment right between their steady blue or green eyes and shoot.

And so, while I've criticized my mother's medium of survival, I haven't men-tioned, not once, until now, that on a visit to Chicago shortly after Tim came forward, it was she alone who stood by my side in candlelight vigil for him out-side Immaculate Conception. She also elected to leave her local parish to attend another. And it was she who elected to tithe to her son instead of the Church for all it had taken from him.

"You think I'm stupid," she said to me once, with three jagged breaths sepa-rating the "stu" from the "pid," at some point when I was a brooding teen. I had her trapped and went in for the kill with an able supply of Advanced Algebra or AP History standing ready to condemn her. I should be able to forgive that teen for lacking the intelligence to recognize that it was she who was the epitome of ignorance and not her mother, but sometimes the poison has to remain, even if directed to the self. Some bitterness, like taking the smallest bit of pleasure for making your mother feel less than, has to be carried forward with you, in a place so raw it rears its stings whenever you become too cavalier. "You were there once, my darling," it snipes. "Don't try that again."

Our actions reveal our faith or lack of faith, I repeat to myself an hour and forty minutes later, walking up Via Claudia. It's ten to ten. The sky is a cloudless blue. A gaggle of American girls walks by me in the opposite direction and I think I hear one saying, "Like, really." *Our inner expectations reveal our hope or lack of hope*, I tell myself, repeating Father B.'s mantra, but my mind speeds to its next thought. I want to yell, "Oh yeah, Father B., what's if it's both? What if I have a lot of faith and just a little, all at the same time? What if hope rises with one step and falls with the next? What do I do then?" I guess the answer is stop, because that is exactly what I do at the park across the road where the miniature dogs are walked. This morning offers up a schnauzer who seems in no more of a hurry to leave than I. *Toss the ball*, his eyes inquire to his owner, who looks instead at a book and drinks coffee through a straw. In surrender, the dog finally rests his head upon his front paws, and I wonder if I should in turn just do the same. Just surrender.

My journal is in hand and I turn to its first dog-ear where I have four pages of questions ready. *This will make Tim whole*, I had told myself last night, preparing questions. In my state of fatigue last night I also thought they would somehow make a difference for Autumn, the long-ago girl from the sentencing hearing, and even for that graduate student Bill; that with them, her quest for survival would grow stronger and his life wouldn't have been in vain. *But how*, my cynic asks. *How could they?* Even if it's remotely possible some benefit can come from this conversation with Ormechea, I wonder how it might with my current state of fear? *I'm on my way to meet my brother's rapist*, I want to cry. Instead of putting in one cup of prosecutor it appears I've added too much chicken shit. Wait a second. Maybe I'll be lucky and he'll be the chicken and refuse to meet with me, just as he did with Reese Dunklin. It's the easiest way out, really, for both of us. Just in case, I take out my letter to Ormechea, tear it to pieces, and start again on the next blank page in my journal.

> Dear Father,
>   I'm writing you in case you changed your mind about meeting me. I had hoped to deliver Tim's message to you and give you perspective to receive it. You're going need it. Without that, I still made a promise; so here it is, enclosed. I also want to tell you something on behalf of my mom. More than any of us, she stands resolute with her faith, but you surely tested it in a way no one should. How she went on, I wish I had that ability. For my part, thank you for the greeting you provided me on Tuesday. It was unexpected.

"You're not done."

"Father B., I'm not going to say, 'journeying toward peace.'"

"Fine. Say what I know you're thinking, even if you don't believe it yet."

"You're lying."

"You can stay tough and still get what you're after, but write it. It at least opens up the possibility, and this is your only chance." A wren swoops by. The schnauzer raises his head toward me inquisitively.

"Okay, I'll try, but even if I write it, don't count on it happening."

"Understood."

And so I add: "Every place must have its start. Although I will *never* forgive *you* for what you did to Tim, I think it is possible that with time I can forgive you for what you did to me."

The Italian wren is chirping, and I can feel the sweat beading down my chest. I gather up my belongings and straighten my hair, dress, and Abbie's bear-stick flower that's in my sweater. I touch Tim's heart again, concealed away in the same back pocket, and make my way up the remainder of Via Claudia.

Would I be lying when I say that while walking up the hill I feel a force in the middle of my back and that when I turn right down San Paolo della Croce I feel it going right through my heart? No, but the only one I can make believe this is me, and, for me, I have to repeat the Second Vatican Council's guidance, "Faith is a supernatural virtue by which we believe to be true those things which have been revealed." Just today, I may be getting a little help.

He's right on time, waiting for me. He holds the second door, the secured one, of the General Curia open. He wears black plants and a beige checked shirt tucked in at the waist. A light tan jacket is flung over his arms that he moves first to his left side and then to his right. It's not until I'm right next to him, after he makes room for me to walk through the door, that I see the tears welling in his eyes. Oh my God. He's crying.

Be careful. He's been an actor all his life.

"Hello," he says.

"You're here. Thank you," I reach my hand toward him.

"You're welcome," he reciprocates. Our formalities are properly performed. As he ushers me into the hallway off the reception area, he suggests, "I thought it might be nice if we spoke in our gardens. The weather seems just right for our visit." We continue walking down a long corridor, and even though there's no particular obstacle, he remarks, pointing to the floor, "Be careful of the marble. It's unique here; like woods in the States. Each has its own catches and creaks. It's easy to slip."

"Okay." I look to my feet, clad in their Mary Jane Tevas, and see sweat stains and grime marking the separation of each toe. Not the image I want, but, knowing Ormechea's attention to women, he won't notice either. Soon he pushes a second set of doors open, and we are outside.

He's right. The Roman sun seems to have only one setting today of bright, warm, and inviting. The doors open immediately onto a palomino-brown clay path that runs parallel to both the northern wing of the Curia and Via San Paolo della Croce. The latter is separated from us by a twelve-foot stone fence I once thought of scaling. Between the building, the pathway, and the fence are two tracks of green lawn. Evenly spaced palm trees, shrubs, and statuary fill their centers at forty-foot intervals.

To break the tension, I suppose, he becomes my tour guide. "This property's been with the Passionists since 1773." He stops, turns, and points to the building wing in front of us. "This is the retreat center. And to your left," he points again, "where we came from, are the Provincial offices."

"The building and grounds are beautiful. How did the Order get the land?"

"I'm fairly sure the pope just gave it Saint Paul of the Cross. And except for a short period of time when Napoleon kicked us out, we've been here ever since."

"That's a lot of history."

"There's more," my tour guide continues, filling the silence between us. "Rumor has it there are rooms and tunnels under this ground that are linked to the floor of the Colosseum's arena. It may have been where the lions were kept." I couldn't help but picture them below my feet, resting and readying for the day when they would be needed again.

While enjoying my "it's-not-too-late" fantasy, I miss what century of history my tour guide has just reviewed, but about halfway down the pathway, he stops. His eyes dart from side to side, and then he turns directly to face me. The welled tears are gone. He was about to start speaking when a delivery truck rolls up behind us. Once it passes, he offers what I imagine he believes to be the most important thing to say.

"First, let me apologize to you, in the place of your brother, and to your whole family."

Let me apologize. The first step to an admission. *In place of your brother.* An acknowledgment.

He's not done, but what he says next makes me wish he had. "I spilled the milk, and I can't put it back in the bottle. I could cry and say I spilt the milk," he brings his fist to his eyes, like he's wiping away fake baby tears, "but that is not going to help any of us."

I sense my outrage building before I can damp it down and say, "Spilled milk? Really Father? That's your comparison?"

He looks as if he might be reconsidering his metaphor, but then he shrugs his shoulders. "There's not much more I can say," he acts flustered. If there were a mosquito to swat away, he would. "You see, I'm still living under a gag order. My mouth must stay closed and my hands are tied." And as he says this, he crosses his arms at the wrist in front of himself. He offers one more thought. "But what I also want you to know is that you don't need me to be miserable for you to be happy. Only you can make your own happiness."

Happiness? It seems such a 1970s me-generation thing to say and an odd choice of words, until I think of something Tim told me a month ago. "I think you'll find him as happy-go-lucky as ever, as if nothing is wrong." Ormechea whitewashed his existence, and, for my sake, he is asking me to do the same.

I wait for him to offer any additional comment, but he just stands there. He had said the three things—apologize, spilled milk, be happy—he thought were the most important to say and, within ten minutes of our meeting, he exhausted them and made it through.

Now it's my turn.

Sympathize, Joan.

"I can't imagine what it's like being unable to speak. It must be a difficult way to live." His shoulders soften and he nods his head. "So I think one goal here today is to find the subjects we can talk about, even if it's only, 'how does it feel to live under a gag order?'"

We start to walk. "My life is not as I expected," he volunteers.

"I can understand that." *Sympathize, Joan.*

"I was at Saint Agnes for ten years without any problems." He speaks like he is a substance abuser recalling his years of sobriety. There's just one problem; he had been at Saint Agnes's for twelve years. "Then, just like that," he snaps his fingers, "I was called to my provincial's office. I think it was Don then. I was shown a letter from the attorney general for Illinois."

"Shauna Boliker."

"I don't recall. I was driven that day to Chicago. I spent a night at a motel. Then I was sent to California the following morning. I went to Southern California first, for a couple of months, and next to Northern California. I stayed at a retreat house there for three months, all while they were trying to decide what to do with me."

How about the guillotine? I did not ask.

I'm conscious for a second that my plan's working. As he did long ago, he still likes the attention and focus on him. So with even greater control, I keep my voice measured and my eye contact direct, but understanding. I know at some point I'll throw in a shoulder pat.

"That must have been awful for you."

The old man's eyelids flutter and he brushes his tanned temple. "Again, not at all what I dah—expected." He caught himself. Had he meant to say deserved? "There was discussion of sending me to England. Then the provincial here in Rome," he signals up to one of the windows above us, "he was good enough to take me in. It took a while to get my paperwork in order, but I was relocated by April."

"Of 2003?"

"Yes."

He makes a shrugging gesture, raising his shoulders, and then shaking his head. "While here, I don't have an active ministry life with the laity." That means us. "But I do get to say Mass inside the community to other priests." He points again, I think in the direction the chapel must be. "Not what I expected for my life, not at all . . ." He adds in a wrist snap as well. "But I am grateful for it." Translation? "I'm happy it's not prison." Then, as if noticing I was here for the first time, he adds, piling it on, "I can understand that *all* of our lives changed in ways we did not expect or want."

If I had time to fully reflect on his words when he uttered them—like giving himself extra points for being good for ten years, the same ten years Tim's life ran off the rails—I would have kicked him in his shins, just as Richard suggested. And the fact he could still say Mass? I'd be on board Dad's solution for the matter: only after castration. But instead the same words come into my head much the same way I repeat over and over again the lap number I'm on while swimming. *Keep him talking. Keep him talking. Keep him talking.*

"You know, Father, other than for Tuesday, the last time I saw you was my wedding day."

He laughs. "That's right. You and Maureen."

What I say next embarrasses me; I'm still playing the old fiddle. "That marriage lasted two years and nine days." He doesn't know where I'm going with this either. "Anyway, it was a priest who helped me through my divorce, and he always reminded me to set the intention for anything major I might be doing next. I think he believed that if we are engaged enough to set the purpose, and then ask God for his assistance in achieving it, we have a fairly decent shot of getting there. So, I'd like to set the intention for our meeting."

Keep him talking. Keep him talking. Keep him talking.

"I pray for understanding," I say.

"For understanding," he repeats. If we had glasses of wine, we would have clinked.

The pathway we're walking ends in a small courtyard. In its center is a white marble statue of the Crucifixion. Including its base, it stands fifteen feet tall. Fully leaved trees and shrubbery are behind it blocking most of the panorama, but the Colosseum rises to the crucifix's right. Three of Rome's hills are beyond it.

"What a view, Father!"

He's back to tour guide mode. "Wait. It gets better."

We walk another fifty feet and stand in a second courtyard. There, a white marble statue of a young Jesus, just about Abbie's age, stands holding his adoptive father's, Joseph's, outstretched hand. The statue makes me feel like we're interrupting a private moment. Jesus looks up to his dad as if he were the best thing that happened to him.

"What do you think?"

Ormechea's right. It got better. At this twenty past the hour, the sun is to our far left, thirty degrees above horizon. It makes this city of two million seem crowned. The horizon also opens up here. I can see the cars roaring round the Circus Maximus and the Parco di Porta Capena (*Hello Egeria!*) to our left. The Roman Forum and Colosseum take up the right portion of the horizon.

"Wow, Father!" I'm calling him that much more than I want. "This view is outstanding." *It is surely not prison.* "I can't imagine what it is like to wake to this every day." *And not prison.*

"Do you see that white building with the black statues on top?"

"Yeah, that's the Wedding Cake. I was there yesterday. The view from top was amazing, but even that doesn't match this."

"The Italians also call it the Typewriter. It was a mausoleum Mussolini built largely to himself. Buildings here aren't supposed to compete with the height of St. Peter's. You see, Mussolini came awfully close."

"Huh, I never knew that."

"And that Italian flag? You see it right there?" He points to a flag jutting out in the distant sky. "That's Quirinal Palace where the president of Italy lives. When the flag flies, it usually means the president is in residence."

"So, he's home."

"Yes."

"Look at all of these hills. How do you drive them during winter?" The practical Alaskan asks.

"Well, first things first, I don't drive here. The driving's too crazy. It gets worse in bad winters. This year we got four inches of snow. It was a good time to stay away from the roads."

"It was like that when I went to law school in Portland. The hills of that city became slalom courses with the least amount of snow. Just like here, no one knew how to drive in it, and treaded snow tires were against the law."

"And where you are, in Anchorage? I hear you had a pretty big snowfall."

"Yeah. We beat the record this year. We got over 117 inches, and we're probably still not done. By the way, how did you know that?"

He doesn't answer. Keeping on the subject of hills, I ask, "Let's see, with the Colosseum there," I point, "that hill just to its left must be Palatine, huh?"

I look at him for any sign of recognition that no matter the beauty of this place, at least he has one small reminder of what he had done. Palatine Hill? Palatine Avenue? Did he get it?

"Yes, that's either Palatine Hill or the Caelian Hill. I get them mixed up."

I didn't say, *I think that would be impossible, seeing as we're on the Caelian Hill*, which makes me think one of two things. Either he's an idiot, highly unlikely, or he knows just what I intended and he's still a liar. I try my best not to smirk and take a second to take stock. What happened to the cup of chicken shit? It seems to have reverted to its more properly measured one teaspoon.

He gestures to our left, away from the view, to a park bench partially in the shade. I sit down first. He sits to my left. When he does, his slacks ride high showing the band of the light nylon socks he wears with his sandals. The Congregation of Discalced Clerks? I wouldn't have guessed Birkenstocks qualify for shoelessness.

He starts first. "I read your letter. Woo! There's a lot of emotion there." I turn to face him, a difficult act in itself, when my instinct is to look away from him like he's a vampire. His glasses are clean. His eyes are only a bit magnified behind them. He's also shaved again and, I believe, is wearing a hint of cologne. He holds his coat over his left arm and taps his watch. I forgot to check for the wedding ring the ordained wear in commitment to God.

"Well"—*do not be sarcastic*—"I wouldn't doubt that. When I wrote it, I had no idea if we might speak. If the letter were my only chance, I had to convey the impact you've had on all our lives, not just Tim's." I tap the edge of the letter he doesn't yet have. It's poking out from my journal. "Still, I know there was a lot in it to take, so I give you credit for meeting with me, especially after having read it."

I feel like a traitor saying that word, *credit*, to a child molester.

"There are things I didn't understand." He speaks in a soft voice that sounds like the voice I remember, although with a creak to it, like an ungreased bike chain.

"Let me try to explain."

"Like the Blue Line. What's that?"

"Oh, my metaphor!" I laugh. "That's one thing you probably don't know about me. I like to write—well, write and read." It feels dangerous saying this, like he might figure out a record is being made. "And so I look for metaphor, the symbol for an experience, like your spilled milk. For me, it came down to our old El line. Tim was traveling on it when he called to tell me what you'd done to him, and, since then, the before and after of our Blue Line call changed the way I looked at my parents, my family, my church . . . even the whole world. Come to think of it, Tim's life changed there too. He kept reading the newspaper about the boys in Boston, and he kept reacting to their stories in ways he didn't expect, like they were hitting too close to home. As soon as he said the words to me, 'what happened to the boys in Boston, happened to me too,' I knew, Father. He didn't even have to say your name. I was a witness too. You were in my brother's room. I saw the closed door. I have no doubt what you did."

"What did I do?" he asks.

I turn to him, speechless. If Tim and Joyce were here, this is when they would have pumped Ormechea full of bullets.

"Excuse me?" My fingers tame their shaking against Abbie's flower. *Hit him with a stick, Mommy.*

He doesn't answer. I look at him dumbfounded, and when I can't any longer, I avert my gaze.

If this were fiction, I could easily tell you what the protagonist would do next. She would stand and berate him, "You offer an apology to me, in the place of my brother, and you ask me to tell you what you did to him? You motherfucker! You cock-sucking, boy-raping, serial-predator, motherfucker. I'll tell you what you did. You may not have penetrated Tim's anus, Father, but you fucked him. You fucked his body. You fucked his eyes. You fucked his ears. You fucked his mouth. You fucked his soul. You fucked his intimacy. You fucked his heart. You fucked his resolve. You fucked his courage. You fucked, fucked, fucked, fucked him! You goddamn, motherfucking fucker! FUCK!"

But I can't say it. Not one word of it. It's as if, when he asks the question, the ingredients switch. Chicken shit is back in control.

"Uh, let me see if I can remind you." My voice? I'm certain it sounds timid. "He remembers you sitting on his bed." I turn my eyes away from him to a gravel pile twenty feet to my right and to a patch of grass just beyond it. I feel the weight on Tim's bed. I see the body lying over him. I hear the groans. I feel his hips grinding. "You . . ." I look right at his eyes and see just one thing. Absence. "You . . ."

One strong, loud voice. Where is it?

"It's too difficult, Father." I turn away, embarrassed at my inadequacy and swing my right leg, like a schoolgirl. Still, I didn't expect the need to refresh his recollection.

I know. Evidence Rule 612! "Any writing or object may be used by a witness to refresh the memory of the witness while testifying."

"I have an idea," I say. "I can go back to my room and get Tim's affidavit. You can read it yourself. And the Boliker letter; I have that too. It states in detail most everything you did, at least to four boys."

He looks at me dismissively, his mouth making a frown and the lines around it that again remind me of a marionette. "I don't think that will be necessary."

His words are a rebuff. Perhaps, he next tries out the lines he practiced for delivery to my parents years ago, in case he ever got caught. "Well, I *did* go into Tim's room, and I remember him getting explosively angry with me . . . twice."

I think of Freddy Thompson and Ormechea's comment to him after the boy told him to get his hands off of him. "Why are you so angry?" It meant Tim wasn't a compliant victim anymore. This would be what the offender would remember. I see Tim growing free and Ormechea still unwilling to confront the reason why. Then Ormechea says, "There are two sides to every story, and I can't talk any more of my own."

Keep him talking. Keep him talking. No, it's my turn. I quickly offer, "Well, let me talk of my side, Father. I was there too. I wasn't behind the closed door, but right outside it. I didn't have to be behind it to know what was going on there was very, very wrong. Who the hell closes a door with a child? And you say twice? I say countless times."

One point to his credit: at least he stays, and I'm not altogether sure why. Perhaps it's just to toy with me. Perhaps, as he had said earlier, it's because I remind him of home. A skinny black cat walks by in my peripheral vision.

Next, I try a different tact. "You remember Charlie Tierney? What you did to Tim was just like what happened with Charlie, but . . ."

"No . . ." He shakes his head and his face sags like a sad clown's. When he turns his chin down, his neck thickens in two rolls.

Finally, I understand. He remembers exactly what he did to Charlie. Mouth on penis, first giving, then receiving, I see a little, black-haired boy's head rising from his lap. Unless mouth is on genitalia or genitalia is piercing an orifice, the act, to Ormechea—the grooming, holding, rubbing, kissing, French kissing, coming into showers naked, teasing, brushing, bear hugging. embracing, pressing harder, even harder, coming, even with clothes between—simply doesn't count. To quote my father from long ago, "He was showing affection, that's all."

"Father," I say, flustered, but it's okay. Chicken shit is going away, "I know we were talking in euphemisms earlier. You have to know, we are not talking about spilled milk. We are talking about boys' lives. Although we can debate physical acts and whether one set of conduct rises above another, in the end, it just doesn't matter what the actual physical act was, because of what *else* you took from these boys. In every case, you took their trust and confidence, their faith in themselves, and their belief in others. You took their parents. My God, Father, you even took their God!"

Unknowingly my comments shift to just our family. "You were our father's friend. Our parents invited you into our home. You even came to my grandparents' home. The way we were raised, you were Jesus walking on earth before us."

"That should have never been."

"At least we agree on that. You're no Jesus and never will be. But when you hurt Tim, for the longest time, it was just like God doing it to the boy. And when that happened, you stole not only us from Tim, but Tim from us. There's a boy we will never know, who will never get to grow up to the man that boy could have been, because of you."

Note to people who are truly remorseful: you don't need me to tell you this. You've thought about it, gone to years of counseling, played it over and over again in your mind, trying, perhaps even, to put *some* of the milk back in the container, to clean up your mess. You live with what you have done and you try to go on, but you do wring your hands over it, because you *want* to be a better person, and you realize you can't be without the community of others, especially those you've hurt so profoundly. You would not be asking them to accept you again, under any circumstance, but you've thought many times about writing to them to give a real, remorseful, down-on-your-knees apology. And never, not ever, would you give an apology and then, within thirty minutes of doing so, ask the victim's bloody sister, "What exactly did I do?"

❧

My face is turning red, and he physically backs away from me. The space between us leaves enough room for me to put down my journal, my letter to him, my sunglasses case, and my phone. I stretch out my arms and knock a kink out of my back. If I had water, I would've taken a drink. I look out toward Palatine Hill. It's green, just like Dad's front lawn. My God? Am I the only one here who can't stand the sight? When I turn back to him, I see he's leaning forward and his toes are curled under the bench. His jacket inches closer to the ground.

"Life just goes on here, doesn't it?" I say.

"It does."

"Is it always so beautiful?"

"Not always."

Daringly, I ask, "Do you know how life has gone on for any of the boys you abused?"

The blank look on his face tells me this is not a conversation with a regular person. He says nothing.

"Well, first off, it's not something they easily comprehended every day of their lives. In most cases, they felt dirty, and less than. They felt that a grime was covering their souls. And, despite the obvious, they weren't exactly sure why. They locked you up with every other inconceivable thought. For Tim, his years of drug use had nothing to do with you. For Charlie, he hid your crimes against him from everyone: his wife, his sister, his friends, and pretty much would've continued to do so until we asked, really begged, him to come forward. Now that his secret is out, he feels like he has no one. He's drinking a lot more. Tim blames himself for that, but the alcohol was always there, well before Tim, but not well before you." I look up at him again. Nothing is registering. "And Greg? He pretends he's doing fine, but look for any long-lasting relationship in his life and you'll come up empty there too. Look at his occupation, and what you'll find is porn producer."

J. B. shakes his head. I see by the look of "I've never heard that before" on his face that he's still in contact with Greg's parents. Or maybe even Greg?

"Really?" he stammers, "I thought he was a . . . a . . . whatever the Hollywood word is for camera operator."

"He has a more acceptable side to his business, but that's not all he does. Some of his 'work,'" I make quote marks in the air, "is right on his web page and Twitter feed. Sex to him is meaningless and degrading of women, I believe, because you degraded him. Like Tim long ago? Maybe still he doesn't see the link. I just don't understand living like that. And as for all of them, even the boys I don't know . . . you say to forget, Father, that I don't need you for my own happiness, and you're right. I don't need you to be miserable in order to have joy in my life. But, I say, Father, that it is in remembering, looking for cause, explanation, and in stopping it from *ever* happening again, that we become better and *more* human, *more* understanding. You just can't do that forgetting. You lock your potential inside and deny progress, not only for yourself, but for those you love and who love you."

His large, still-soft hands curl into fists and then stretch out again. Before he can enter any counterargument, his cell phone, buried in his front pocket, rings.

"*Pronto.*"

"*Arrivo? A hora?*"

"Okay."

He hangs up and says a deacon and his son (I wonder how old) have arrived at the main house, and he needs to go check them in. "But I still have more time to sit," he offers.

I lull him into easier conversation. "What's it like to speak Italian?"

"You heard it; that's just about it." He gives a long, hard exhale. "After the years here, I still don't really speak the language." What he just admitted doesn't register, not yet.

I look toward the black cat. She's now curled in a ball on the warm soil, right next to young Jesus and his dad. I point, "Lots of cats here."

"There are over three hundred thousand of them in Rome. Most here come up from the Colosseum."

"That's a lot of cats." I'm not sure why I make the connection, but ask, "How many priests are in your community now?" The change of subject gives me a chance to take deeper breaths.

"There used to be 120 of us, but now there are just sixty. One good thing; they've remodeled the monastery, knocked out rooms and made them bigger. Two priests now share one bathroom." Something about his response makes me think of his genitalia, hoping, that it isn't in working order anymore.

"Do they know why you're here?" *Lukas? Orven? Enno?*

"Some do; some don't. They give me a lot of support now. I also have a moderator I check in with every thirty days or so. I let him know how I'm doing."

"You'll probably want to talk about this meeting next time," I laugh.

So does he, "Yes, yes I do." Seeming to gain some confidence, he adds, "I disagree with something you said in your letter."

"What's that?"

"It's your belief or thought that God doesn't forgive. I do believe God forgives everything. Everything!"

"You'll have to forgive me yourself, Father, but *that* belief can easily serve as a license to continue to do wrong."

"No, it doesn't work that way. Forgiveness comes when you learn from your conduct and you don't repeat it."

"And that's what you're doing?"

"Yes," he says, resolutely. If it's a lie, he's good. Nothing about his statement or his eyes indicates falsity.

Thinking of Father B., I offer up, "A good friend of mine would agree with you. Although he might debate my ultimate conclusion as well, a major reason for his theory was Jesus's statement, 'Father, forgive them, for they know not what they do.' My friend would say that is why we need to ask God for the gift of forgiveness, so we might forgive as Jesus did on the cross. In your case, even if you had or have some kind of disease, Father, you *knew* exactly what you did. It may be harsh to say, especially as I sit right next to you talking, but I don't see God forgiving you, especially when what you did, you did in his name."

To my statement, he remains defiant and repeats himself, "I hope you'll understand this, for your sake as well. God forgives everything."

ॐ

We're in a standoff, me hoping that punishment would remain his course, and he, just as Tim predicted, sure of his get-out-of-eternal-damnation card. And in truth, because I lack any clarity of what remains after an earthly existence, I could never win this point. To believe in the afterlife is one thing I can accept, but the Devil? Unless he was right in front of me, not so much? The most I could wish J. B. is an absence from God, and judging by his incomprehension or lack of continuing care for his victims, I'm certain he already suffers from that.

We're both silent for a while longer, and I have the sense it might be time to help out that deacon. As if on cue, he states, "Listen, we should probably head back. If you have more questions, we can continue to talk after I've helped the deacon to his room."

"I'd like that. I actually haven't asked you any of my questions yet."

When we stand, so does the cat. She stretches her front paws out in a downward-dog position and next makes a fast getaway, in the opposite direction we're going, toward the bushes and Palatine Hill. Despite my last statement, every part of me, managers and all, wishes that I could just leave with her.

❧

The walk back to the Curia to assist that deacon and his please-don't-be-too-young son finally gives me the opportunity to open my journal.

"You know, I'm a preparer," I say. "I always have been since I was a young child, and I have this list of questions to ask you. I see the first question I've written is, 'How are you?'" *Ah, no litigator here, just the pretend-all-is-well, heartfelt inquirer.* "How are you, Father?"

"I'm well. Shocked to see you." He laughs a coroner's laugh, as if it were improper for the occasion.

"I know. I could say the very same thing. Even if I found you, everyone's guess was that you'd refuse to speak with me." They assumed, of course, I'd tell you what I was doing with your confession. "Okay, second question. What are your days like?"

He doesn't seem embarrassed when he says, "I work in the order's archives most mornings with ancient and old documents."

"What do you do with them?"

"Mostly, when people need things copied, I get them for them."

"And in the afternoons?"

"Well, you saw I work the front desk in the afternoons, starting at three."

Making copies in the mornings, answering phones in the afternoon. Instantaneously, I think of the control he once had over church finances. But like his lack of command of Italian, it doesn't register yet how important my register of his powerlessness will become.

"Is the work challenging for you?"

"I make the best of it." *Read, no.*

"Well, the work must do you well. Either it does or it's the Italian sun. You look good." My voice rises at the *good*, to emphasize what? I'm not sure. "May I ask how old are you?"

"I'll be seventy-five on June 3."

"That's a landmark. Congratulations." I guess he has about another ten healthy years in him.

"How's your brother? Jean, I think. I remember him from his time at Immaculate Conception." Jean had also been a Passionist priest. The one thing I recall about him, besides how tall he was compared to J. B., was his choice of singing the entire consecration of the Eucharist, from the "On the night he was betrayed," all the way through, "All glory and power is yours, almighty Father. Now and Forever." He made Jesus sound like a rock opera. Then again, one had been out about that time.

"He's doing fine; he's living in Arizona."

"I heard he left the priesthood." Does he wonder how I know this? Passionistsglobalnetwork.org was good for these tidbits.

"Yes, that's true."

"That had to be a difficult choice."

"Perhaps. I could see he was unhappy, but I never asked why."

I don't mention my astonishment that when his little brother was in obvious distress over a major life decision, he didn't even ask why he was unhappy. But it's not off his mark, is it? Failing to comprehend the suffering of others?

"Is he your only family?"

"No, I have two older sisters."

"They're both alive?"

"Yes, and doing well. I see them when I return to California for visits."

For a second, I wonder if he regrets telling me this. I feel my face turning red again. The asshole gets to go home on work release.

Calm down. Maybe they can arrest him in California.

"Oh, you get to go back to the States?"

"For vacations, once a year," and then he tries to course correct. "And only to the retreat house in Southern California, where I'm supervised. I visit my sisters from there."

Keep him talking.

"I remember your mom and still recall that awful day she fell getting out of your car right in front of our house. My dad was so upset. He blamed himself, of course, for not warning you about the pothole at the curb's edge. It was a long time before he forgave himself for her broken hip."

The mention of my father and his contrition also raises no response. No, "How is Walter?" or, "I seriously hope he doesn't blame himself for Chicago street maintenance." The priest, for that is what he still is, just silently leads us through a different door that opens to the interior of the Curia. We walk down yet another long, marble-floored hallway. As if he forgot his first caution, he says again, "Watch the tile. It's unique here. Like woods in the States."

"Thank you, Father, I will."

Perhaps he noticed when he looked up to speak. "You sure are tall. You must have played basketball at I. C."

Now I laugh, "I would have, but I was blind as a bat and had terrible hand-eye coordination. Just ask Mr. Carco."

The mention of my former gym teacher's name makes him smile, whether or not he liked the guy, and my recollection is he did not. I could keep saying names like Carco, Corso, Murphy, Duffy, and Lennon. I start to believe the familiarity of them alone will be enough to permit me to stay.

A group of three people, a woman and two men, are ahead looking up at a broken transom. They stop their conversation when we walk by. Ormechea nods, but no words are exchanged.

I think of saying, "If Dad were here, he would fix that. It wouldn't take three people to get it done." But, I'm not bringing up Dad again until we have more time to discuss him. Ormechea is already opening another door to our right. He signals for me to step in.

It's a small dining hall. A table large enough for twenty or so people is in its center. I sit at a smaller round table to its right, closest to what looks like a door to the kitchen. There are two armless wooden chairs, and I take one. On the wall to my right is a painting of a young priest in a Passionist's black robes doing nothing but standing there, facing out from the canvas. Mountains are behind him. To my left is a dark oil painting of Jesus. He's on the cross.

"I shouldn't be long," Ormechea says, still standing at the door. "I just have to help them find their room. Can I get you anything? Water? Coffee?"

❧

"Senora, would you like some *caffè* with your tiramisu?"

For the last three courses, Giancarlo's been especially solicitous. I've been sitting at one of his checker-clothed tables, third over, closest to the curb, for nearly two hours. Each course, the selection of Latium cheese, then the rigatoni, followed by the rabbit, he placed gently to the side of my pen and paper, and as for my water glass, to avert any spills, he makes sure it stays appropriately out of reach.

"Yes, thank you. One macchiato, *per favore*," I throw in the please just to show I can.

I'm still busy writing and rewriting every moment of my conversation with Ormechea, trying to remember what came first. The conversation about monastery renovations or forgiveness? And was "gaffer" the word he was trying to remember for Greg's camera-operator occupation? As for the spilled milk comment and asking me to repeat action by action what he did to Tim, I remember those sentences verbatim. Writing them down now had made me sick to my stomach. "Hello, little rabbit, for a second time."

What stopped me while sitting on that park bench from saying exactly what he did to Tim or even from slapping him, I can't say. All I can admit is my embarrassment. The taskmaster is trying to have a field day. "Some prosecutor and tough litigator you are!" she says. But each time she tries to attack, something more centered in me shushes her. How dare she, on one of my braver days. And as for what came next, I hope I made some amends.

❧

"No, thank you. I'll be fine," I reply. As soon as Ormechea leaves, I grab my journal to write the snippets of what I'll record in greater detail later. I write: "I know I spilled the milk," "ten good years," "they didn't know what to do with me," "I'm living under a gag order," "doesn't drive, doesn't speak Italian." Then I add my observations: "ancient steps," "lions of the Colosseum," "we are in the Garden of Gethsemane," "palomino-brown pathway," and "warm April sun." With each word comes power.

I have to admit, part of me feels caught in my own trap. In acting polite, I become it. In questioning, I'm concerned. But that's why when I write these words down, I feel I regain my mission. "Keep him talking," I think, "so I see what I'm up against." Now decode what he has said. "I apologize to you, in the place of your brother," came out no more remorseful than if he had backed into our family car. "Gag order" is code for continuing control over this conversation.

"You don't need me to be miserable to be happy" just as easily means "nothing about your state, or your family's, or the other boys' I took controls mine." I knew it before, but witnessed in actual presence and not in memory, Tim is again correct. Father John Baptist Ormechea is a living, breathing sociopath.

I put my pen down. The Passionist priest in the painting looks amused and Jesus is befuddled. And just before the door opens, I offer them both, with raised hands in each of their directions, one comfort, a promise even, "Don't worry, I've got this covered."

Halfway through my tiramisu, I overhear a conversation between Giancarlo and a couple behind me. They're from Norway and recently married, just two weeks ago. This trip to Rome is a long weekend getaway and another honeymoon is still to follow. I like the couple. They're both so athletic and pretty, she with long blonde hair and eyes that are feverish for him, the way mine once were for Richard, and he, with soft lips and a day's worth of unshaved whiskers. When I turn, smile, and offer a "congratulations," the new husband says, "I've been watching you. Are you a writer?

"You're still here," Ormechea announces from the open doorway. He walks to my table, and when he pulls his chair back to sit, the legs creak against the marble he said to watch.

"It's good to see you," He does smile.

"That's hard to believe." I don't give him an explanation.

"So I wanted to ask you. No person came for a tour of the church on Tuesday. Was that you who called?"

"Ah," I laugh and feel a bit of pride even as my ears turn red. "I see you've caught me in my lie. Yes, it was. I hope you understand that, as I said on Tuesday, I came here to Rome for one specific reason: to find you. I spent Monday sitting up at the park, Celimontana, trying to find the right words to explain the reason for my visit. On Tuesday, I knew I was going to deliver my letter to you. But I had no confirmation you were actually here in Rome and not on vacation somewhere." *Like California.* "And I thought, if he, I mean you, were here, and this was my one time to see you, I had to find a way. That's why I invented Abigail Sheehan and told the woman who answered the phone I was from America, Pennsylvania to be exact, and hoping an English speaker could give me a tour of the basilica. I hope you can imagine my shock when the receptionist told me an American priest named John Baptist would be available and that, of all places, you worked the reception desk. As for my lie? I do apologize to you," I say, lying. "It was wrong."

"That's okay," he offers.

"Listen, in the garden, I can see that you and I have some disagreement as to the value of remembering. I say that without remembrance and acknowledgment, history will soon repeat itself."

"And my concern is, if you don't let go, the past can drag you down."

"Well, maybe some of us are made to remember and speak about our loss, maybe even write about it," I'm growing bold, "so that others can forget." I think of Tim and Charlie and Greg. "I think I might be best tasked as one who remembers."

Did I say, "as one who remembers" or "best tasked as a rememberer," a made-up word, a silly word with its er-er ending. For a moment, I regret the choice I made back in that Passionist dining room not to hit the microphone icon on my iPhone and create a voice memo of our conversation. I had the opportunity to do so when Ormechea was helping the deacon. When he came back, all I had to do was cover my phone with a piece of paper or my sunglasses to avoid detection. He would have had no idea what I was up to.

Did I not hit record because the Alaska Rules of Professional Conduct ban a lawyer from taping a conversation without the other participant's consent? I think I can argue this rule shouldn't guide my conduct when I'm outside its jurisdiction. *The Good Wife* successfully tried that approach just the other night. But I know the rule had nothing to do with my choice. Neither did the fear I might be found out. My reason was simply this. I wanted my memory to serve as witness, nothing else. I wanted *it* to decide what was most important and most meaningful. This choice is the reason I've been sitting at this table at Il Bocconcino, a restaurant that Lorena from the Lancelot had recommended, going on three hours, writing, sometimes in the right order, sometimes not, what came next. So which was it, "one who remembers?" Or that silly word?

❧

He repeats his defense. "The problem is I *can't* speak of it. I'm not allowed to talk. My hands are tied," again he raises them as if he's in handcuffs, "by the provincial and by the moderator."

You mean, my adversary, by the lawyers. "I wonder what they would think of you meeting with me now? I meant to add in my letter, you were welcome to have anyone you would like join us."

"I think it's better this way."

Hmm, he doesn't want them to know . . . "Well, if I may, let me go through my list of questions. There may be some you can't answer, and I'll respect that. Some of these you've answered already, but not this one. Do you miss home?"

"Yes, yes I do," a moment of truth. "This isn't home. As I said, I was called to the Provincial's office in December and shown the AG's letter and I moved that day. After that my life changed in an instant."

"What was your biggest adjustment?"

"Everything happened so quickly, I don't really think I had time to adjust?" The truth again.

"That reminds me, Father. At some point prior to December 2002, do you recall calling Timmie at his home?"

"What?" I can't read his face.

"Some time in the fall of 2002, when the state's attorney was investigating the charges and your superiors were already aware of her potential case, Tim got four phone calls from a number with a Louisville, Kentucky, area code. Besides you, he didn't know anyone in Louisville. Were you trying to reach him?"

"No," he denies. "That couldn't have been me. I didn't know about the investigation until I was called into the provincial's office."

"Not a thing?" I ask, not believing the answer. Who else could have been calling Tim? Surely, Father Higgins could have given the priest a heads-up.

"Not a thing," he repeats stalwartly.

"Let's go back a little further. Before all this happened to any of the boys, do you think there was anything else people could have done to help you?"

"I think they gave me the support they knew how to give at the time."

"Which was not getting you out of the ministry and away from kids. Did you wish you did anything differently?"

"Yes, I do." I wait for him to expound, but he says nothing.

"Did you have an addiction to substances. Alcohol? Drugs?"

Again, the marionette frown comes to his mouth and a knitted look eats up his forehead. He doesn't respond.

"Was it easy to get away with harming a child?"

He twitches in his seat and crosses his arms.

"Did this happen to you as a child?"

He seems to look not past but through me, as if my questions might be staining this "it's too good to be true" reunion.

"Do you think you might be suppressing memories?" "Why only boys?" "Was it easy in a family like mine?" "How close did you come to being caught?"

Not once does he answer. Finally, he offers, "I have a hard time answering these questions because they assume things I cannot answer."

"Yes, Father, they do." When I look at him, I sit up straight and feel my shoulders square.

His next response makes me sit even taller. "I bet you're a good lawyer."

I know I look him in his eyes. They're not tearing up any more. In fact, under the slight magnification his glasses bring to them, I can tell he's not having fun. "Yes, Father," I say, "I am. And if anyone were to try to deny he harmed my brother, you can bet the cross-examination would start."

"I see," but he doesn't. He averts his eyes from my gaze and looks to the painting of Jesus on the cross. "And of everything you have said or not said here today, the hardest thing for me to hear is that you have no recollection of hurting Tim. I hope you know how preposterous that sounds."

"Well, beyond the attorney general's letter, I don't know a lot."

"You were there, Father. You think you need a letter or affidavit to remind you?"

As if he might be prosecuted further, he exercises the right to remain silent, but he also issues no denial.

"How did it make you feel to put a child's penis in your mouth? Did other priests join you? What thoughts went through your mind when Loretta Finger caught you with Greg? Who was your intended next victim? If you had admitted you were gay and found a loving adult relationship, do you think you still would've chosen child victims?" Knowing these and others questions like them that I'd written down would only be met with silence, I choose not to ask. I close my book and instead query, "Father, do you want people to forgive you?"

He doesn't pause, "Yes."

"How can they do that when you say nothing to them?"

"I'm not sure."

"Father, one thing they told us after your removal is that they sent you here to get you away from children. But there's a playground right down the damn street. Tell me! Are the children of Rome safe from you."

"Yes, yes they are." His mouth drops as if he might be sad about the point. "As I said," he even chooses to laugh, "I don't speak Italian."

❧

"I think you would enjoy an aperitif."

"Yes, thank you, Giancarlo. And please, get two for the newlyweds. Any kind will do."

As Giancarlo walks inside to the bar, I write out, "I don't speak Italian." "I don't drive." "I make copies and answer the phone." I also write, "Stay put, Mary. I'll go check on Tim." "Eddie, with Helen out of town, I can get Charlie from soccer." And "Don't get up, Vicky. Greg will drive me home."

Because he doesn't know how to ask, to compliment, to groom; because he can't drive to get them; because he doesn't have the money to ply them with gifts, the score can conceivably be Italian Children 1, Predator Priest 0.

I look up to the shade starting to grow on the other side of Via Ostilla. I may, in fact, be done.

❧

"That's it, Father. Those are my questions. I know you've answered what you can." *Only what you're willing to offer up.* I give him a smile. It's time to let the tables turn. "Do you have any questions for me?"

After a brief silence he says, "It's better this way, isn't it?"

"What do you mean?" I'm cautious, not sure where he might be taking us.

"Talking. The provincial doesn't understand." He points outside, as if gesturing toward Saint Peter's. "Neither do the big guys. What we need instead of silence is opportunities like this, to communicate."

I give a half smile. *I don't disagree, if you can consider what you've done communicating.*

"And what the Vatican is doing to the American nuns," he sighs, as if in solidarity. "It's terrible."

This time, it's me that's silent. I'm not taking his "I'm on the woman's side" bait.

He thinks of a next question. "How is Father?" He doesn't say Walter.

"Suffering."

"Did he have cancer?"

"Yes, twice. He's had prostate cancer, then kidney cancer, heart disease, and a triple bypass. He has high cholesterol, low blood pressure, poor pulmonary functioning from all those years fighting fires, neuropathy, and also diabetes. He's pretty much bedridden. It's just a matter of time, but how much time, I don't know."

"I read your father's note."

"Good, he'd like that."

"I disagree with the statement I was in league with the Devil."

"Then who were you in league with?"

He doesn't answer.

"You don't understand, do you? By linking you with Satan, Dad's saying the Devil was responsible for your actions. Not you. I think that was gallant on his part." Ormechea smirks and crosses his hands over his chest. He's not buying it, so I continue, "If you think about it, it's even forgiving on his part. Of course, the one person he can't forgive is himself. He chose you over his son. It's why I think all this not getting better is him giving up on living." *Unlike some of us.* "He's doing his penance here on earth."

"Could be."

"He considered you his friend. Were you? Or did you just use him to get to Tim?"

"He was a friend. I also remember him as a workhorse."

As he says this, a short video of Dad plays in my brain. It's eight thirty in the morning, and he's just returned from the firehouse. He's changed out of his uniform and into paint-covered jeans and a clean white T-shirt. He puts on his old gym shoes. Mom brings his coffee and wheat toast with jelly. After a quick kiss goodbye to the two of us, he's off again, in the church's red pickup truck. He's going back to work with less than one hour between jobs.

"After forty years, he's done working," I say.

"How is Mother?" Again, not Mary.

"Mom's wonderful. She's about to turn eighty, and she still volunteers non-stop. She brings communion to the homebound, volunteers at the Norwood Park Senior Home, watches Joyce's kids, and still manages to exercise regularly at the Senior Center."

"That's great. "

"Of all of us, she's the faith source. She doesn't let events conquer it. Frankly, I think her way of survival requires cutting out pieces of history and that's not honest to me. But still, we all rely on her."

"I think she has a point." Ah, he appreciates it.

"As you can see, I take the opposite approach." I grab my journal again, turn to a blank page, and write the words, "cut, cut, snip, snip."

"Well, be careful, that's how they kill monkeys?"

"Kill monkeys. I have to write that down too. What does that mean?"

"You don't know that story?"

"No."

He's getting excited, as if he's reaching for an old homily. He gets to preach. "Well, to catch monkeys, somewhere in Africa, the tribesmen take long tubes and put a banana at the end of the tube. When the monkey reaches his hand through and grabs the banana, the band tightens around his arm." Ormechea mimics the action. "The only way the band will loosen is if the monkey lets go of the banana. But, the monkey doesn't want to let go, so he hangs on, is caught, and killed."

"Are you saying I'm killing myself?"

"Not exactly, just be careful, though, because not letting go can hurt you. Then there's the story of the scar."

And here comes old homily number two. "What's that?"

"Well, we have scars sometimes to remind us of injuries." He points to one on his left hand. "But if we keeping picking at the scar, we injure ourselves again."

"Or gain greater discernment."

He laughs, "I have a feeling neither of us is going to convince the other."

I laugh too, but only at how immutable he and I both are. "You are right."

"Tell me, and how is your aunt?"

I know he's speaking of Lorraine. "She is doing remarkably well as well. She's been in the convent sixty-five years now. I went to visit her in Cincinnati a couple of years ago and had dinner with some of her friends, all sisters over eighty and former teachers. They were a kick."

"And your sisters. "

"Joyce is a Chicago cop." That seemed to get a reaction. He pushes his chair farther back. "Julie is in restaurant hospitality. Maureen is a stay-at-home mom, and Teresa, she's still struggling after her divorce. As for me, I'm back in private practice after a stint as a prosecutor."

Does that get a reaction too? Now he leans back in his chair, likely wondering if this was a good idea. To soften the blow and make him think I'm a friend to all defendants, I cover. "I was not a good prosecutor. I couldn't see the world in black and white as my colleagues did. I wanted to know how people chose a life of crime and what, if anything, I could do to keep the person from committing the next one. Those were the people I tried to help the most. The next victim." *Like any child here in Italy.*

Our time is going quickly. Next, we run through more parish names. Duffy and Stanton, Brander and Devine, Mulcrone and Urqhart, and with each offering, I can tell, he wants to tell stories. He wants to be home. Then he asks of Alaska and what life is like there. When I tell him I found God more in the mountains than in any church, he goes back in homily mode and remarks, "That's where you find God; in the *G-O-D*, Great Outdoors." When I show him a photo of Richard he offers up that he looks Italian. When we speak about Abigail, he agrees. She sounds like a miracle. I only bring her up because she's a girl and he's no threat.

Our conversation slows.

"Are you sure I can't get you some coffee?"

"No, I'm fine."

"How about that tour of the cathedral?"

"No."

I can tell he doesn't want me to leave. He needs more home.

"Lunch?"

"No, Father. You already gave me the opportunity I sought: to tell you, 'we are still here, and we still matter.' But there is something I want to give you."

"Check, please, Giancarlo, and do me a favor. Take all the drinks off the newlyweds' bill and put them on mine. Please don't tell them who paid for them. Or if you do, wait until I leave."

I reach for my sunglasses case. Distinctive to the Juicy Couture brand, it's big and hard covered. Something much larger than sunglasses can be kept inside it. I wonder if that's a flinch I see coming from him, and if he's concerned, just for a second, whether a paring knife or something more destructive is within. But, without knowing when it occurred, I'm done with "It's not too late." I don't even need it in fantasy mode anymore.

When I open the case, all it contains is what I placed inside it while Ormechea was dealing with the deacon. I had moved it from my back pocket.

"My daughter," I said, holding up the red painted heart, "gave this to me in preparation for this trip. It was just a small act. While I wasn't looking, she took it off her bedroom shelf and hid it in my backpack. I asked her about it during a phone call. She said it was her way of saying, 'don't forget me.' This entire trip, this heart"—*Tim's heart*—"has given me the courage I've needed for this visit. Not that I need it for this next reason, but it also reminds me how much I love her." *And why I've been so damn kind to you. I want to go home.* "I give this to you as a small token of my gratitude for you agreeing to speak to me."

I see what looks like tears return to his eyes. Is that even a finger brush to his cheek? "Thank you! Thank you very much." He takes it and turns it in his hand, just as I often did.

"You're most welcome,"

"This is God's work."

"I know."

"You're a beautiful person."

I smile. He doesn't know why, "Now, you're being too kind."

As he walks me toward the front door, he asks if I'd changed my mind about the coffee.

"No, I've taken enough of your time." *I don't need any more.*

"Where are you off to next?"

"I'm not sure, but tomorrow I'm set to go to the Vatican." *There's something I need to do there.*

"Have you been to the Spanish Steps?"

"Yes, a couple of days ago. I enjoyed it there. It was so beautiful . . ." I'm about to say, "seeing all those young people," but I stop myself for their protection. I don't want his thoughts on any of them. "To see the gorgeous potted, purple azaleas," I cover.

We make it to the doors that open up onto San Paolo della Croce when I turn, hand him another envelope, and say, "I have one more thing for you. I wrote this letter to you in case you changed your mind about meeting me. Inside it is also a letter from Tim that I've transcribed. His words are harsh. Despite this meeting, I believe you deserve them from him, and I will defend his right to believe and say them to the very end."

"Like I said," he remarks, "you're a good lawyer."

"We already covered that," I laugh, "but you might want to add a good sister."

"I can do that."

"Goodbye, Father, *Adios.*" *Intended translation: Go with God, but only if God lets you.*

I'm not sure of his reply or of how long he might have stayed there at the double set of doors watching me leave and thinking of home. I do know I made my way down the Curia's ramp and the following set of stairs observant to each foot fall at a slight jog. When I reached the bottom of the stairs and walked through its still-open gate, I looked up to the noon-high sun and never turned back.

What I didn't say:

Dear Father,

    I hope you know by now that the heart I gave you was not one of gratitude, but instead . . . can you guess? . . . one of remembrance. You see, each day that heart sits on your shelf; each time you might mention it to your moderator or others in the know; each passing thought you might have of it and how it and my visit might give you hope; when these things occur, Father, my purpose is fulfilled. You are remembering that the hearts of those you defiled keep beating.

    Journeying toward peace for their sake and mine, this time for real,

    Joan

What Tim did say:

Ormechea,

    I'm trying to understand the saying, "everything happens for a reason." Did I draw a number before birth, a fucking lottery quick pick? Hey, you win years of sexual abuse as a child that will haunt you until you die? I wanted to put something on paper for you, shithead, but I decided not to waste my time. Scum of the earth should be placed in prison, not given an office with a view. But you should know, you DID NOT win.

    I am happy to be clean again, including free of the shit you and your employers shove down people's throats. I relish the fact my children will never be forced to endure your egotistical self-prescribed drug. In my opinion, from Satan all the way down to the pope and his peons, you're all part of one big drug cartel. You serve no purpose. I don't need to pray for forgiveness for believing this. I don't need to be part of an organization. I choose to be good and to help my kids make good choices.

    Know one more thing. IF I EVER SEE YOU AGAIN, I WILL NOT HESITATE. Have a paralyzing stroke old man so nobody has to listen to your crap anymore.

    John Baptist Ormechea, cp = child predator

WHAT IS MINE

Friday morning

I have come to say

Colosseo, Cavour, Termini, cambiare per la linea rossa.

The Red Line. Red. Red means "Stop." This is what two Metro police officers ask me to do. No, not stop planning a murder, I'm done with that, but stop taking photos of commuters with long vanilla-white sweaters and bright pink purses; of a steep stairwell, which causes an elderly woman to hold tightly to its handrail; of a *Show True Independence* billboard, advertising *Made in the U.S.A.* Fruit of the Loom underwear; of subway car graffiti, including the one covered with the word *POISON*; of bearded men on subway platforms; of signs to Anagnina and Battistini.

Red. To the officers, I mean potential danger. I'm studying the access routes, plotting some cardinal offense, planning to take the beautiful and bloodied innocents with me. But they don't know, all I want to take is what's already mine.

"Senora, no. No photos."

"Who? Me?" Yes, thank goodness, I'm an American. Yes, I smile. *See me, officers, clad in a powder-blue skirt, the color of the Virgin Mary herself. Look at my yoga-insignia T-shirt and at my headband. Even that has a dove on it? No, officers. There's no danger here. No reason to stop me. Take my camera, if you must. Delete the images you find offensive. What is it? The sign to Linea A? The escalator to street top? Smile now, gentlemen. They're yours. Send me on my way, for I shall do no harm.*

La Linea Rossa. La tappa successiva è Repubblica, all'uscita per il Teatro dell'Opera di Roma, Barberini, e per la Fontana de Trevi, Spagna, Flaminio, la

Piazza del Popolo, Lepanto, apparentemente nulla da vedere, e Ottaviano. L'uscita è a sinistra.

By now it's old-school. Exit to the right, my child.

May the long-time sun

Il Ponte Sant'Angelo. In a Jeopardy-styled answer, "What Via Ottaviano is not." Not a single Bernini-inspired archangel leads me to my destination. Instead the four-block and four-lane right-of-way to the Vatican City's wall is the opposite of angel inspired. It's like Christmas without Christ and a Charlie Brown's Thanksgiving without thanks. It's commerce. Columns of clothing outlets and cantinas, pharmacies and bakeries fill the street's storefronts. Tour buses inch their way from the Metro Station to the Piazza Risorgimento. And on a Friday morning, just past ten, the street merchants hawk their wares.

"Avoid the lines at the Vatican Museum, Miss," one tour operator calls out in English. He's short and has a mane of dark hair and a well-trimmed beard. I shall call him Luca. "You'll be waiting three hours, unless you come with me," Luca says.

Yet today, Rome fits snugly like the ski jacket I've been wearing for three Alaska winters. I reply comfortably, "Oh no, *signore. Non può dire? Io sono dale Germania.*" "Go forth and prosper," *Drivetime Italian* CDs. Today I'm from Germany.

An Australian woman offers, "G'day. Won't you come with me, Miss. My tours are in English."

And to her I say, "No, thank you. My English is terrible."

I swipe away those who follow with similar responses, "Isn't this the way to the Eiffel Tower?" "No, I have a private invitation from the Pappa himself." Sometimes, I give an honest answer. "No, thank you. I made a reservation for the Vatican Museum online." Whether doling out fact or fiction, one thing seems certain. I'm in command. Not even il Pappa could slow me down. But, hold that thought. One thing can. While I've succumbed to Rome's happy-hour wines, I've avoided her pastries. One of my favorites is in the window of La Ottoviano's Dolci. And when I order *"una cannoli e una acqua, non gassata,"* even the postcard version of the Italian grandmother standing next to me doesn't raise one criticizing eye.

shine upon you.

Last night, I had a chance to start again. The dinner guests at the Lancelot's tables were all new and fresh to the city, wanting to speak of their Thursday treks to the Jewish Ghetto and the Villa d'Este fountains in Tivoli. Not once in our conversations did I mention that it was Giacomo Mattei, son of Muzio, who had one of the few set of keys to the Jewish Ghetto, who installed the obelisk in Celimontana, under which I almost wrote my letter to the priest who abused my brother, until that cute high school boy sent me on my way. Nor did I even think to question the American woman, Susan, who went to Tivoli, on whether she was aware its Artemis-of-Ephesus fountain was commissioned by the son of Lucrezia Borgia at the same time he served on the College of Cardinals or that the statue once held a central location in the gardens until it was deemed too pagan, probably, no doubt by some child-abusing-hiding bishop.

No. Last night, I was the perfect American tourist spending a carefree week in beautiful Roma. I had seen many things—the Trevi Fountain, the Villa Medici, the Spanish Steps, and even a door's eye view of the Pantheon. "Tomorrow, on Friday, I have just one site left to see, the Vatican," I said. And, "No, I really didn't want a travel mate." Especially you, Penelope, lady from New Hampshire whose partner just died and who was taking this trip, even though she and he had booked it together, and though she was still really sad, she owed it to him because he was a history professor interested in debunking Christian myths. "Thank you, however, for the kind offer." And, "No, thank you," you shouldn't ask me again. And, "Yes, you'll be fine touring by yourself." "I've been doing it all week. Even the Metro is safe. Don't believe whatever guidebook has terrified you. No one will attack."

When I heard Penelope would be joining Susan and me on Faris's "Magic Night Tour" of the city later last night, I must admit I thought of cancelling. But this was Faris we were talking about, my one-degree removed Anchorage friend and closest Roman ally. I could handle a little Penelope. I could handle many things, I knew by last evening, because I already had.

Before dinner, I had made my way back to the small rise by the Colosseum and tried to get a view that was the direct opposite from the one I held this morning. Yes, on that hill, the one covered in shrubbery, was the crucifixion statue, and, if I looked just fifty feet to its right, Jesus was there with Joseph looking in my direction at a sun that was setting, this time in red. The black cat might've already made her way down the hill toward me by then. She felt peaceful, I believed, and, oddly enough, so did I. But the peace wasn't for me. It wasn't even for Tim.

It was the unintended comments, the "I don't drive," and "besides, I don't speak Italian," that still meant the most to me. Without the command of the Italian language, without a way to enter a home, without a means to charm a parent, without the money to buy a television set, and without the desire to drive to the Rossi's, the Bianchi's, the Esposito's, or Lombardi's, the monster that is Ormechea is deactivated. Yes, he could still sit and watch the children play at the Parco Giochi in Celimontana, and even, perhaps, fantasize about their young bodies, but on the whole, he had been neutralized. The Italian children were just what Tim had asked for them to be. Safe.

All love surround you.

Just past the buses, the insistent tour operators, and the kiosk on Piazza Risorgimento that sells a bobbleheaded Benedict is a more subdued street called Viale dei Bastioni Michelangelo. A bed-and-breakfast is here. So, too, is an ice cream shop. Those with earlier reservations than mine for the Vatican Museum turned right a block before, and those on their way to Saint Peter's Square had no reason to stop.

"I'm not ready."

"Then don't go."

I sit. My photo album is with me. After a bite of the cannoli, I turn to the picture I seek. In it, there are eight candles in total. Subtract the one for good luck, and it's October 22, 1971, my seventh birthday. A smiling girl, with a mop of golden hair and the short bangs she appears to have cut herself, sits cross-armed. She wears a tomato-red sweater with a gold ring at the end of its neckline zipper and sleeves pushed up to her elbows. On her parents' dining room table, her birthday cake is still in its eleven-by-nine pan. The cake is smothered in chocolate frosting. The words "Happy Birthday" are spelled out in the hard confectioned candies that I'm certain her mother bought from the neighborhood Jewel Grocers.

The long right arm of the mother is to the little girl's left. Always present, as it always will be. And to her right, is a six-year-old boy. His larger-than-life right ear is in full view as he tilts his head toward his left shoulder. A white T-shirt peeks out from under his brown, yellow, and white striped sweater. His fingertips are touching, and, he smiles a toothless, beaming, full, lovely, chocolate-transfixed smile.

I intend to leave them here, the girl, her brother, and the always-present arm of a mother. I intend to find some crack under a statue of angels in which to stow them as reminders, very much like Ormechea's now-beating, red-porcelain heart. But they cannot go alone. Charlie, Greg, Kurt, and the rest of the boys must go too.

It will take a number of tries to get the inscription intended for the back of the photo right, and so I test out, "We are the forgotten children, now in adult bodies. The once victims of your excesses." And "Boys touched by priests in a way no child should experience. Girls, sisters of those boys, without the power to stop it." Then there's, "We once ate your body and drank your blood, and now you leave us to starve." No, they're all too melodramatic and give them more power than they deserve.

Do words even matter? Can they stop the inevitable? Or is their only purpose to make an adequate record of our journeys, to be, as Aristotle said, the scribes of our souls? Either way, are my words the best they can be? Have they fulfilled their promise? Are they good enough for remembrance? Can they save one child, say, one Autumn? Will she know she matters and she needs to keep choosing survival? We didn't get here soon enough for the graduate student, but did we, for her? That's all Tim and I have ever wanted.

"*Sorella*," "Sister," a blond boy no older than twenty calls out excitedly to a nun who's just left the ice cream shop, chocolate gelato cone in hand. He's bringing her change. Behind him, the sun gleams upon Saint Peter's cupola to the point it blinds.

And the pure light within you

Saint Peter's cupola by rose garden, Saint Peter's cupola by orange grove, and next through the keyhole gate of the Grand Priory of Malta—although the Piazza Mattei's turtle fountain and *Roman Holiday*'s Bocca della Verità attempt to round out Faris's Magic Night Tour, from Aventine Hill to Janiculum, from Palatine to Quirinal, from what Bramante had intended at Saint Peter's Montorio, to what Maderno's nave had obscured from all places but the distant, Saint Peter's Basilica was Faris's Night Tour's Holy Roman epicenter. "To understand Saint Peter's, you must see it as we Romans see it," Faris seems to have said, "as possible, through vantage points of great beauty."

"Close your eyes."

"What?" Penelope had asked. After dominating the last thirty minutes of conversation with talk of the Great Hoax, that Jesus's body was simply taken from his grave by his friends, the command, "close your eyes," must have sounded foreign to her.

"Do what? Why?" she asked again, even more flustered. She placed her small shamrock-green silk purse with embroidered flowers on Faris's dashboard with a thud, as if it held too much change.

"Just for a moment, close your eyes," Faris implored softly, trying to tame the Caterina Sforza, the Tigress, among us. Penelope remained resistant, even as we took a left onto the Vittorio Emmanuel bridge and crossed the Tiber. Whether she eventually acquiesced, neither Susan nor I could say, because when my backseat mate shut her eyes, I did as well. All that remained was the sound of the accelerating engine, the fall of Penelope's purse, her loud exhale, and the brush of wind coming in from the half-open rear window.

❧

"Close your eyes."

"What?"

"Close your eyes, Joannie. It's time to sleep."

I had decided to stop feigning sleep but to still be quiet and not point out the sleeping dogs, Crayola crayons, or yucca plants I still saw in the Wyoming night sky. The stars filled our station wagon's windshield and circled around us as Long Pockets accelerated the engine, no gumballs in sight. A slight breeze from the air conditioning vent brushed against my knees.

"They'll be back tomorrow, I promise," he next said. "We'll watch them from our campsite. I'll have a fire going and you can let me know everything you see."

"Then they won't be as bright."

"A small fire will do no more damage than these headlights, Pumpkin. Trust me."

I turned my body from right to left and leaned against him, his flannel shirt soft and spongy as a pillow. And when he said that, "trust me," I knew I always should.

"Okay, Dad." I exhaled. He was right. I was so tired.

"Oh, and one more thing, pumpkin. Thanks for your help. I don't know what I would have done without you: I probably would've made a wrong turn back there and missed Route 287 altogether. You're a great navigator, Joan, always keeping us going the right direction. Now, close your eyes."

❧

"And, open!"

The car's engine was silent. Even Penelope was quiet. In fact, the only audible sound was the water bouncing up from Bernini's and Maderno's fountains. Faris had driven us as close to the barricades of Saint Peter's Square as possible, trying to give us, "the experience pilgrims had here, before Mussolini constructed Via Della Conciliazione. Like the way you fall upon the Trevi Fountain now? Almost by mistake? Saint Peter's used to appear just like that too." He snapped his fingers and said, "Just like magic," on this magical night tour.

Like my command to the children of Parco Giochi, I looked up. Three-quarters of the moon hung high in the sky, just to the right of Saint Peter's cupola. The planet Venus rose perpendicular to the northern corner of the basilica, rising between Saints Peter and Matthias as they surround a hand-outstretched Jesus on the basilica's rooftop. Between the moon and planet, the night sky was empty, but beyond them, the stars rose up. Quickly, I could tell you, I saw a send-in-the-clowns balloon emptied of its helium, a birch tree that lost its cascading leaves, and a little girl blowing out her birthday candles.

"We are stargazers," I think I might have said to Dad, more easily and truthfully than I ever said, "We are Roman Catholics," after chastising my father that we were Irish and German, not Roman. But standing there, on Saint Peter's Square, beneath stars, and under my own inquisition, I realized, as if for the first time, we were all these things.

"You can leave the Catholic Church when Jesus does, Joan."

"Yes, but even if I leave before then, Father B., can it ever leave you?"

Guide your way on

During the Church's Jubilee Year in 2000, a group of Catholic women theologians issued the Madeleva Manifesto. It was in honor of Sister Madeleva Wolff, a graduate of Berkeley, an Oxford student, and president of Saint Mary's College in Notre Dame, Indiana, from 1934 to 1961. "To women in ministry and theological studies," the Catholic women offered, "reimagine what it means to be the whole body of Christ. The way things are now is not the design of God."

"To women looking for models of prophetic leadership," they further opined, "walk with us as we seek to follow the way of Jesus Christ, who inspires our hope and guides our concerns." To women "tempted by the demons of despair and indifference" over their current state in the Church, they offered, "reimagine what it means to be a full human being made in the image of God, and to live and speak this truth in your daily lives."

They kept going. "To women who suffer the cost of discipleship, we say: you are not alone. We remember those who have gone before us, who first held up for us the pearl of great price, the richness of Catholic thought and spirituality." To women younger than me, they urged, "carry forward the heritage of biblical justice." To all, they implored, "look for the holy in unexpected places," and "imagine the great shalom of God." As such, the Madeleva Manifesto asks of Catholic women what is ingrained in the life of any Cubs' fan: persevere, at all costs, persevere.

Every guidebook and travel website is correct. To avoid the Vatican Museum's queues as well as the plethora of tour operators, buy your reserved tickets on-line. Security check your bag, pull out your iPad for your Musei Vaticani audio tour, take the spiral staircases up to a glass-covered gallery, with a view of Saint Peter's Dome and the Belvedere and Pigna courtyards below, and begin.

The thought of a museum was born as one of Pope Julius II's "sudden inspirations." According to *Vatican City*, the official city-state publication, "the gruff and abrupt pontiff would look out with pleasure across the long garden that dropped off in gradual descent" from his palace "before rising again to the distant Palazzetto del Belvedere," and think, "we don't need a park there. We need a building, one with two long corridors linked together at all levels by two additional buildings in such a way that I never need to walk down a flight of stairs again." As for what green remained in outer courtyards, Pope Julius also offered his acquired statuary collection. The *Laocoon,* the *Apollo Belvedere*, the *Venus Felix*, and even, upstairs, in the Gallery of the Candelabra, dear *Diana/ Artemis of Ephesus* are here for my viewing, all because of him.

I know I'm supposed to be grateful. Without the humanist popes, who saw godliness in all human creativity, the works of prior civilizations may have gone the same way those civilizations did. But still? One blowjob equals one thousand euros? Full-on penetration equals two? Every time the church puts a price on its priests' crimes, I want to call out, "Sell this, the *Belvedere Torso*, and give the proceeds to the children you have raped. And this, *La Nicchione della Pigna*? Tear it from its precipice. Where it once stood, on stairs flocked with peacocks and lions, pharaohs and spheres, make a shrine to the children victims, each and every one of them. If they will allow, list their names before they fall away. Add their ages—twelve, eleven, eight—when a priest indelibly changed their lives, killed their souls. Make it a Vietnam Wall of remembrance, an Armistice Day retreat. Display your crimes just as surely as you display your treasures, because you forgot the most important treasure you ever held was someone else's kid."

A future pope will say, "I want a poor church." I will want him to know one thing in response. "Until you take full cognizance of your Church's crimes, including your continued harboring of abusers and those who protect them, until you truly remember and wholeheartedly beg, on your knees, each victim for forgiveness, not simply offer up one grand apology as part of a homily or meet with a selected few as even your predecessor had done, you already have one."

For Timothy Nockels

"Did you rip his mask off?" Abbie asked. It was after 1:00 a.m., Rome time, but I knew Richard would be off with her on some midafternoon adventure. That's why it was difficult to hear her over the roar of small children climbing the inflated slides at Bouncing Bears. It sounded like a mosh pit.

"What, darling?" I yelled.

"The bad man's mask. Did you take it from him?" I was intrigued. Her reference to beating him with a bear stick had disappeared, and I immediately appreciated the metaphor in her question.

"You know, darling, I hadn't thought about it that way, but I think I did pull his mask off."

"Did it hurt him when you pulled?" I couldn't tell if she had wanted it to hurt, so I was cautious about my answer.

"Well, I didn't have to pull too hard. It came off pretty easily."

"But did it hurt, even a little? Did he say, 'Ouch'?"

"No, darling, but I think that's because he doesn't know how to hurt. Either that, or he still doesn't know I took it. His mask, you see, looked an awful lot like his face."

"He had a face-face mask?"

"What?"

"One that looked just like him, but wasn't him?"

"Yeah, you could say that," out of the mouth of babes, my babe. "He had it for a lot of years and fooled many people with it, including Grandma and Grandpa."

"Including," she said the word like an expert, "Uncle Tim?"
"No, darling, he never fooled Tim."

Dear Tim,

There's a statue of Jesus in the Vatican Museum's Modern Religious Art collection. It's made of tarnished metal, copper, maybe bronze. The important part is nothing about the man shines. He has spindly legs and bone-thin arms. A rough cloak covers half of his body. Thin sandals barely protect his feet. His right hand crosses his torso. With each finger extended, he balances a canteen against his bare chest. This is somewhat surprising because, by the look of things, I'd have guessed the canteen is empty. Each of Jesus's ribs is visible. The indentation at his belly evidences a long-time hunger and thirst. So too do his sunken cheeks and the shoulder blades that poke out like two ends of a coat hanger.

Low to his hip, lower than one might expect, his left arm carries and cradles a sickly, sleeping lamb whose little feet curl up, staying, as best as they can, out of Jesus's walking way. It looks like they have far to go. No open-country, verdant pastures or resting ninety-nine are anywhere in sight. Nevertheless, perhaps you would expect Jesus would be glowing, so happy to find his lost charge, but this Jesus doesn't look triumphant. He looks as if it took all he had, every bit of his strength, to bring his one lamb this far. He also looks worried that his effort will never be enough to bring that lamb all the way home and back to good health.

I'm no expert on Jesus, I'm no expert on a lot of things, including what I'm currently doing, but I know what it's like to lose someone that was trusted to your care. I know that first sense of panic when your arms are empty, when what was supposed to be between them is not. I know what it's like to stand in the woods, in the darkness, in the beyond-freezing cold, to call out his name, time after time. I know what it's like to listen and hope for a response but hear nothing but the crack of ice and the hiss of a returning wind. I know what's like to sink to my knees with those empty, empty arms and beg and pray for forgiveness, guidance, hope, anything that will bring that little one home.

Like Jesus, at times, brother, I've been lucky. I've found that lost creature, dog, cat, chicken, horse, whatever it might be, the equivalent of a wet and tired lamb, covered in mud, barely breathing, ready to give up, but still harboring the ability to come back to some semblance of life. And in that moment of find, the feeling isn't triumph. It isn't even joy. It's just a prayer. *Stay with me, stay with me, stay with me as long as you can.*

You told me once that when you least expect, when you hurt the most, when you're ready to call it a day, something in you will carry you forward and will help you decide that no matter what happens or happened to you, you're worth more. You told me "that" something was God. But you didn't tell me how it feels when

God can't bring you all the way back. When there's no saving you from touches that feel like flames or no way of giving you hope that your financial future is going to be okay. God can't take away this fact. You were harmed, gravely harmed, and most painful of all, under God's watch and name. Do you know this? El, our abbreviation for our Blue Line Elevated, the place of our connection, means "God" in Hebrew? Even still, even there, God could do nothing.

I came to Rome with great hopes this visit might somehow help you; that an admission from J. B. would right some of the wrongs. Yet when it came time to speak your name, to list his crimes against you, even I failed you. If pushed further, if one denial came from his lips, I know this, I would have bludgeoned him, but he didn't and wasn't.

If it is any recompense, he is a tired, lame, old, old man whose heart and conscience is a shadow of yours. Just as he doesn't know remorse, he can never know true joy or true love. And that, my brother, is what I believe, through your story, the world needs to know. Thus, my only offering to you is this, this Book of Timothy, this promise, this prayer: I will stay with you, stay with you, stay with you, as long as you allow.

For Charlie Tierney and Greg Conrad

In 2011 five million people visited the Vatican Museum. So assuming the same number of visitors for 2012 and an equal number of tourists on the six days the museum is open each week, excluding Italy's eleven public holidays, 16,611 people walk through the Pio Clementine with me today. Along the way, they each stop to admire the *Belvedere Torso*, just as Michelangelo once did. Some crowd around Constantia's purple porphyry sarcophagus, looking for the peacocks and wine, the symbols of early Christianity. Few know to link her to the saga of two brothers, upon whose graves a Celian Hill church was built, one I once hoped to burn down.

We rest together in the Cortile della Pigna to seek shade from an early afternoon's sun. We take espresso at the cafeteria nearby the Pinacoteca. And when our time comes to take the quarter-mile-long march, past the statue of Diana, the huntress, and Raphael's tapestry of a resurrected Jesus, whose eyes seem to follow us, we'll still go forward, shoulder to shoulder, locked in stepped time, toward the sacred of sacred, the Sistine Chapel.

None of them, however, will deviate with me when I see Penelope across the way in the Room of Maps buying jigsaw puzzles and poster reprints—I suppose, of Anubis and Thoth—from a nearby kiosk. Our night together had ended cordially, just after midnight. While I knew she would be here, I thought the chance of running into her had to be low, at least one in 16,611 people low.

Despite the odds, I also run into the newlyweds from yesterday, whom I'm more than happy to see when they each tap my shoulder in the room of tapestries and thank me for the purchased drinks. Why can't I be the same for Penelope? Without much more effort, I can see, like me, she's a woman in mourning. She's owed sympathy. One hand on her shoulder, one smile might have softened her. Yet I hide. I don't want to brighten her day for fear it might darken mine.

Last night, after my call with Richard and Abbie, I had opened my hotel room's window to the inner courtyard and waited to hear voices. Perhaps they would be those of Helen and her best friend or of Faris feeding overdue treats to his little dog, Mister Red. But it was quiet, not a voice, not a bark to be heard, until it wasn't.

Then, the rain fell thick and heavy and even felt like it was falling on the Hotel Lancelot alone. It fell in pellets on tiled patio squares, gray cobblestones, iron gates, marble statues, and metal gutters. *Una pioggia italiana*, an Italian rain, I thought, for its distinct sounds and the scent of garden flowers, whose names I still didn't know, that reached upward to me. It reminded me of what my mother told me long ago when a storm like this came so suddenly. The angels must be crying.

Maybe, for Penelope, she also thought it was a sign, that her beloved waited for her evening's sojourn to complete before turning the cobblestoned sidewalks with their raised edges into miniature streams suitable only for stiletto heels. I hope that for her this was the case. She deserved it to be so. For me, I was equally lucky. It drowned out all voices, including my one. Sleep, for the first time in a long while, came easily.

Dear Charlie and Greg,

Right before I fell asleep last night, I recalled the revelation I had midway through my conversation with Ormechea. It was right after talking about your drinking, Charlie, and your career choice, Greg. Frustrated, I looked over to Ormechea for any sign of understanding that his actions mattered and, that while he may not be able to put milk back in the bottle, he should still suffer the pain of conscience.

It was then I realized without question I was looking at a man incapable of either understanding or conscience. He could say the right words, but he couldn't feel the feelings behind those words. And that was when the anger I harbored toward him all these years lifted. It was replaced with the one thing I never expected, and the one thing he was completely incapable of giving: empathy. My heart went out to a man without one.

That's when I thought—although it's terrible to say and perhaps wrong of me—it was so much better to be his victims than to be him. You both have hearts you need to protect from burden. You both have pain you need to banish to survive. But you are so much more than that miserable man can ever be.

Now, of course, as Tim has cautioned, I've become a source of great trouble for both of you. I've asked and even begged you to re-experience a time in your lives that you want left behind. I've commanded and asserted that only when you dissect, only when you see how you both continue to relive the past through your addictions or avoidance measures, will you be capable of healing. But why do I say this? Can't it be just as helpful to compartmentalize and lock away the experiences that are too much to handle, so you can feel joy, so you can trust love? Maybe we all don't need to hit the replay button. Maybe we just need to wake up, day after day, ready to experience, as fully as we can, what each new day holds. For each of you, I hope it is promise: great promise. You also have this: my heartfelt, no statutes-of-limitation-tolling goodbye.

For Kurt Wilowski

This is La Capella Majora. It was renovated under the direction of Pope Sixtus, hence, its other name, the Sistine Chapel. Initial artists, including Botticelli, spent three years painting the first frescoes nearest to the altar. The frescoes tell the stories of Moses and Jesus. Upon their completion, Sixtus dedicated the chapel to the Virgin Mary, and the first Mass was said here on her feast day, August 15, 1483, in celebration of her assumption into heaven; that is, if she didn't die, body and all, in Ephesus.

No doubt, it's Michelangelo's work that predominates. He spent four years, from 1508 to 1512, on his back and on his often-mentioned self-designed scaffolding, taking permitted artist's license with his original commission to paint just the twelve apostles. Instead, more than three hundred figures cover the ceiling, many of them in the series of nine paintings showing God's creation of the world, God's relationship with humankind, and the inevitable fall from God's grace, precipitated, Michelangelo might seem to believe, by one woman's defiant act.

It wasn't until 1537, twenty-six years after the ceiling's completion and at the close of the Italian Renaissance, that Michelangelo was recommissioned to paint the walls behind the altar. The subject was Christ's second return, when he takes the good, on his right side, to heaven, and casts the sinners, to his left, to hell. With exposed genitalia, both female and male, Michelangelo had no problem depicting brute human nature. However, after the Council of Trent criticized nudity in public art, let alone a chapel, the Church commissioned Tuscan-born artist Da Volterra to cover all exposed genitalia in loincloths and to repaint Saint Catherine and Saint Blaize so it wouldn't look like the two were about to have sex.

That this is called the pope's private chapel is one thing, but how he might have a minute alone here is hard to believe, especially when we pilgrims take over the place. In name, this chapel functions as the entire papal household's place of worship. This group includes a cast of potential sinners for Michelangelo's attention, the almoner, the secretary for relations with states, the chaplains of "His Holiness," the general counselor for Vatican City, and the equivalent of the pope's men-in-waiting. Pope Benedict is said to still officiate Mass here. In November 2009, he invited five hundred artists to this room to discuss how art might bring us closer to God. More than half the invitees declined.

I will wrongly believe the next time this room will be put to use for a papal conclave will be upon the news of Pope Benedict's death. It's too soon to know how Father B.'s last offering to me, the appointment of a Jesuit as pope, will fare in bringing about my return. But I will correctly surmise, at some future time, the smoke will rise from here, in either black or white, to tell us whether or not we have a pope. *Habemus papam.* Is it wrong to have wanted for Benedict's death so we might see him replaced by someone with actual sympathy for victims? Who doesn't think we are out to steal Church wealth or to wrongly disparage the Church's name?

Strangely, though I'm surprised by the absence of these thoughts, for they are not my sentiments upon stepping into the Sistine Chapel. We shuffle in, me and the five hundred people who join me this hour, and find our place within the crowd. We gawk, looking from guidebook to hand of God, back to guidebook, then in search of Botticelli's Moses. And where is Michelangelo's portrait of himself among the damned? He's right to consider himself like the rest of us: flawed. The crowd hums as friends and strangers begin to talk. I make out a few words, *meraviglioso, einzigartige,* and *fantastico.* Once our combined utterances reach a certain decibel, however, one of the eight security guards who patrols the room claps and yells, "*Silencio!*" We are being reminded. "We are in a church!"

I need no reminder. I walk to the altar, fall to my knees, raise the photo of

Tim and me, and begin to recite my inscribed words, "May the long-time sun shine upon you . . ."

ॐ

Dear Kurt,

It wasn't until I wrote Tim's name, then Charlie's, and then Greg's that my pen stopped. Shall I add you, because, I then realized, he never denied you? He asked for a refresher course on how, exactly, he defiled Tim and disputed my father's assertion he was in league with the devil, but not once did I receive his surprise or derision that he might somehow be responsible for a boy's death?

Recognition by omission, dear Kurt?. Is that enough? Perhaps so, especially when combined with Mrs. Sprague's and Father Edison's observances of the car, the speed, and the no reason for you to die. Just in case, please forgive this indulgence. If you were never in harm's way, know that it is only out of love that I connect with those who were. And if you were, I'm sorry, so very sorry, you felt so alone. Let me speak out for your grief. Let me add you in remembrance.

Some things you need to know. I never knew you, but I know, from one sister, your younger brother still thinks often of you. Your parents established a scholarship in your name at your old high school. Your mom said it was because it felt like home to you, and, because of that, you are still there for her. She added that you always brought out the best in her.

For the boys I do not know

From the roof of Saint's Peter's, along the spiraling staircase to the top of the cupola, over Saint Peter's Square, and then upon it, with my mother's image of John Paul II, and then without it, I call out their names. "For Timothy Nockels, for Charlie Tierney, for Greg Conrad, for Kurt Wilowski, and for the boys I do not know," I sing the words of an old Celtic song my Irish charmer mother once taught me.

I'm not loud. Most times, I speak in a whisper, not wanting to draw undue attention to myself, especially from the *"Silencio"* guards. I also have no intention of impacting the visits of any member of this traveling throng. If they are here in pilgrimage, I will be their good pilgrim. If it is only the antiquities that delight, nothing about me will get in their collective antiquity ways. But to come so close, and not speak in remembrance?

It's not that any of them, especially the men I don't know, need me to do so. Except for Tim, they've lived their entire lives without me. Judging by Charlie's and Greg's experience, they're likely better off for doing so as well. But, if the few are to be remembered, so must the all. I bow and ask God to give them His eternal good company.

For Joan Nockels Wilson

"Describe one of the happiest moments of your life," Marsha suggested in the counseling session I've skipped over recounting, the one that took place the week prior to my burn-down-the-Vietnam-village phone call with Tim.

I didn't hesitate. "That would have to be the moment we adopted Abbie."

"No, I want you to go back further than that, to a time in your life when the world didn't count on you for success or responsibility, even great ones like taking care of your daughter. I want you to try to find a moment when you were authentically Joan and none of your managers—the taskmaster, the rescuer, the angry teenager—had to take care of a situation. What can you recall?"

"It was summer, either that or a bright spring day. The sun was streaming in through our dining room window, which was a normally a difficult thing for it to do since the window looked out to a narrow gangway. I'm not sure why, but I was lying on my stomach, under the dining room table of all places. I was flipping through the pages of a book my godmother had given me, a book I really wanted. It was the story of Jonathan Livingston Seagull. And Neil Diamond's soundtrack for the story was playing on the record player. I think that record had been a gift from my godmother as well."

"How old were you?"

"Eight, maybe nine."

"What else do you remember? Close your eyes."

"The images of sea gulls on the pages, lots of seagulls and words that made me feel beautiful. Also Neil Diamond singing." In my mind's eye, I could hear myself singing to the soundtrack, something about dreaming, but when I looked at Marsha again, I could tell it hadn't been out loud.

"Have you read *Jonathan Livingston Seagull* lately?"

"Not since I was a kid."

"What do you remember about the story?"

"All possibility is already within you. You just have to believe it's there first and still your mind from the naysayers."

"What else do you remember about that happy centered moment sitting under the table with your book and your music?"

"I told you about my hair, right? How because I couldn't see well I had no idea how dirty it was."

"You've mentioned it a few times," Marsha made a note. Probably something like, "need to revisit and remove stigma."

"Well, that day, I remember my hair. It was clean and light, and long strands of it were draping onto the pages of my book. When the bright sun hit them, I thought I was looking at gold."

She didn't need to find the metaphor for me, because there I was, feeling the sun turn my hair into something precious and believing that all possibility was already within me.

"This is who shall go to Rome," she said, also not needing any response. We were done here.

❧

Except the story was more than that, I realized, again, after finding another 1973 edition of *Jonathan Livingston Seagull* in a used bookstore shortly before flying to Rome. Jonathan was having problems with his flock. More accurately, he was the bane to it.

> "Jonathan Livingston Seagull," said the Elder, "Stand to Center for Shame in the sight of your fellow gulls!" . . .
> . . . ". . . for his reckless irresponsibility," the solemn voice intoned, "violating the dignity and tradition of the Gull Family . . ."

When given the choice to either atone or pursue a higher purpose for himself, Jonathon sets off alone and toward the sun.

❧

In answer to the question, "Why do we stay Catholic?" Madeleva Society theologians have a common response. Sister Chris Schenck, who has lectured extensively on the silencing of women within the Church, still has confidence, "The institutional church *will* change." Other Madeleva theologians espouse, "This is my church as much as it is Pope Benedict's." "I love it too much to leave it." And, my personal favorite, "I'm here, deal with it."

But I wonder if they ever tire of derision. I wonder why, in the twenty-first century, we are still debating whether women somehow hold less intelligence or virtue or skill to turn bread and wine into the spiritual manifestation of a loving God. And I see I'm getting on my soapbox. In 2011 and well into 2012, the Church spent months preparing the laity, homily after homily, for changes in the Catholic liturgy's wording. The goal, church leaders propounded, was to bring the colloquial American edition of the Roman missal, in place since 1971, closer to the original Latin text. Thus, when peace is wished to us, we must no longer respond "and also with you," but "and with your spirit." Words like "incarnate" and "consubstantial with the Father" are to roll from our tongues during the Nicene Creed. The changes were important and vital, we were consistently reminded week after week because? I could never figure that out. Yet in comparison to this weekly teaching, not more than twice in ten years (including, I must add, from Father B.) have I heard a homily regarding the Church's degradation of its own children. Frankly, I'm not consubstantial with that.

Back before entering the Sistine Chapel, I kept hiding from Penelope. Even if I could have moved quickly forward, I realized I kept my advantage by giving her the lead. So, when she stopped to buy her jigsaw puzzles just past the Raphael tapestries, I made my way to the window in the opposite direction from her.

The lawn and trees of the Belvedere courtyard were below, but it was the pattern on the sun-washed clay-tiled roof across from me that held my attention. All the tiles seemed braided together in a thick rope I might be able to grab. After a few minutes lost in nothingness, I turned to check on Penelope's progress. She was at the cashier's desk and close to closing the deal, but then she must've requested something else because the saleswoman left her to look through a row of books. In a little while, she handed Penelope two of them for inspection. I had to admit, the thought of Penelope buying a Pontifical Commission—endorsed keepsake was throwing me off balance. She couldn't have an interest in religious art. So what was it? The Antiquities? A history of the Etruscans? What was she buying?

That's when it must've landed, the glaucous-winged gull. When I turned to look at the roof again, he was standing motionless on a pile of rounded rocks, just outside the windowsill. Grass seedlings peeked out between his long yellow toes. Except for the plate glass window between us, the tomato-red dot on his beak's bottom mandible was close enough to touch. As long as he would allow, I watched him. And then, as if he had no more to foretell, he flew away, toward the sun, I suppose.

Your forgotten children, no longer in need

When Tim was four years old, he went missing. My mother wasn't sure how she could've lost him. Except for Dad, who was at the firehouse, we were all home together in the morning. There was no school and no other place to be or go. She could only think that he slipped out the front door while she was upstairs feeding the baby, this time, Joycie. After fifteen minutes of nonstop calling for Tim, after checking at neighbors', and along the curbside for one "don't let it be true" curled body, she called the Crystal Lake Police.

Even in 1970, long before the days of Amber alerts or even parents walking their kindergarteners to school, the squad car arrived at our house quickly. I hid behind my mother when she opened our dark-cherry-red front door to a tall man dressed in light brown and wearing a hat that looked like Smokey Bear's.

"May I come inside," the patrol officer asked, "and take a look around?" Mom and I stepped back like we were one body. When the officer's police radio spoke, I grabbed her right leg tighter. He took off his hat and placed it on the small octagonal side table we kept next to our living room couch. At the time I remember it was the big tall man with a scary-looking crew cut in our house that frightened me more than Tim's disappearance. Despite my devotion to this one little brother, I was at the remarkable age where bad things hadn't yet happened, firemen always came home and death hadn't vanquished anyone I knew. Heck, even the birds that hit our living room windows or the salamanders running dry in basement window wells could be breathed or moistened back to life.

The officer inspected each room of our house for another ten minutes, rechecking the spots Mom said she had certainly searched. Except for this: well under the double bed in the guestroom off our downstairs den, in the same place where Cha once hid her newborn kittens, the officer found one small boy, sleeping.

The officer joked how no words could rouse Tim from his slumber. He only began to wake when the officer pulled him out from under the box spring by one of the small boy's gym shoes.

The last thing I distinctly remember was this. Only when her boy was back in her arms again did my mother's tears unleash. Her fingers pawed at his eyes and her soft, rapid kisses washed over his cheeks. "He was lost and is found," she might have even said. And so, like the prodigal son and his father, they began to celebrate.

ঽৣ

That's been the problem for the ten past years. But for changes I can never see coming in the Church or, frankly, in me, in my lifetime, reunion between us seems impossible. Celebration is a moot point.

We hold more power and love than you will ever know

It's 5:45 in the afternoon and Mass, the last service of the day, is about to start. By this time, I had already stood in black shoes and dusted dirty socks on the porphyry circle where Charlemagne was once crowned king. I'd seen Michelangelo's *pieta*, kissed Saint Peter's toe, searched for the story of a Barberini childbirth on Bernini's spiraling *baldacchino*. I had inspected the Door of Good and Evil and its neighbor, the Door of Death. I looked into human-sized angels' eyes and stood awestruck as white rays of light moved over the S. PETRI GLORIA inscription on the edge of the Michelangelo-designed interior dome.

I was pilgrim and tourist, expeditioner and critic. Pope Sixtus left his name here, inscribed just as large as the words, "In glory to Saint Peter." That's some manifestation of self-importance. But most of all, and yet again, I was stalker.

I asked this question: "Where could I leave us?" This photo of Tim and me, with Charlie's, Greg's, and Kurt's names written upon it. Could I attach us with votive candle wax to an interior fold of the maroon velvet cloth that cordoned off church seating? Or perhaps, could I slip us under the statue of Saint Veronica's raised toes.

I could conceal us, I supposed, straight and thin into the crease of some wall where wood met marble or a painting of a crucified Saint Peter. Or we could become mosaic. I could fold and crimp us into the size of a single tesserae tile and make us, like my once gleaming hair, the color of gold. For two hours it seemed, I pondered and searched, wondering how to keep us undiscoverable.

I wanted Tim, the boys I knew, those I didn't, and me to stay here in Saint Peter's. Granted we would be just as silent as all the dead pontiffs' tombs, but, absent official shrine, we could be our own memorial, our own wailing wall, bearing witness. And if anyone asked for directions, I could tell them the tale of how to find the forgotten. Such as this, "look for Canovas's statue of the winged angel grieving. A headband circles her long wavy hair and a silk cloth is folded around the wrist that leans against her cheek. Face the direction she faces and, next, "turn right" or "left" or "back" or "look down." "Take twenty paces," "thirty," "forty," "two." "Look there. Do you see us?" "In the folds," "in the corners," "in the mosaic." "This is where you shall find us. And when you do, say a silent prayer."

Once victims of John Baptist Ormechea, cp, child predator,

After announcing myself as *peregrine*, "pilgrim," and not *turista*, to the *gendarmerie*, who, in their blue-and-gold-striped ties, just like Matthew's, have let me through a roped barricade, I'm sitting in the seventh row back from the altar. In front of me a woman with a bald spot and gold hoop earrings wears her gray sweater inside out. The organist starts to play something rich in drama, like the opening to *The Phantom of the Opera*, but more churchlike, like "O Holy Night," except it's not Christmassy, not even close. Before a tenor voice accompanies the rich, diminished minor chords, a high sad crucifix passes, carried in the hands of one altar boy. The near-death Jesus pauses at the center aisle's obsidian circle. When a small, tanned, sixtyish priest in white vestments reaches the stalled crucifix, the procession of two altar boys and one additional concelebrant, all male, of course, moves forward. They cross a clay-colored, octagonal floor detail, walk up two small steps between long, unused communion bars, and reach the altar. It's Bernini's Altar of the Chair, which, legend says, enshrines a small wooden stool that once belonged to Saint Peter.

I've listed my reasons and joined my causes, one fragment of outrage to the other, a treasure chest of wrongdoings to ultimate remedies that cannot be made right, at least in my lifetime, to the point where there can be no dispute. I've decided my own course and wrote my own walking papers.

And, therefore, *Dear Ladies and Gentlemen of the Jury,*

[say it again, slowly, quietly]

Dear Ladies and Gentlemen of the Jury,

Why, standing here, do I tremor? I can't logically understand my own reaction.

"When was this ever about logic?" either Father B. or the poetry book in my prosecutor desk drawer responds.

"Nel nome del Padre, e del Figlio, e dello Spirito Santo," the high priest with frameless eyeglasses welcomes in a soft caressing voice, and I feel like I did the first day I walked to St. Peter's Square, drawn into those fishing nets and not away from them. I feel like I'm home. I cry and by that I mean brush dewdrop-sized tears flowing from my still wetting eyes. I'm overreacting, I know,

perhaps just to the idea of attending Mass here in Saint Peter's, this ultimate spiritual home of all Catholics, but I'm also in some kind of fight, flight, or freeze mode where my centered, this-person-shall-go-to-Rome self, dear Marsha, is not engaged.

Here's what concerns me. Despite difficult experience, despite the molestation of my brother, I *want* to find solace here and be part of this crowd of easy believers. I *want* it to not matter to me if my sweater is on backward, or if it does, to have it be my largest concern.

"*La grazia del Signore nostro Gesù Cristo, l'amore di Dio Padre, e la comunione dello Spirito Santo sia con tutti voi,*" the priest says. And before I respond, "And also with you, I mean with your spirit," I pray. I beg, "Dear Lord, have pity on me. Allow me to have the courage to stay and follow all the living examples I have before me; those, like the Madeleva scholars, who recognize they receive much more from this Church than what it takes. Please Father, give me more."

"Our actions reveal our faith or lack of faith."

And just as that prayer passes, I'm brought again to a different recognition. "What you are in love with are its people and not its policies." Perhaps it's the photo still in my hand that's said so. "Don't confuse the two," it adds.

"Our inner expectations reveal our hope or lack of hope."

All is going way too quickly. The *Kyrie*s and *Gloria*s are soon over and the Liturgy of the Word starts. I even Google translate the Gospel, the Book of John, chapter six, verses fifty-two to fifty-nine, to look for a sign. In it, Jesus says, "Those who eat my flesh and drink my blood abide in me, and I in them. Just as the living Father sent me and I live because of the Father, so whoever eats me will live because of me."

Is it one? A sign to go? Because beyond my own personal commitment that I'm just as deserving of the Eucharist as any other sinner, this Church won't officially let me take Communion. And here comes the anger, the indignation, the righteousness.

"*Calm down, Joan.*" I right myself from these uneven moorings and return to solid, slow breaths. There, I let each word of the homily wash over me, as if they were sent for my personal well-being. *Tutti, momiento del cuerpo, del uni, del regalo.* List them before they fall away. *Andale el miso, sacramente la Christo, frequente, domenica.* Words I take as an offering. *Pan, il frutti, siempre, la futura, commune con Cristo.* "The Eucharist," I should have thought to say to Ormechea, "is a two-thousand-year-old remembrance." *Lo unitare, lo spirito, uni state de grazie.* "We are united, united in spirit," I translate. But can this be enough?

I haven't forgotten Tim. I've raised our image at least twice and muttered my protestation so softly, not even the inside-out sweater lady heard. "I've brought you here, brother. I've said in my own small way, your story matters." And when I rise for Communion, the Communion I'm not supposed to have, but take, willingly, I carry you in my hands. We bow before acceptance, right under the yellowing light issuing from Bernini's alabaster dove. And before I raise the bread to my lips, don't tell anyone, I lower it to yours.

"The body of Christ, we are."

Kneeling back at my pew, it's an unexpected father, not God or Father B., who comes to still me. "Choose a direction," Dad says, "even if it's the wrong one. It's the standing still that will kill you." I audibly laugh and, I'm not kidding, the sweater lady hushes me. Our Mass has five minutes to go.

"Reimagine what it means to be a full human being made in the image of God, and to live and speak this truth in our daily lives," the Madeleva scholars have said to women like me, those in despair over the current state of a Church we've, despite its faults, somehow grown to love. They ask us to stay and, like my long-ago patron, to join them in battle. "Look," they might add, "the Church that burned Jeanne d'Arc has made her a saint. Once persecuted, Galileo is redeemed. To those who lost their way, including its Renaissance popes, it offers derision, and to Luther and the Holocaust Jews it didn't protect, it now apologizes." But as someone who has spent years nailing top grades, *magna cum laudes*, prestigious jobs, and, hell, even Boston Marathon qualifying times to prove that I matter, I still have to ask, "At what cost? And aren't I worth more than sorrow and battle wounds? Must I forever hold my breath over what a diocesan priest may say next? And, by staying, aren't the odds just as good that I'll be just as defeated as the bevy of women who reached out to Father Sebastian, but never once thought to call the police? Aren't I smarter than that? Shouldn't I be?"

"Il Signore sia con voi," the priest announces. "The Lord be with you."

"And with your spirit," I say, the one time I can remember.

❧

A tear, and by that I mean not a cry, but a rip, a fear, a prayer, a slash, a song.

Once, as one seagull named Jonathan flew too high toward the sun, Neil Diamond sang about a page that needed a word to speak for everything that joins us. If there is such a page that needs such a word, it is this one, the page right in front of me. But it can't find that union, not anymore. I finally know without waver, my word is goodbye. There is no more to give; and it can't have her.

Dear Abbie,

The night before you joined our family, the moon went into a total eclipse for the first time on a northern winter's solstice since 1638. Three hundred eighty-four years ago. Can you even imagine that? Probably not, since we're still working on counting past fifty-nine. Then, Rembrandt and Rubens were still in their prime. The great Shakespearean tragedies, *Hamlet*, *Macbeth*, *King Lear*, were a little over forty years old. The steam turbine was a new invention.

Between then and today, generation after generation of people have celebrated Christmas, Hanukkah, or Ramadan, lost loved ones, invited births, and made their way, day by day, year by year, hurt by hurt . . . When you were adopted, December 21, 2010, our earth turned back toward the sun, and so did I.

Since that day, my life has turned, opened, redirected, found new meaning, and gone through every thing and cliché you can imagine. Ah, yet another cliché. How could it have not? I know, when you grow up, your plan is to be a dragon. You've already instructed me to stop pretending to eat ice cream and instead to pretend I'm not on a diet. And according to you, I should never be sad to know someone I love is in heaven. In fact, you've said when you were in heaven resting on a cloud, you waited and waited for a mommy whose name started with a "J." I thank you for that, and, although I believe your standards should've been higher, I'm abundantly glad I qualified.

But here's the thing; actually one of the thousands of things that worry me now that I am your mother (one additional worry—when I write that I sound like mine). I ask myself how do I bring you to God, at least until the time when you can make up your own mind about a higher being. Despite all this travail (I'll fill you in later), I can tell you this. I was brought to God by the Catholic Church. I sat in its pews, rose and kneeled, kneeled and rose again. I listened to the Gospel and found Jesus to be, most of the time, an amazing person. That's right, not to deny the Trinity, but it was Jesus's humanity that kept me spellbound: his ruthless honesty, his justified anger, his friendships with the scorned, and his love of telling stories. More important, I wanted to become his friend.

That friendship still required sustenance and example. I met Jesus again through my mother saying her rosary, my father seeking a living penance, my aunt grateful for her pain, even a priest who taught me to feed the good dog and not the evil one.

I can list its failures: its false hierarchy, its degradation of children, its illogical stance toward women. But without the Church, how do I give you this? Jesus as a friend?

Even though kindergarten is still a year away for you, one way was in the application I've already considered for you to attend St. Elizabeth Ann Seaton's Catholic School. Don't tell anyone, but before I left for Rome, I went to the open house, met your one-day potential teacher, and really liked her. Yet, what I loved most were the things that felt most familiar, like seeing the crucifix on the classroom wall, Mary with her hands raised (she and I still have issues, but she was a good mom), and knowing that you would begin every day in prayer. That felt comforting to me, like I would be giving you a pair of wool socks to keep you warm.

But, darling, the cost of using my route and that of my brother's to make Jesus your friend? The knowledge that in Church eyes you will never be an equal. While I might get you qualified for Communion, so you may choose a community with Jesus on your terms, beyond that, you are too precious to me to sacrifice. So my promise to you is this. I'll find another way. Until then, there is love.

and those who hid him in plain sight.

"You are in my heart, in my heart, in my heart." I repeat to Jesus, after Mass has ended. I'm on my knees, right where I belong. "Not in my pocket, and I will beg like a leper. I promise. I will ask, hope, and expect great goodness from you." I know that something beyond me is happening when I add, "Father, there's one last thing; pray for him to have the gift of understanding." It's highly unlikely I'll ever forgive Ormechea for all he has done and even continues to do, but there is at least this, a little step, a prayer with his name on it that doesn't involve Hell.

If there's anything I can say thank you for that's sprung from my forty-seven years of being a Catholic, minus two as an atheist, it's that this church has been my window to the light, and I wouldn't have had that light available to me without it. Today, as if in metaphor, the sun behind Bernini's dove is everything I once imagined. It's glorious and transcendent, quieting and peaceful. And, I just noticed, it's the outstretched hand of a young girl that comes closest of all the gilded figures surrounding the dove to reaching it. "A champion she is," I think, "even if she comes up short." But I have a pretty good feeling about this. That light and dove are coming directly toward her.

I finally rise and turn to leave. The open door to the portico is visible, although it's two football fields full of church away. Yet, despite efforts of the *gendarmerie* to empty the basilica before its 7:00 p.m. closure (*"in questo modo si prega di signora,"* "this way please, madame," they say), I saunter. I touch everything they let me: communion banisters, gold crosses across crypts, and wings of curly headed baby angels with dimpled arms and thighs I equally want to squeeze, softly and kindly, as if rubbing my old dog's ears. I reach with each rounded and spread toe through my too-thin Tevas and toward the smoothness of marble underfoot. I feel the cool of ancient columns against my ears.

"Mi scusi, per favore," the guard's arm points to the open door. It's from here, just shy of the portico, that I raise my brother's and my image one last time. I take out my mother's copy of the *Catholic New World* as well and add her image of John Paul II to the blessing or, shall I also say, protest.

May the long-time sun shine upon you, all love surround you. And the pure light within you guide your way on. For Timothy Nockels, for Charlie Tierney, for Greg Conrad, for Kurt Wilowski, for all the boys I do not know, and for Joan Nockels Wilson. We hold more power and love than you will ever know. Once victims of John Baptist Ormechea, cp, child predator, and those who hid him in plain sight.

The light from the nearest open archway to Saint Peter's Square provides a Halloween glow to Giotta's *Navicella*, a gold-and-blue mosaic in the roofed portico that captures the moment Saint Peter decided to get out of the boat. Seconds later, when Peter noticed a strong wind and began to fear for his safety, Jesus would both hold him up and admonish, "You of little faith, why did you doubt?"

Despite the chastising, I'm hoping this will be the story for me. I hope that from today to my last there will be twenty times twenty moments when I at least have the courage to get out of the boat, and, even if I can't make it to shore alone, I hope I have enough faith to know this: I will be held up.

Outside, the sun hangs low in an early evening's sky and I know from several vantage points, orange fields, rose gardens, piazzas, and even key holes, the pilgrim and the poet, the protester and the purist look west, waiting for the highest copula on the horizon to shine. Whether that's still my hope for the religion that calls this place home? That it will, perhaps for the first time ever, shine? Of course it is. As a Madeleva scholar has said, "This is my church as much as it is any pope's." But, for the time being, I'll have to watch from the distance. The view from even there, I know, can be quite compelling.

❧

There is one last thing. Before slipping the photo of Tim and me back into its protective, plastic case, I pondered my ability to hide us in the portico, perhaps in the high statue of Justice's—*Aequitas's*—scale or in Faith's—*Sola Fide's*—defiantly raised chalice. Both women, I love that, but there was no turning back from what had been my final decision. The surveillance cameras are too numerous. The cleaning crews must know every place to look, each scale and chalice to scour. They must sweep and peel, scrape and examine all centimeters of their protected, sacred ground. And when found, this silent act of protest on the back of a photo that holds my brother's visage? There could be only one expected consequence. We would be examined, and then swept, peeled, and scraped away with the rest of their garbage. To my brother, I promised him this: never again.

I'll be taking with me all that is mine.

PURE SOUL

August 10, 2012

"Take the Blue Line to Addison."

"I know, Ma." I'm sitting in Dad's high back chair in the living room. "Not everything's changed since I moved away, you know. I know how to get to Wrigley."

"Well how about this? You don't need a transfer slip anymore, just a CTA card. Take mine. I get a senior discount anyway." With a summer tan and even just a little more weight on her frame, she looks healthier since the last time I saw her, just before Rome, a few months ago. She's wearing the new light green shirt Joycie got her for her eightieth birthday, which we just celebrated four days ago, in combination with Abbie's fourth.

"That's okay, I bought one at O'Hare," I point over to Julie who is on the couch across from me putting on makeup. Abbie's helping her by holding the compact mirror at just the right angle. "It's got enough on it to get the three of us to the game, maybe not back, but we'll take care of that later, especially since we need to catch the plane home tonight."

"The game starts in two hours," Ma says.

"I know."

"So when you get off at Addison, take the stairs, not the escalator, they're faster." Something dawns on her. Her palm is to her forehead. "But what am I thinking? It won't matter because the 152 bus will be too full to get a seat anyway." Mom looks at my sister, "You might as well drive, Julie. If there's no room to park at the firehouse, you'll have to pay, but that's better than a crowded bus in August, especially in this heat with Abbie."

"Grandma? Are we going to see baby bears?" Abbie·asks. Frosting from the chocolate donut Mom bought for her at Oven Fresh, on the way home from morning Mass, is still in the corners of my girl's mouth. I'll have to take care of that.

Mom and Julie audibly gasp.

"Jeez Joan!" Julie says as her mascara applicator hits the carpet, "*What* are you doing to my goddaughter?"

"I've already explained this to her a couple of times."

"Well, not very well," Julie shakes her head and turns to Abbie. "Abbie, the Cubs are people."

"Do you know how crazy that sounds?" The Diet Pepsi I just drank goes up my nose.

"The Cubs are people," my little girl repeats with a mysterious look on her face. This is a strange concept for an Alaskan four-year-old.

I chime in, "Well, remember when you woke up, I told you we were going to meet Uncle Tim at a baseball game?"

"Yeah?"

"The people play baseball. They're on a team called the Cubs. They're Mommy's favorites."

"Oh, well, Julie," Abbie says, "Mom told me they play baseball, but I didn't remember."

"You forgot?"

"Yeah. They play baseball." We've got her dressed in a shirt with smiley faces, hearts, and stars. It matches her teal shorts, the closest color I have for her to Cubbie blue. I've borrowed one of Julie's Cubs shirts. It reads, "1908 World Series Champions."

By the look on Julie's face, I see she intends to test the sufficiency of my explanation. "Abbie," she turns her toward herself, "do you know what baseball is?"

Abbie pauses a beat too long and looks my way. I turn my head to the open front door. No one, especially not long-gone Bucky, is coming in for the rescue. Abbie finally asks, "What's baseball, Aunt Julie?"

Now Dad, who's making his way from his bedroom to the living room couch with his walker, gets into the mix. He's dressed in his new pink polo shirt, the one that Mom bought him for the party, and a nice pair of shorts. He looks happy too. "Joannie," he lisps, "she doesn't even know what baseball is?"

"No, but she knows what an Arctic Cat is and how to club a halibut." They all ignore me and focus attention jointly on their pupil.

"Abbie, come here. Grandpa has something to tell you." Once he's sitting, she leans against his knee, just as I once did with my grandfather. Mom hands Dad his bridge, which he puts it in, before saying, "Abbie, baseball is a sport." His *s's* come out perfectly now.

"What's a sport? What's that?"

"For Christ's sake?"

"Crying out loud."

"Joan!"

The three of them have it in for me just like Gaston and the townspeople do for the Beast—*Beauty and the Beast* being my point of reference lately. I wish I had my phone out to record this. I need evidence of this prosecution.

"A sport means it's athletic," Dad offers up.

"Like the Olympics," Julie says.

"Hmmm . . ." *Uh-oh.* "What's Olympics?"

And, again, an eagle-eye descends.

"We don't have live TV, Jules." If there's any ground for excommunication from the Nockels, it's this: no TV. I look to Abbie. "Athletics is like when you and I go running at the track."

"Oh."

Julie takes over. "In baseball, there's a ball, there's a bat, and then there are gloves."

"You are losing her at the gloves," my voice rises. "She's thinking either princess outfits or playing outside in the winter." Despite the Diet Pepsi I have on the side table, Mom hands me a cup of the Starbucks and pretends to thud a finger into my temple for my poor schooling of my daughter in important matters. I laugh and squeeze her hand before she makes her way to Abbie's mouth with a clean, wet washcloth.

Julie continues. "So you throw the ball, you hit the ball, and you catch the ball?"

"And you run around the bases," Mom says.

"And you run around the bases!" Julie repeats. Each hold and move their arms quickly, mimicking running. Except for the forty-year age difference between them, they're practically Mary Martin twins.

"Oh, so we're going to watch baseball," Abbie concludes, facing her judges.

"Yes!" Dad responds, once again in relief.

"Well, do they put on costumes, like the bad man? Mommy took his mask, you know."

And again I'm faced with three stares. "I know, I know, I say too much."

"Stop it, for her sake," Mom pleads.

"I will." It's not a false promise, but one I'll break time and time again.

Julie takes on Abbie's question. "Yes, they put on their blue, pinstriped Cubbie uniforms."

"Oh, like unicorns; I'm going to be one for Halloween."

"Joan Mary," Mom says, announcing the conversation's end. She's handing Julie her keys and the "Go Cubs Go" poster Julie had made for the last game she attended. "It's time for you all to go. Take Peterson to Clark. It'll be faster."

ঐ

"It's one thirty. Where did you tell him to meet us?" I ask Julie. "The game's already started." My taskmaster is out, I can tell. She hates being late.

"It's the end that matters with the Cubs, never the beginning," Julie says. "I told him to meet us by the bleacher entrance, by the Harry Caray statue. A one . . . a two . . . a Abbie! Get back here! Jeez! She keeps following Mister Cubbie Bear!" By that she means the man dressed in a bear costume. He's also wearing a blue Cubs jersey and batting helmet.

Abbie turns back toward us, waving goodbye to Mr. Cubbie. "I wonder if he's even official," I say. "The beer cooler he's carrying for tips says, 'Be cool. Billy's hot!' You think that's Billy?"

"Or creep-o in a costume?"

"We've seen that before."

And here we go. *Before . . . then After.*

"Does he look the same?"

I know *who* she means. "Pretty much. A little older, better glasses, and no bad combover."

"Does he act the same?"

"I think the answer to that question is no. It was why I didn't go to the police back in Rome. I would've sworn I would've done that. All I had to do was leave them a few newspaper clippings, and they would know I was authentic. But after I figured out he couldn't groom families anymore, I was largely satisfied. I don't know. Do you think I went too easy on him?"

"That's not for me to answer." She switches her eyeglasses out for her sunglasses. "Do you think you went too easy on him?"

This is a question I've asked myself often, especially after my strong, loud voice faltered in the face of his, *"What exactly did I do?"* question. Who knows. Maybe some sick part of him wanted me to describe his sexual acts, to remind him of the excitement that once filled his groin, and to let him linger over that long-ago contact. But it's my fear I remember, not whether his eyes lit up like they used to when young boys were around. I've been both punishing and then justifying myself ever since. Still, the answer I'm about to give Julie is the truth.

"Well, there are many days I think I should've been more forceful with him and not let him hide behind this idea that he couldn't speak. But then, it wasn't his words that mattered. I got the most out of him when he thought he wasn't saying anything. On the days that I remember this, I feel pretty good. I'll feel even better when I send him an autographed copy of my book."

"He's gonna kill you!" Her voice gets sing-songy, in that Johnny Cammareri tone.

"It'd be one way to finally get him in prison."

"Joan!"

"I'm joking. I came home for Abbie. No one's taking me from her."

"You know Dad's told everyone what you did?"

"He doesn't get out much anymore. Who could he have told?"

"He sits on the front porch like he's king of the neighborhood. So he's told the Branders, the Antkoviaks, the Stantons, and the guy across the street who works for the Secret Service."

"Did he also happen to mention to him that I love the president? I don't want that guy thinking there's a cyber stalker across the street."

"Not sure it came up. Anyway, word's spread since then. Joan Troka knows. Mrs. Tierney does too. He's just proud of you. Let him be."

I don't tell her what I'm feeling, that this has always been what I wanted, to make Dad proud. And I also don't mention the twenty dollars and the note Mom's slipped into a side pocket of my computer bag, which I don't think she wanted me to find until my plane ride home. It read,

Dear Joan,

I want you to know that we think you are awesome and many other adjectives that one can think of. Never giving up is a great one too. You have a gift and I hope you know it. Enjoy your life with your family and know we are always thinking of you, always and always.

M.O.M.

I also haven't told Mom how, since my return, I've been trying to craft a reverse skill: the ability to forget and get on with it. Ormechea, I would have to admit, might be a little proud as well and think his homily may have worked, because I'm trying to let go of the damn banana.

"Hey Julie," I point down Waveland Avenue to the tallest white guy walking toward us, about fifty yards away. "That can't be him. Can it?"

Julie laughs. "You mean that guy wearing an Oakland A's jersey and ball cap. At least it's not the Cardinals. That is TIMMIE!" She waves wildly and yells loud enough for him to hear and, once he gets close enough, for Abbie to go running. Before I know it, she's swept up in his hands, *PURE SOUL* and all.

Bottom of the First

"It's beautiful from behind centerfield. It looks just like a field of dreams."

"You always loved that movie," Tim says.

"And Kevin Costner," adds Julie.

"No, at the time it was Ray Liotta. I wonder whatever happened to him. Probably drugs. His face changed from his innocent days as Shoeless Joe."

"That's oxymoronic," Julie chortles.

"Yours has too," Tim says at the same time. I know he's referring to the still-embedded creases on my forehead. Our feet are on the bleacher ahead of us. I notice, as if it makes peace for his wardrobe selection, that at least our Vibram soles match.

"Thanks, brother."

"Mommy's old," Abbie adds.

"Thanks, honey. Have a peanut."

Soriano grounds into a fielder's choice. DeJesus scores.

"We're winning!"

"It's one to zero at the bottom of the first, Joan. Don't get ahead of yourself."

"Back to Liotta. What's your proof that he's taking drugs?" Tim asks.

"He just looks different. I rest my case."

"Foul," Julie says.

"Where's Joycie? She'd believe me."

"She's working or she'd be here. Besides, Chicago cops believe everyone's either a murderer, thief, or drug addict," my sister says.

"Then ask Maureen."

"She's too nice. She'd support anything you said," adds Tim.

"So I'm ahead."

"Nope, Julie and I want more proof. You're tied, including your own vote, two to two."

"Can we call Carole?"

"Only after you ask Terri. Sister-cousins can only break full-sibling dead-locks."

"That's not fair. How is she?"

"Carole or Terri?" asks Tim.

"You mean Teresa," Julie says. "That's the name she goes by."

"Terri, I mean Teresa," I say. "I thought you changed your last name and not your first after a divorce. How's she doing?"

Tim looks away and Julie sighs. I take a swig of a newly poured PBR.

"What? Still the divorce? It's been five years."

"She's not digging herself out," says Tim.

"Neither has Dad," Julie adds.

I'm surprised. "He's been good this week. He's got up every day I've been home."

"He's tried a little more, probably so you don't nag him. But, he's sinking too. The two of them are a pair."

"What can I do to help?"

Time for death stare number four from my left and right. Abbie joins in, and, as the closest witness, perhaps she should.

"Wait! Don't answer that! I can't do anything. Can I?"

"Ding, ding, ding!" Julie announces, "We have a winner!"

"No we don't," Tim chimes in as the Bleacher Bums boo. "The Reds just scored; it's two to one."

Beside my grandfather's dress uniform hat and the gathered plaster-of-paris hel-mets stood a miniature of a horse-powered fire wagon, not unlike a stagecoach. A black-and-gold steam-powered water pump filled its berth. A fire chief with raven black hair and mustache sat high on the wagon seat above it. He held tight to long gold slicks of rope linked, in turn, to six black-beauty stallions.

As a young girl, there wasn't a time, on my excursions to my grandfather's shelf, I didn't inevitably reach for that wagon. I ran my fingers along its polished corners and traced the spokes of its fire-engine-red wheels. Imagining how fast the chief must be telling the horses to go, I tested the lines to ensure the pump wouldn't fall and tried to brush away the imaginary water sloshing out of it and onto the chief's back. Then, like Gulliver to a Lilliputian, I traced his nose and mouth and neck and moved next to his shoulders and down to his arms. When I reached his hands, I held them in my own and whispered in a frantic child's voice, "Hurry, man! It's time." The lead horses were next. I wrapped my hands around each of their midsections, kissed the top of their manes, and spoke, again in a soft whisper, "Come on, guys, let's go! We have to get there. The people need us!"

Where *there* was could have been anywhere, but there was one common denominator. People, in all cases, my family, must be in need. For most of my life, only one strong, loud voice propelled me forward, always, toward the flames. Why? That's just what firefighters do. We get up and go. We climb the ladder and step on the roof. We hear of injustice and start calling out against it. We get on the plane. We track the bad man down. We take his mask. It's natural. It's even necessary. Until, of course, we see that we never had a concrete plan with which to begin, not ever.

The truth of the matter is my nine-year-old ghost, the justice warrior, wrong righter, peacemaker, brother's keeper, whoever she was, took on such big roles, roles she was never equipped to handle, for only one reason. She was taught that's what love was for, but somewhere on the journey from childhood to adulthood, she missed the signposts that read, "Proceed Cautiously," "Give no more than you are able," and "Not everything is your fault." So, instead, she jumped. She battled. She used love, the best excuse ever, to try to make situations right. And isn't that worth something? To say, by word and action, she loved?

Bottom of the Sixth

"This is weird."

"What? That Julie volunteered to take Abbie to the gift store? You know she's gonna spoil her. We don't get to see her that often." Tim crossed his feet at his ankles and looked to centerfield.

"No, it's not that. It's that I'm talking to you in person. I feel like I should have a phone."

He laughs.

"But maybe it's no different. I can't see your eyes behind those reflecto-sunglasses of yours."

He takes them off. His eyes still look like Mom's. "Is that better?"

"Much," I pull his whiskers. "I like the goatee. You didn't have it the last time I saw you."

"I started growing it after the downsize."

"How's that going?"

"Not too bad, yet. I'm filling in for a buddy of mine on the floor for the next three weeks. But after that, it's slim. Pit trading is going away, and I'm going away with it."

"Can you do computerized?

"For half the money and that's after the thirty percent pay cut I already took."

I'm getting nervous, "Are you going to lose the house?"

"Not yet."

Scared for him, I turn to concentrate on the game. "How did this happen? Cincinnati eight, Cubs three," I scoff. "This must be why Julie calls them her bad boyfriend."

"And why she hightailed it for the gift shop. She didn't wanna see the slaughter. They've only won one of the last nine games. It's the errors killing them today."

"Castro's up. That's good."

"One of their better hitters, but still less than a .300 average."

"How do you know that, A's fan?"

"Uh . . . it says right there." He points to the scoreboard at third-base side.

"Jerk," I hit him in the arm and keep my hand on his bicep for just a second. He's real. He's here. "Okay this is when he's gonna hit a home run. Right now. Are you ready? This is when he's gonna . . . this is when he's gonna hit a . . . wait. No! That was not a home run. That was a . . . that was a what?"

"They struck him out." It sounds like Tim's whispering.

"They struck him out? Dammit?"

"Yup."

"So why are people applauding? This is Wrigley Field. They should go home if they don't want the Cubs to win."

"Joan, this may be a foreign concept to you, but do you see those people in red? They can actually drive here from Cincinnati."

"Well, if that's the case." I yell. "Hey, people in red! GO HOME!"

"You go home!" a voice yells from behind. I think it's the guy four rows back with the red polo and a lawyer's haircut. And can you believe this? I raise a middle finger. What's happened to me? Cubs fans are supposed to be polite.

"And now you're a troublemaker," Tim scorns.

"Brother, when it comes to protecting my own, when was I not?"

Like Mom and I long ago, Tim and I know we're no longer talking about baseball.

"Hey, I want you to know something," I say. "It took me some time, but I figured it out from your note to Ormechea. When you were talking about the Church's self-prescribed drug..."

"What?"

"You don't believe in God anymore, do you?"

He turns to me and furrows his forehead. He looks apologetic, like he's letting me down. "I'm sorry," he says. "I don't. I think when we die, we just die. And I think when we live, we should make it worthwhile, no holding out for some eternal happily ever after."

"Even if there's no happily ever after," I try to offer, "it doesn't have to mean we're going through this life alone. I tend to think we're not. In my life, I even think I have proof."

"Are you gonna try to change my mind?"

"No. I just feel sad. I hoped you'd feel someone was always on your side, especially when things get bad."

He puts a hand on my knee and says, "I do."

᎒

Top of the Seventh

"Ice cold beer. Get your ice cold beer, here!" The concessioner flips his cooler's lid and calls out his sale. "Beer" and "here" sound as if the Pepperidge Farm man is saying them. I raise two fingers and send over the twenty Mom gave me down the crowded row of patrons, all of whom, I can see, are Cubs fans. And as if there's no reason not to trust, back comes two full sixteen-ounce cups and four singles. I hand a cup and the four singles to Tim.

"Four bucks?" He laughs. "Really, Joan?"

"I can make it more. Things are always tight at home, but I can make it more."

I feel a cool hand on my shoulder. "Joan, I'm scared, but I believe this, I'm gonna be okay."

I turn to the subject of our elephant. "I didn't get him."

"Not in the traditional sense. He's not in jail, and you were right to leave Greg alone, even if you could convince Shauna to prosecute after all this time. It's his decision. Not ours. But you told me J. B.'s life is a joke, he has no power. Unless he's buying a boy on some corner, he's not finding his way into Italian families and getting to their kids. Even those kids in the playground you told me about? I think they're okay too. As long as they're safe, I'm good."

"From where I sit," I make our shoes touch, "it's always been about you." I think to myself, *honey-made.*

"Well, that's got to change too."

He points to Abbie walking by the soda stand and coming our way. She's holding Julie's hand. Between the two of them, they have a new Cubs hat, which is on Abbie's head, a giant "We're Number One" foam finger, a key chain, a bobblehead of Castro, a pink Cubbie bear, and peanuts, hotdogs, nachos, and ice cream. Abbie, I see, is in charge of the ice cream.

"This doesn't mean I'm ever giving up on you. If you ask, I'll answer. But, promise me, if you get afraid, you'll ask."

He doesn't answer.

❧

Seventh inning stretch

"Okay, Chicago, let me hear you! A one, a two, a three," the guest singer, I wish I heard who it was, announces as thirty-eight thousand people sing "Take Me Out to the Ball Game" in a mixture of flat, off-key, and who was that screeching? Oh, I think it was me. After the cheers, I say to Abbie, "You're now official. What do you think of that?" I hand her the certificate I picked up that identifies this as Abbie's first Cubs game.

She looks and then hands it back, not as impressed as I am. "Is it time to go home, Momma?"

"No sweetie, that was just the seventh-inning stretch. We're Cubs fans. We only leave when the game is over."

"What's a stretch?"

Tim jumps in, "It's when I do this to you." He grabs her by the waist, bounces her in the air, but soon stops. "She's feeling pretty sweaty to me, Joan. Abbie, are you getting hot?"

"It's only seventy," Julie says.

"Which is like one hundred to an Alaskan." I feel her stomach and tend to agree with Tim's assessment. "Sweetie, can you answer Uncle Tim?" I ask.

"Yes, I'm hot."

"Maybe we should go."

"Let me try something else," Tim says. "Abbie come with me."

I watch from a distance. After getting a cup of ice, the two make their way to the shade under Wrigley's still hand-changed scoreboard. Julie hands me another beer.

"I should go with them."

"They're fine. Have a drink"

"You're trying to get me drunk?"

"You betcha!"

"Don't say that. It still makes the hairs on the back of my neck go up."

"You have to get over Dad's girlfriend." This is Julie's reference to Sarah Palin.

"I know."

"Okay. Change of subject. If you had a choice of dinner with David DeJesus, Darwin Barney, or Starlin Castro, who would you choose?"

"That's an odd selection."

"No, it's not. Two are on base. Castro's up to bat."

"Is David related to Ivan? He was one of my favorite Cubs."

"To humor you, let's say yes."

"Well, I like Darwin, he sounds evolutionary. And then there's Castro. He sounds so revolutionary, but dang, he just let the grounder slip through his legs. That's a dealbreaker. I'll take David."

"I knew you would."

"How?"

"Nostalgia, baby." Julie raises her hand as if she's going to give me a high five. "You always go back to the old days."

"At least you didn't say good old days."

"Most of the time they were. I think you forget that too." Castro doubles. DeJesus and Rizzo score. "Atta boy! Makes up for your error. Eight to six. Now we're getting somewhere," Julie adds, but I respond to her last point.

"I know it seems that way a lot of times, but really Julie, I remember more."

??

List them before they fall away. We were the children of Clarence, Palatine, and

Hartzell Avenues, of firefighters and police officers, sanitation workers, painters, plumbers, and carpenters. Our houses carried names like Cape Cod and Tudor, nothing befitting our immigrant roots, for we were the children of the rougher class, the Irish, the Polish, the Italians, and the Germans. Children of parents who loved us, but, please forgive them, who also sought the last bastion of Chicago neighborhoods free of others who didn't look like us.

One-car garages were in the alleys, and we jumped from their rooftops into backyard, aboveground pools just four feet deep. *"Be careful or you're going to break your neck,"* a mother would cry. Once safely in, we made whirlpools and called Marco Polo until the ice cream truck summoned us to Good Humor.

I remember, Julie. We played Red Rover. *Let Mollie Come Over.* We kicked dodge balls in alleys and ran from front doors in unending games of ding-dong ditch. On warm evenings, we gathered on front porches. Inevitably, it seemed, Dad joined us, guitar in hand, and we sang.

Night came. The stars rose. And so did our voices. God listened to us. We were certain of this. I remember.

❧

Our last chance
From the poet's desk: "Analysis of Baseball" by May Swenson

> It's about
> the ball,
> the bat,
> the mitts,
> the bases,
> and the fans.
> It's done
> on a diamond
> and for fun.
> It's about
> home, and it's
> about run.

It's the bottom of the ninth. Our rally caps are on. Tim taught Abbie what a rally cap was. The two runs the Cubs got in the eighth brought us close to a tie, but with a Cincinnati score in the top of the ninth, we're still two runs behind. It's Cincinnati ten, Cubs eight.

"Hey, hey, what you say? The Cubs are gonna win today!" Someone tries to start a rallying cry. I know I should join in and that my focus should be upon Soriano, Castro, and Vitters, who are the next at-bats, but the game between Tim and Abbie, who are back in the stands with us, a cooler Abbie now in my presence, is more interesting. Tim's reaching a finger into Abbie's stockpile of shelled peanuts and pretending to take her collection from her. The game expands until every nut is covered under Tim's *PURE* tattooed and literal hand. Abbie has no idea until he lets her see just where they all have gone. She laughs and pokes Tim in his belly. He laughs and it sounds just as I remember. "Like a spring of fresh water in the desert."

❧

We Nockels are hangers-on, never quitting in our allegiance to our team. We wait for that final out in the bottom of the ninth and cheer on our boys, our oh-so-bad boyfriends. Despite five errors, count them, five, in one game and, now, nine losses in ten, we still cheer, "That's okay, guys, we'll get 'em tomorrow." We believe in them. They're family.

The four of us—Tim, Julie, Abbie, and me—make our way out the way we came in, down the spiraled ramp to the Harry Caray statue exit from the stadium. We walk together under Waveland Avenue's arching trees and then turn west to walk down Addison. I turn to take a photo of Wrigley's famous red marquee. It says, HUNT'S: OFFICIAL KETCHUP OF THE CHICAGO CUBS. It's at Racine Avenue that I embrace Tim and ask him to give the boys a hug from me. To this day, it's never a kiss for them. I say my goodbye, and bless him, again and again in my mind. Abbie, I see, holds on to him even longer than I do.

It's here at Racine that he crosses to the south side of Addison to get to his car. With Abbie, Jule, and I on the north side of Addison, we all still walk together westward, although with two lanes of cars between us. We each wait for the light to turn green at Magnolia. As we stand on the shaded side of the street, Abbie looks across it and says, as if his face were a surprise, "Look, Mommy! It's Timmie, my favorite uncle."

When I look up, I see Tim has changed his mind. Rather than cross Magnolia along with us, his back turns, and he walks south down Magnolia instead. And this, I swear. He's taller and straighter than any of those around him. Only on him does the late afternoon sun seem to shine.

I think of what Tim wrote on the last February 1st anniversary, "I made it, Uncle Dan . . . I know you're proud of me."

And just like that, the Blue Line passes, fades away really, no longer seeking division. Although we part, we both know this. Our hands won't slip, and we'll never let each other go.

EPILOGUE

Late October, 2012

The autumn following my return from Rome, the Chinook winds revisited Bear Valley even earlier than they had the year before. More surprisingly, the snow beat them. Richard and I weren't ready. Before the close of September, seven inches piled up on the roof of our house, shed, and chicken coop, well before any of them had been winterized or garden hoses put away or tires changed over.

Cletus loved it.

"That's right, old boy," I remember saying to him on a recent Saturday morning after opening the front door for him to go outside. "We get another winter together." At least part of one, I thought. I watched as he rubbed his tired back into the coolness, and when he returned, the snowflakes that lingered on his muzzle and ruff melted at my touch. Clete had seen me through everything: the end of a starter marriage and then the beginning and decade-long hard work of a real one; the mourning for five lost embryos and the celebration for one found child; and, finally, the Blue Line call from a brother and the visits to Rome and Chicago that brought us closer to whatever we have now. Peace? Such a strong word that's not really fitting. Acceptance? That might be better.

As I've said, I named him Cletus so he would remind me that whatever strong, loud voice I knew my grandfather had, I had as well. It's why I believe that in the early hours of Sunday October 14th, when my dog's stomach twisted and with his body so ravaged surgery would be difficult, that maybe both my dog and my grandfather thought I no longer required the reminder.

At 2:45 a.m., after Clete's heart took longer than usual in most cases of euthanasia to stop beating, and I had sung his soul to the long-time sun and lavished his neck in tears and kisses, and Melissa, his vet at the twenty-four-hour clinic, asked what should be done with his body, that I answered, holder-on as I am, "I'll take him with me. It's the only place he belongs."

Later that morning, with Richard and Abbie laughing about a made-up game in our master bedroom, I poured myself a cup of coffee and walked to a living room shelf. It held Clete's framed photo. It was summer in the picture. A long, tall stick of birch tree was between my dog's front paws. The bigger, the better had always been his choice. There hadn't been a day on long, narrow trails when I didn't have to jump out of his way to avoid being thwacked by whatever tree monstrosity was in his grip. Clete's head was high as usual too. Those brilliant brown eyes of his looked right into the camera and had come out without one stroke of flash. He looked real. Unlike what waited for me in the back of my Honda Element, he looked alive.

Despite this seized vivacity, though, it wasn't the photo that left me outside of myself, but what was next to it: a copy of Antoine de Saint-Exupery's *The Little Prince*. Because it had been well read and marked, I knew the two sets of dog-eared pages had been my doing. In the first, the fox told the prince, "If you tame me, then we shall need each other. To me, you will be unique in all the world. To you, I shall be unique in all the world." This was exactly what Cletus, a dog whose bite was often the first thing to meet other canines, and I, a woman who did the same to her kind, were to each other. I like to think that together we grew to calm. In the second dog-eared page, the fox lets the boy with hair the color of wheat in on this secret. "It's quite simple," he said. "One sees clearly only with the heart. Anything essential is invisible to the eyes." *Be awake and alive.*

"Richard," I asked when his and Abbie's game of wind tag, won by blowing hair off the other's face, was over, "did you place this book here for me?" He said he hadn't. And neither had I. I hadn't seen the book in months. I knew this because I'd been searching for it, looking forward to reading those very dog-eared pages to Abbie.

Okay, Mr. Maher, and now, even my brother, have at it. World-champion inquisitor within me, do the same. Give me an explanation. Was my husband forgetful? How about me? Maybe in my grief and inconsistent rest that morning (I had checked Cletus's body three times) I had sleepwalked? If so, I must have somehow known right where the book had been and moved it to where my conscious self would later find it. What else? Maybe it had always been there? I just missed it the four or so times I dusted. Though none yet knew of Clete's death, perhaps it was friends. How about intruders or aliens?

I well understood my doubt. Since returning from Rome, I'd looked for every reasonable explanation of my experiences there. "No big deal," I'd thought, that Faris had an aunt in my home city. "Of course," I've justified, "Ormechea's superiors had no better place to put him than working the front desk." But it was always the Book of Timothy that confounded me. First, because it came at confession, and second, because it surfaced on the plane. But what about what happened next? How could I explain that away too?

I had been faithful to the promise I made in Saint Peter's aisles to walk away from the Catholic Church. Even a pope named for the patron saint of animals hadn't tempted me back to full-time communion. But some moments, I just missed it. So, like the old, bald man in the back of Santi Giovanni e Paolo, I returned to it once and kneeled in a hidden pew. I stayed through a Sunday Mass's Liturgy of the Word. The second reading was this: a reading from the second letter of Paul to Timothy.

For my benefit, and no else's, I have to ask. How could I explain this third outreach of The Book of Timothy? And add to it this *Little Prince* finding, other than for this? God had upped God's game, finding me both through my brother and through a book that held his laughter right by a photo that took away my bite.

By midafternoon on the Sunday that Cletus died, Richard returned home with a backhoe he rented to dig a grave under my birch tree, the one with the squirrel-less drey. It wasn't the first time he had done so. In September, Emma, the dog who looked at me like she had met me before and was just waiting for me to realize it, died of cancer, ten years, seven months, and five days after her six-month prognosis.

Perhaps it had been our fault to dig her grave so close to the roots of the birch tree. Perhaps, also, it had been the weight of an early snow on overwhelmed branches that had not yet lost their leaves, for when the Chinooks returned, ninety miles per hour in gust force, the tree I once thought could take anything didn't. It split directly in two, the defeated side lying down, its fallen canopy directed toward Denali and the vertical portion still pointing up to our far northern hemisphere stars.

"You're not going to cut it down, are you?" I asked Richard. His jeans were coated in dirt and the flannel shirt that brought out his Tahitian blue eyes was torn from an unexpected run-in with a branch. He had just jumped out of the backhoe's cab, but he left the *ca-hunk-a-hunk*, ready-for-work rattling of its diesel engine going. The shovel itself was turned downward and lowered to the ground.

I had wanted a smooth resting place for Clete and didn't want his legs to be too confined, as it seemed they had been for Emma. So I laid myself down, four feet into the earth, where his body would soon be, stretched out, and felt for every potential place of discomfort.

When I stood again, Richard was bending down at the grave's edge. He had already lifted a jilted rock I had left for him and tossed it a literal stone's throw away. "I can, if you'd like," he offered, his voice sounding hoarse from a cold. "I'd need help removing the trunk, but we could chainsaw right here." He pointed to the lowest point in the vertical crack. He made a promise that the following summer we could put something else, "maybe a whistling aspen like we planted on Serenity" in its place. I liked this about him. No matter how difficult this past year had been between us, there was always, for him, at least I hoped, going to be a next summer, and I knew one more thing for certain. I wanted that next summer with him too.

I remember next being on my knees again and spreading the browning petals of the garden flowers, the delphinium and lily, the petunia and foxglove, Abbie had collected for Cletus's grave. At least for a short time, just like Clete, the late-summer flowers had survived the early snowstorm. I spread the petals layers deep in hope the earth would be as welcoming as it could be to my dog's soft fur and even softer brown eyes that wouldn't close, no matter how hard I tried.

❧

Within the earth, all was silent. The laughs, the cries, the winds, the storms, the working diesel engines; they were all out of earshot. And gone, just as well, were the four-alarm calls of fire, family, church, and Chicago. Here, in this sacred ground, I expected fur to one day pull away from skin, and skin, in turn, from muscle, and muscle from bone, and organ from fascia just as well, until this singular body of a singular creature I have loved purposefully and with abandon has vanished. I know a church-taught saying came to mind.

Ashes to ashes.

Dust to dust.

All that is not of God must die.

"But the inhabitant of this dog's body is of God," I also knew enough to think. And so, dear prosecutor and dear brother, am I. That's just how, I believe, we all must be: humans, dogs, trees, even chickens. Halved from our bodies, and the rest . . . peacefully with God.

And so, under a setting sun that turned Mount Susitna the color of the Little Prince's hair, I did rise to graveside, lower a corpse to earth, and, because I was alive and grateful for it, rise to surface once again. I did wish for my brother my constant hope for his peace and prosperity. I did kiss my husband and hold my daughter. And I did wish at that singular moment for my singular dog that I could be enough to teach Abbie of a love that pierces the soul and keeps it reaching skyward. And last, I would answer my own question of Richard about that tree. Of course, it would stay just as it was: half of earth, where we anger, lament, love, laugh, and die, over and over again, and half of the sky, reaching just as gloriously toward the ever-connected stars and the heavens beyond.

Always we would remain, in the constant presence of the other.

ACKNOWLEDGMENTS

This book began with a promise that took me many years to keep. So, there are many people to thank. To my first teachers, Sherry Simpson, Eva Saulitis, and Derick Burleson (all gone too soon) and to Judith Barrington, Peggy Shumaker, Jo-Ann Mapson, Zack Rogow, Ernestine Hayes, Kathleen Tarr, and David Stevenson. To my first readers, Scott, Michael, Jason, Jessica, Eric, Sara, Megan, Maureen, Margaret, Mari, and Kate. To fellow Bear Valley neighbor and exceptional writer Don Rearden, for awarding a pre-Rome version of this story the Jason Wenger Literary Prize. To the Rasmuson Foundation for awarding an individual artist's grant that permitted me to take a sabbatical from the practice of law to finish this telling. To the Breadloaf Writers Conference, the Kachemak Bay Writer's Conference, and the Tutka Bay Writers Retreat. To Dawn Marano, who had a vision, to Joeth Hall, who had a keen eye, and to all at Red Hen Press (Kate, Natasha, Rebeccah, Monica, and Tobi especially), who put this book in front of you. To Brooklyn Social Media (Louise, Linda, Emma, and Ed), my publicists, for ably spreading the word.

To my parents and my aunt Sister Ann Carolyn Blackburn, S.N.D. Even as they died, they taught me how to forgive. To all my sisters, Teresa, Julie, Carole, Joyce, and Maureen, minor characters here, but not in my life. To Richard, my husband, and Abbie, my daughter. You two are my world.

The name of only one survivor is in these pages. I have done my best to make the other men unrecognizable while preserving their truths. To them I say Sláinte and continued healing.

And last, to Tim, my first-memory brother. Whether together we achieved your wish and ended clergy abuse of children? We're both realistic enough to know the answer is no, but I can say this. Because of you, there is at least one child who never lost his laugh and there will be many more. I'm sure of it. So smile on, and I'm still not letting go.

With a boundless love,
A Joyous Cubs Fan

BIOGRAPHICAL NOTE

Joan Nockels Wilson is a writer and lawyer. A native of Chicago and a for-ever-learner, she has studied at Northwestern University; University of California, Berkeley; Lewis and Clark College; and the University of Alaska. She holds a Master's of Fine Arts in creative nonfiction, is a Rasmuson Foundation Individual Artist award winner, and is a member of the Breadloaf community of writers. Her work has appeared in literary journals and audio shows, most recently *Cirque* and *Arctic Entries*. She lives with her husband, daughter, and a vizsla named Vivian in Anchorage, Alaska. This is her first book.